Nutshell Series

of

WEST PUBLISHING COMPANY

P.O. Box 3526

St. Paul, Minnesota 55165

May, 1983

Administrative Law and Process, 2nd Ed., 1981, 445 pages, by Ernest Gellhorn, Dean and Professor of Law, Case Western Reserve University and Barry B. Boyer, Professor of Law, SUNY, Buffalo.

Admiralty, 1983, approximately 325 pages, by Frank L. Maraist, Professor of Law, Louisiana State University.

Agency-Partnership, 1977, 364 pages, by Roscoe T. Steffen, Late Professor of Law, University of Chicago.

American Indian Law, 1981, 288 pages, by William C. Canby, Jr., former Professor of Law, Arizona State University.

Antitrust Law and Economics, 2nd Ed., 1981, 425 pages, by Ernest Gellhorn, Dean and Professor of Law, Case Western Reserve University.

Church-State Relations—Law of, 1981, 305 pages, by Leonard F. Manning, Late Professor of Law, Fordham University.

Civil Procedure, 1979, 271 pages, by Mary Kay Kane, Professor of Law, University of California, Hastings College of the Law.

Civil Rights, 1978, 279 pages, by Norman Vieira, Professor of Law, Southern Illinois University.

Commercial Paper, 3rd Ed., 1982, 404 pages, by Charles M. Weber, Professor of Business Law, University of

I

Arizona and Richard E. Speidel, Professor of Law, Northwestern University.

Community Property, 1982, 423 pages, by Robert L. Mennell, Professor of Law, Hamline University.

Comparative Legal Traditions, 1982, 402 pages, by Mary Ann Glendon, Professor of Law, Boston College, Michael Wallace Gordon, Professor of Law, University of Florida and Christopher Osakwe, Professor of Law, Tulane University.

Conflicts, 1982, 469 pages, by David D. Siegel, Professor of Law, Albany Law School, Union University.

Constitutional Analysis, 1979, 388 pages, by Jerre S. Williams, Professor of Law Emeritus, University of Texas.

Constitutional Power—Federal and State, 1974, 411 pages, by David E. Engdahl, Professor of Law, University of Puget Sound.

Consumer Law, 2nd Ed., 1981, 418 pages, by David G. Epstein, Professor of Law, University of Texas and Steve H. Nickles, Professor of Law, University of Minnesota.

Contracts, 1975, 307 pages, by Gordon D. Schaber, Dean and Professor of Law, McGeorge School of Law and Claude D. Rohwer, Professor of Law, McGeorge School of Law.

Contract Remedies, 1981, 323 pages, by Jane M. Friedman, Professor of Law, Wayne State University.

Corporations—Law of, 1980, 379 pages, by Robert W. Hamilton, Professor of Law, University of Texas.

Corrections and Prisoners' Rights—Law of, 2nd Ed., 1983, approximately 365 pages, by Sheldon Krantz, Dean and Professor of Law, University of San Diego.

Criminal Law, 1975, 302 pages, by Arnold H. Loewy, Professor of Law, University of North Carolina.

Criminal Procedure—Constitutional Limitations, 3rd Ed., 1980, 438 pages, by Jerold H. Israel, Professor of Law, University of Michigan and Wayne R. LaFave, Professor of Law, University of Illinois.

Debtor-Creditor Law, 2nd Ed., 1980, 324 pages, by David G. Epstein, Professor of Law, University of Texas.

Employment Discrimination—Federal Law of, 2nd Ed., 1981, 402 pages, by Mack A. Player, Professor of Law, University of Georgia.

Energy Law, 1981, 338 pages, by Joseph P. Tomain, Professor of Law, Drake University.

Environmental Law, 1983, approximately 332 pages by Roger W. Findley, Professor of Law, University of Illinois and Daniel A. Farber, Professor of Law, University of Minnesota.

Estate Planning—Introduction to, 3rd Ed., 1983, 370 pages, by Robert J. Lynn, Professor of Law, Ohio State University.

Evidence, Federal Rules of, 1981, 428 pages, by Michael H. Graham, Professor of Law, University of Illinois.

Evidence, State and Federal Rules, 2nd Ed., 1981, 514 pages, by Paul F. Rothstein, Professor of Law, Georgetown University.

Family Law, 1977, 400 pages, by Harry D. Krause, Professor of Law, University of Illinois.

Federal Estate and Gift Taxation, 3rd Ed., 1983, 509 pages, by John K. McNulty, Professor of Law, University of California, Berkeley.

Federal Income Taxation of Individuals, 3rd Ed., 1983, approximately 425 pages, by John K. McNulty, Professor of Law, University of California, Berkeley.

Federal Income Taxation of Corporations and Stockholders, 2nd Ed., 1981, 362 pages, by Jonathan Sobeloff, Late Professor of Law, Georgetown University and Peter P. Weidenbruch, Jr., Professor of Law, Georgetown University.

Federal Jurisdiction, 2nd Ed., 1981, 258 pages, by David P. Currie, Professor of Law, University of Chicago.

Future Interests, 1981, 361 pages, by Lawrence W. Waggoner, Professor of Law, University of Michigan.

NUTSHELL SERIES

Government Contracts, 1979, 423 pages, by W. Noel Keyes, Professor of Law, Pepperdine University.

Historical Introduction to Anglo-American Law, 2nd Ed., 1973, 280 pages, by Frederick G. Kempin, Jr., Professor of Business Law, Wharton School of Finance and Commerce, University of Pennsylvania.

Injunctions, 1974, 264 pages, by John F. Dobbyn, Professor of Law, Villanova University.

Insurance Law, 1981, 281 pages, by John F. Dobbyn, Professor of Law, Villanova University.

Intellectual Property—Patents, Trademarks and Copyright, 1983, approximately 410 pages, by Arthur R. Miller, Professor of Law, Harvard University, and Michael H. Davis, Professor of Law, University of Tennessee.

International Business Transactions, 1981, 393 pages, by Donald T. Wilson, Professor of Law, Loyola University, Los Angeles.

Introduction to the Study and Practice of Law, 1983, approximately 400 pages, by Kenney F. Hegland, Professor of Law, University of Arizona.

Judicial Process, 1980, 292 pages, by William L. Reynolds, Professor of Law, University of Maryland.

Jurisdiction, 4th Ed., 1980, 232 pages, by Albert A. Ehrenzweig, Late Professor of Law, University of California, Berkeley, David W. Louisell, Late Professor of Law, University of California, Berkeley and Geoffrey C. Hazard, Jr., Professor of Law, Yale Law School.

Juvenile Courts, 2nd Ed., 1977, 275 pages, by Sanford J. Fox, Professor of Law, Boston College.

Labor Arbitration Law and Practice, 1979, 358 pages, by Dennis R. Nolan, Professor of Law, University of South Carolina.

Labor Law, 1979, 403 pages, by Douglas L. Leslie, Professor of Law, University of Virginia.

Land Use, 1978, 316 pages, by Robert R. Wright, Professor of Law, University of Arkansas, Little Rock and Susan Webber, Professor of Law, University of Arkansas, Little Rock.

Landlord and Tenant Law, 1979, 319 pages, by David S. Hill, Professor of Law, University of Colorado.

Law Study and Law Examinations—Introduction to, 1971, 389 pages, by Stanley V. Kinyon, Late Professor of Law, University of Minnesota.

Legal Interviewing and Counseling, 1976, 353 pages, by Thomas L. Shaffer, Professor of Law, Washington and Lee University.

Legal Research, 3rd Ed., 1978, 415 pages, by Morris L. Cohen, Professor of Law and Law Librarian, Yale University.

Legal Writing, 1982, 294 pages, by Dr. Lynn B. Squires, University of Washington School of Law and Marjorie Dick Rombauer, Professor of Law, University of Washington.

Legislative Law and Process, 1975, 279 pages, by Jack Davies, Professor of Law, William Mitchell College of Law.

Local Government Law, 2nd Ed., 1983, approximately 345 pages, by David J. McCarthy, Jr., Professor of Law, Georgetown University.

Mass Communications Law, 2nd Ed., 1983, 473 pages, by Harvey L. Zuckman, Professor of Law, Catholic University and Martin J. Gaynes, Lecturer in Law, Temple University.

Medical Malpractice—The Law of, 1977, 340 pages, by Joseph H. King, Professor of Law, University of Tennessee.

Military Law, 1980, 378 pages, by Charles A. Shanor, Professor of Law, Emory University and Timothy P. Terrell, Professor of Law, Emory University.

Oil and Gas, 1983, approximately 365 pages, by John S. Lowe, Professor of Law, University of Tulsa.

Personal Property, 1983, approximately 318 pages, by Barlow Burke, Jr., Professor of Law, American University.

Post-Conviction Remedies, 1978, 360 pages, by Robert Popper, Professor of Law, University of Missouri, Kansas City.

Presidential Power, 1977, 328 pages, by Arthur Selwyn Miller, Professor of Law Emeritus, George Washington University.

Procedure Before Trial, 1972, 258 pages, by Delmar Karlen, Professor of Law, College of William and Mary.

Products Liability, 2nd Ed., 1981, 341 pages, by Dix W. Noel, Late Professor of Law, University of Tennessee and Jerry J. Phillips, Professor of Law, University of Tennessee.

Professional Responsibility, 1980, 399 pages, by Robert H. Aronson, Professor of Law, University of Washington, and Donald T. Weckstein, Professor of Law, University of San Diego.

Real Estate Finance, 1979, 292 pages, by Jon W. Bruce, Professor of Law, Vanderbilt University.

Real Property, 2nd Ed., 1981, 448 pages, by Roger H. Bernhardt, Professor of Law, Golden Gate University.

Regulated Industries, 1982, 394 pages, by Ernest Gellhorn, Dean and Professor of Law, Case Western Reserve University, and Richard J. Pierce, Professor of Law, Tulane University.

Remedies, 1977, 364 pages, by John F. O'Connell, Professor of Law, Western State University College of Law, Fullerton.

Res Judicata, 1976, 310 pages, by Robert C. Casad, Professor of Law, University of Kansas.

Sales, 2nd Ed., 1981, 370 pages, by John M. Stockton, Professor of Business Law, Wharton School of Finance and Commerce, University of Pennsylvania.

Secured Transactions, 2nd Ed., 1981, 391 pages, by Henry J. Bailey, Professor of Law Emeritus, Willamette University.

Securities Regulation, 2nd Ed., 1982, 322 pages, by David L. Ratner, Dean and Professor of Law, University of San Francisco.

Sex Discrimination, 1982, 399 pages, by Claire Sherman Thomas, Lecturer, University of Washington, Women's Studies Department.

Titles—The Calculus of Interests, 1968, 277 pages, by Oval A. Phipps, Late Professor of Law, St. Louis University.

Torts—Injuries to Persons and Property, 1977, 434 pages, by Edward J. Kionka, Professor of Law, Southern Illinois University.

Torts—Injuries to Family, Social and Trade Relations, 1979, 358 pages, by Wex S. Malone, Professor of Law Emeritus, Louisiana State University.

Trial Advocacy, 1979, 402 pages, by Paul B. Bergman, Adjunct Professor of Law, University of California, Los Angeles.

Trial and Practice Skills, 1978, 346 pages, by Kenney F. Hegland, Professor of Law, University of Arizona.

Trial, The First—Where Do I Sit? What Do I Say?, 1982, 396 pages, by Steven H. Goldberg, Professor of Law, University of Minnesota.

Unfair Trade Practices, 1982, 444 pages, by Charles R. McManis, Professor of Law, Washington University, St. Louis.

Uniform Commercial Code, 1975, 507 pages, by Bradford Stone, Professor of Law, Detroit College of Law.

Uniform Probate Code, 1978, 425 pages, by Lawrence H. Averill, Jr., Dean and Professor of Law, University of Arkansas, Little Rock.

Welfare Law—Structure and Entitlement, 1979, 455 pages, by Arthur B. LaFrance, Dean and Professor of

Law, Lewis and Clark College, Northwestern School of Law.

Wills and Trusts, 1979, 392 pages, by Robert L. Mennell, Professor of Law, Hamline University.

Hornbook Series

and

Basic Legal Texts

of

WEST PUBLISHING COMPANY

P.O. Box 3526

St. Paul, Minnesota 55165

May, 1983

---

of Law, University of Illinois and Peter Hay, Dean and Professor of Law, University of Illinois.

Constitutional Law, Nowak, Rotunda and Young's Hornbook on, 2nd Ed., Student Ed., 1983, approximately 1100 pages, by John E. Nowak, Professor of Law, University of Illinois, Ronald D. Rotunda, Professor of Law, University of Illinois, and J. Nelson Young, Professor of Law, University of North Carolina.

Contracts, Calamari and Perillo's Hornbook on, 2nd Ed., 1977, 878 pages, by John D. Calamari, Professor of Law, Fordham University and Joseph M. Perillo, Professor of Law, Fordham University.

Contracts, Corbin's One Volume Student Ed., 1952, 1224 pages, by Arthur L. Corbin, Late Professor of Law, Yale University.

Contracts, Simpson's Hornbook on, 2nd Ed., 1965, 510 pages, by Laurence P. Simpson, Late Professor of Law, New York University.

Corporate Taxation, Kahn's Handbook on, 3rd Ed., Student Ed., Soft cover, 1981 with 1982 Supplement, 614 pages, by Douglas A. Kahn, Professor of Law, University of Michigan.

Corporations, Henn's Hornbook on, 3rd Ed., Student Ed., 1983, approximately 1167 pages, by Harry G. Henn, Professor of Law, Cornell University.

Criminal Law, LaFave and Scott's Hornbook on, 1972, 763 pages, by Wayne R. LaFave, Professor of Law, University of Illinois, and Austin Scott, Jr., Late Professor of Law, University of Colorado.

Damages, McCormick's Hornbook on, 1935, 811 pages, by Charles T. McCormick, Late Dean and Professor of Law, University of Texas.

Domestic Relations, Clark's Hornbook on, 1968, 754 pages, by Homer H. Clark, Jr., Professor of Law, University of Colorado.

Environmental Law, Rodgers' Hornbook on, 1977, 956 pages, by William H. Rodgers, Jr., Professor of Law, University of Washington.

Estate and Gift Taxes, Lowndes, Kramer and McCord's Hornbook on, 3rd Ed., 1974, 1099 pages, by Charles L. B. Lowndes, Late Professor of Law, Duke University, Robert Kramer, Professor of Law Emeritus, George Washington University, and John H. McCord, Professor of Law, University of Illinois.

Evidence, Lilly's Introduction to, 1978, 486 pages, by Graham C. Lilly, Professor of Law, University of Virginia.

Evidence, McCormick's Hornbook on, 2nd Ed., 1972 with 1978 Pocket Part, 938 pages, General Editor, Edward W. Cleary, Professor of Law Emeritus, Arizona State University.

Federal Courts, Wright's Hornbook on, 4th Ed., Student Ed., 1983, 870 pages, by Charles Alan Wright, Professor of Law, University of Texas.

Federal Income Taxation of Individuals, Posin's Hornbook on, Student Ed., 1983, approximately 421 pages, by Daniel Q. Posin, Jr., Professor of Law, Hofstra University.

Future Interest, Simes' Hornbook on, 2nd Ed., 1966, 355 pages, by Lewis M. Simes, Late Professor of Law, University of Michigan.

Income Taxation, Chommie's Hornbook on, 2nd Ed., 1973, 1051 pages, by John C. Chommie, Late Professor of Law, University of Miami.

Insurance, Keeton's Basic Text on, 1971, 712 pages, by Robert E. Keeton, Professor of Law Emeritus, Harvard University.

Labor Law, Gorman's Basic Text on, 1976, 914 pages, by Robert A. Gorman, Professor of Law, University of Pennsylvania.

Law Problems, Ballentine's, 5th Ed., 1975, 767 pages, General Editor, William E. Burby, Late Professor of Law, University of Southern California.

HORNBOOKS & BASIC TEXTS

Legal Writing Style, Weihofen's, 2nd Ed., 1980, 332 pages, by Henry Weihofen, Professor of Law Emeritus, University of New Mexico.

Local Government Law, Reynolds' Hornbook on, 1982, 860 pages, by Osborne M. Reynolds, Professor of Law, University of Oklahoma.

New York Practice, Siegel's Hornbook on, 1978, with 1981–82 Pocket Part, 1011 pages, by David D. Siegel, Professor of Law, Albany Law School of Union University.

Oil and Gas, Hemingway's Hornbook on, 2nd Ed., Student Ed., 1983, approximately 507 pages, by Richard W. Hemingway, Professor of Law, University of Oklahoma.

Poor, Law of the, LaFrance, Schroeder, Bennett and Boyd's Hornbook on, 1973, 558 pages, by Arthur B. LaFrance, Dean and Professor of Law, Lewis and Clark College, Northwestern School of Law, Milton R. Schroeder, Professor of Law, Arizona State University, Robert W. Bennett, Professor of Law, Northwestern University and William E. Boyd, Professor of Law, University of Arizona.

Property, Boyer's Survey of, 3rd Ed., 1981, 766 pages, by Ralph E. Boyer, Professor of Law, University of Miami.

Real Estate Finance Law, Osborne, Nelson and Whitman's Hornbook on, (successor to Hornbook on Mortgages), 1979, 885 pages, by George E. Osborne, Late Professor of Law, Stanford University, Grant S. Nelson, Professor of Law, University of Missouri, Columbia and Dale A. Whitman, Dean and Professor of Law, University of Missouri, Columbia.

Real Property, Burby's Hornbook on, 3rd Ed., 1965, 490 pages, by William E. Burby, Late Professor of Law, University of Southern California.

Real Property, Moynihan's Introduction to, 1962, 254 pages, by Cornelius J. Moynihan, Professor of Law, Suffolk University.

HORNBOOKS & BASIC TEXTS

Remedies, Dobb's Hornbook on, 1973, 1067 pages, by Dan B. Dobbs, Professor of Law, University of Arizona.

Sales, Nordstrom's Hornbook on, 1970, 600 pages, by Robert J. Nordstrom, former Professor of Law, Ohio State University.

Secured Transactions under the U.C.C., Henson's Hornbook on, 2nd Ed., 1979, with 1979 Pocket Part, 504 pages, by Ray D. Henson, Professor of Law, University of California, Hastings College of the Law.

Torts, Prosser's Hornbook on, 4th Ed., 1971, 1208 pages, by William L. Prosser, Late Dean and Professor of Law, University of California, Berkeley.

Trial Advocacy, Jeans' Handbook on, Student Ed., Soft cover, 1975, by James W. Jeans, Professor of Law, University of Missouri, Kansas City.

Trusts, Bogert's Hornbook on, 5th Ed., 1973, 726 pages, by George G. Bogert, Late Professor of Law, University of Chicago and George T. Bogert, Attorney, Chicago, Illinois.

Urban Planning and Land Development Control, Hagman's Hornbook on, 1971, 706 pages, by Donald G. Hagman, Late Professor of Law, University of California, Los Angeles.

Uniform Commercial Code, White and Summers' Hornbook on, 2nd Ed., 1980, 1250 pages, by James J. White, Professor of Law, University of Michigan and Robert S. Summers, Professor of Law, Cornell University.

Wills, Atkinson's Hornbook on, 2nd Ed., 1953, 975 pages, by Thomas E. Atkinson, Late Professor of Law, New York University.

Advisory Board

XIV

CRIMINAL PROCEDURE
IN A NUTSHELL

CONSTITUTIONAL LIMITATIONS

By

JEROLD H. ISRAEL
Professor of Law, University of Michigan

WAYNE R. LaFAVE
David C. Baum Professor of Law,
University of Illinois

THIRD EDITION

ST. PAUL, MINN.
WEST PUBLISHING CO.
1980

Library of Congress Cataloging in Publication Data

Israel, Jerold H   1934–
    Criminal procedure in a nutshell.
    (Nutshell series)

    Includes index.
    1. Criminal procedure—United States. I. LaFave, Wayne R.,
joint author. II. Title.
KF9619.3.18   1980   345.73'05   80-23164

ISBN 0-8299-2107-9

Israel & LaFave Const Limit. 3rd Ed.

2nd Reprint— 1983

PREFACE

This brief text is intended primarily for use by law students during their study of the ever-expanding field of criminal procedure. In preparing these materials, we have attempted to set forth as succinctly and clearly as possible an analysis of difficult problems of major current significance. In doing so, however, we have not wavered from our firm conviction—which we believe is manifested in our casebook on *Modern Criminal Procedure* (with Professor Yale Kamisar)—that there is no substitute for in-depth study of the basic sources: the leading cases in the field, and the critical and extended analysis of the cases to be found in the legal literature. Rather, we have undertaken this work on the assumption that the diligent student might also profit from a less cluttered look at some of the principal problems in the field. On the basis of our own experience with students and that reported to us by other teachers of criminal procedure, we believe this assumption is valid—that at some point it is useful for the student to examine only the forest and not the trees.

This is not a text on criminal procedure, but rather about *constitutional* criminal procedure. As anyone who has followed the work of the Su-

preme Court in recent years well knows, we have
about reached the point—to borrow Judge Henry
Friendly's phrase—where we may view "the Bill of
Rights as a code of criminal procedure." Whatever
one may think of this significant development, it is
apparent that most of the difficult problem areas
in the field of criminal procedure are now constitutional in dimension. In concentrating upon the
"constitutionalized" parts of the criminal justice
process, we have avoided the task—almost impossible for a book of this size—of describing the
various non-constitutional standards applied to the
criminal justice process in the 50 states and our
federal system. Those standards are treated in
much larger works, such as *Modern Criminal
Procedure* and local texts.

In Chapter One of this book, we have attempted
to trace the development, noted above, whereby the
Bill of Rights has attained foremost importance in
criminal procedure. In the course of this analysis,
we have briefly reviewed the many different procedural steps which are now subject to constitutional limitations. In the later chapters, we have
again found it necessary to be selective in our
treatment, and we therefore have undertaken a
more detailed analysis of only certain steps in the
process. We have limited ourselves to the "most
pervasive right" to counsel and the various rights
which the suspect possesses vis-a-vis the police (including a discussion of the scope of the exclusionary rule sanction used to protect those
rights), on the ground that these are the areas in
which a student in a basic criminal procedure

course is likely to desire some supplementary reading. We conclude with a chapter on the procedures for raising constitutional challenges. Special emphasis is placed on habeas corpus because we have found this increasingly intricate subject a particularly troublesome one for law students.

For the sake of brevity and ease in reading this text, we have departed from the traditional citation style for cases. Where it would not be ambiguous, we have used abbreviations for the name of the governmental unit in the case name (e. g., U.S., N.Y.), and also have shortened the oft-used Commonwealth, People, and State to C., P., and S., respectively. We have cited only the official reporter for Supreme Court decisions, and only the regional reporters for state cases. As to the latter, the court of decision is indicated in parentheses with the date; only the state is indicated when the case was decided by the highest court in the state. A previous discussion of the same case (or, occasionally a subsequent discussion) is noted by a page reference within parentheses; thus, all citations in the form of (p. ___) refer to the pages of this text. Traditional introductory signals ("see", "see, e. g.", and "accord") have been omitted where the case supports the text either through direct ruling, dicta, or the decision's general treatment of a particular issue.

Space limitations have also caused us to cite only leading, recent, and other illustrative cases. This, we again emphasize, should not be taken to mean that secondary sources—books, law review articles, commission reports, and the like—cannot be of considerable use to the student. Those secondary materials which we have found most challenging and helpful are cited in *Modern Criminal Procedure.*

This text includes cases decided by the United States Supreme Court through July 2, 1980, the conclusion of the October 1979 Term.

J.H.I.
W.R.L.

September, 1980

OUTLINE

OUTLINE

CHAPTER 2. ARREST, SEARCH AND SEIZURE

OUTLINE

OUTLINE

**CHAPTER 3. WIRETAPPING, ELECTRONIC
EAVESDROPPING, AND THE USE
OF SECRET AGENTS**

CHAPTER 4. POLICE INTERROGATION AND CONFESSIONS

OUTLINE

CHAPTER 7. RIGHT TO COUNSEL

CHAPTER 8. RAISING CONSTITUTIONAL CLAIMS

TABLE OF CASES

For Commonwealth v. _____ , People v. _____ , State v. _____ , and United States v. _____ , see the name of the opposing party. For Application of _____ , Ex parte _____ , In re _____ , and In the Matter of _____ , see the name of the party. For People ex rel. _____ , State ex rel. _____ , and United States ex rel. _____ , see the name of the first party.

A

TABLE OF CASES

TABLE OF CASES

C

TABLE OF CASES

TABLE OF CASES

D

TABLE OF CASES

E

TABLE OF CASES

TABLE OF CASES

TABLE OF CASES

I

TABLE OF CASES

J

K

TABLE OF CASES

TABLE OF CASES

TABLE OF CASES

TABLE OF CASES

N

O

TABLE OF CASES

P

TABLE OF CASES

TABLE OF CASES

TABLE OF CASES

TABLE OF CASES

U

V

W

TABLE OF CASES

TABLE OF CASES

CONSTITUTIONAL—CRIMINAL PROCEDURE

CHAPTER 1

THE CONSTITUTIONALIZATION OF CRIMINAL PROCEDURE

1. INTRODUCTION

The criminal law "revolution." Few, if any, areas of the law have undergone such significant revision over the last twenty years as has criminal procedure. Indeed, the change in criminal procedure has been so rapid and far reaching that some commentators have characterized it as a legal "revolution" (although others prefer to view it as merely "accentuated evolution"). The United States Supreme Court has been a key participant in this "revolution". During the 1960's, almost every Supreme Court term was marked by one or more decisions announcing significant new developments in the field of constitutional criminal procedure. While the Court's rulings during the 1970's contained fewer dramatic innovations, they provided a substantial body of law illustrating the varied applications of the new developments of the 1960's. The end result, for many areas of criminal procedure, was a major restructuring of the governing legal requirements. Of course, many important changes also were instituted by legislation, but very frequently the impetus for those changes also could be found in Supreme Court decisions.

The Constitution and criminal procedure. The Supreme Court's substantial role in the development of criminal procedure over the past twenty years is a product, in part, of the special emphasis upon criminal procedure in the United States Constitution. Of 23 separate rights noted in the first eight Amendments, 12 concern criminal procedure. The Fourth Amendment guarantees the right of the people to be secure against unreasonable searches and seizures and prohibits the issuance of warrants unless certain conditions are met. The Fifth Amendment requires prosecution by grand jury indictment for violation of all infamous crimes (excepting certain military prosecutions) and prohibits placing a person "twice in jeopardy" or compelling him to be a "witness against himself." The Sixth Amendment lists several rights that apply "in all criminal prosecutions"—the right to a speedy and public trial, by an impartial jury of the state and district in which the crime was committed, notice of the "nature and cause of the accusation," confrontation of opposing witnesses, compulsory process for obtaining favorable witnesses, and the assistance of counsel. The Eighth Amendment adds a prohibition against requiring excessive bail. Finally, aside from these guarantees directed specifically at criminal procedure, the Fifth Amendment encompasses the criminal justice process, along with other legal processes, in its general prohibition against the "deprivat[ion] of life, liberty or property without due process of law."

Of course, the provisions of the Constitution are not self-defining. Their impact upon criminal procedure depends in the end upon the Supreme Court's basic approach in determining their content. Interpreted narrowly, the constitutional guarantees would have a minimal effect on criminal procedure; they would govern only limited aspects of the total process and impose restrictions of minor significance in those areas. On the other hand, if the broadest conceivable interpretations were adopted, and were supported by various specific rules designed to secure their implementation, the constitutional guarantees would provide a comprehensive code that would govern almost every aspect of criminal procedure. The degree of current constitutional regulation lies somewhere between these extremes. Several aspects of the criminal justice process remain largely untouched by Supreme Court decisions, and several others have been subjected only to restrictions of a rather limited scope. For many others, however, the Court's decisions have established comprehensive sets of governing principles that substantially regulate the process.

Recent trends. The decisions of the past twenty years, while not pointing entirely in one direction, generally have moved towards promoting further "constitutionalization" of criminal procedure. The pace of this movement has, of course, varied with the composition of the Court. The Court of the middle and late 1960's tended to move faster and towards more extensive constitutionalization than the Court of the 1970's. The general direction of the movement, however, has been persistent throughout the entire period. Admittedly, several rulings of the 1970's retreated from the broad implications of certain major decisions of the 1960's. Yet, the decisions of the 1970's also moved toward further constitutionalization in many other areas of criminal procedure, and in some instances, did so quite dramatically. The very recent Supreme Court decisions of the 1980's suggest, moreover, that this overall pattern is not likely to change in the near future.

The movement towards further constitutionalization has been reflected primarily in two doctrinal trends—(1) the extension of the application of the Bill of Rights guarantees to the states via the Fourteenth Amendment, and (2) the expansion of the interpretation of individual guarantees both to cover additional aspects of the criminal justice process and to provide greater regulation of those aspects previously covered. The sections that follow seek to explore, in a general fashion, the development of both of these trends.

2. APPLICATION OF BILL OF RIGHTS GUARANTEES TO THE STATES

Introduction. The first 10 Amendments were enacted as limitations solely upon the federal government. *Barron v. Baltimore*, 7 Pet. 243 (1833). The adoption of the Fourteenth Amendment in 1868, however, significantly extended federal constitutional controls over the action of state governments. That Amendment provides, inter alia, that no state may "deprive any person of life, liberty and property without due process of law." From the outset, the Supreme Court has been troubled by the relation of the Fourteenth Amendment limitation upon the states to the Bill of Rights limitations upon the federal government. At least four separate views of the appropriate relationship between the respective Amendments have been advanced by various members of the Court. These views have been debated at length, usually in concurring and dissenting opinions, over the years. Among the most notable discussions are those found in *Adamson v. Cal.*, 332 U.S. 46 (1947); *Pointer v. Texas*, 380 U.S. 400 (1965); and *Duncan v. La.*, 391 U.S. 145 (1968).

The fundamental rights interpretation. The relationship between the Fourteenth Amendment and the Bill of Rights was first considered by the Supreme Court in the criminal procedure context in

Hurtado v. Cal., 110 U.S. 516 (1884). The Court there adopted the "fundamental rights interpretation" of the Fourteenth Amendment's due process clause, an interpretation that prevailed until the early 1960's and is still advocated by some members of the Court. The fundamental rights interpretation finds no necessary relationship between the content of the Fourteenth Amendment and the guarantees of the Bill of Rights. The due process clause is viewed as simply incorporating all principles "implicit in the concept of ordered liberty." *Palko v. Conn.*, 302 U.S. 319 (1937). As applied to criminal procedure, those principles require that the state afford the defendant "that fundamental fairness essential to the very concept of justice." *Lisenba v. Cal.*, 314 U.S. 219, 236 (1941). While a state's violation of a procedural right noted in the Bill of Rights is viewed as a likely indicator that fundamental fairness has been denied, it is not necessarily conclusive. Similarly, the absence of a specific Bill of Rights guarantee prohibiting a particular practice does not necessarily mean that the practice complies with fundamental fairness. The due process clause of the Fourteenth Amendment, like the due process clause of the Fifth Amendment, can reach beyond the specific guarantees.

In support of the fundamental rights interpretation, it frequently is argued that not all Bill of Rights guarantees necessarily reflect in all their aspects that process needed to achieve basic fairness. Some reflect only the "restricted views of Eighteenth Century England regarding the best method for the ascertainment of facts." *Adamson v. Cal.*, supra (Frankfurter, J., con.). Others encompass fundamental rights, but do not do so in every aspect of the guarantee. For example, the Fifth Amendment double jeopardy clause prohibits the Federal government from retrying a previously acquitted defendant both where the government's justification for seeking a retrial lies only in its interest in gaining a second chance to prove guilt and where its justification is based on a trial error that tainted the jury verdict. Several authorities have suggested that basic fairness is violated only in the former situation, since only there has the government had a fair opportunity to present its case. Proceeding from the independent perspective of the Fourteenth Amendment, a court could readily rely upon this analysis to find that a retrial prohibition ordinarily is fundamental (and therefore applicable to the states) only where there was no error in the first trial. Indeed, it could even shape its ruling to the facts of the particular case before it. Thus, while state retrials of acquitted defendants might ordinarily be acceptable where justified by trial errors, exercise of such retrial authority in a particular case, taking into consideration the "totality of the circumstances" (e. g., whether the prosecution "invited" the trial error), could still constitute a denial of due process.

While the fundamental rights interpretation prevailed from *Hurtado* until the early 1960's, its application can be divided roughly into two periods. Prior to the early 1930's, the Supreme Court reviewed comparatively few criminal cases arising from state courts and generally ruled against Fourteenth Amendment protection of interests encompassed within the specific guarantees of the Bill of Rights. Although these decisions usually dealt with a single aspect of a general right, the opinions often seemed to characterize all aspects of the right as "not fundamental." Thus, a decision dealing with prosecutorial comment upon defendant's refusal to take the stand was commonly characterized as holding that due process did not guarantee any element of the privilege against self-incrimination. The early 1930's, however, marked a change in direction. The Supreme Court began to display increasing interest in state criminal procedure and state criminal cases soon occupied a significant portion of its docket. During this period the Supreme Court held that elements of several rights guaranteed by the first eight Amendments were also fundamental rights protected by the Fourteenth Amendment. In *Powell v. Ala.*, 287 U.S. 45 (1932), for example, the Court recognized that the indigent's right to appointed counsel, an element of the Sixth Amendment guarantee of assistance of counsel, was a fundamental right as applied to certain types of state cases. At the same time, the Court rejected claims that elements of several other guarantees were fundamental. Most of these decisions, however, were carefully limited to the particular problem before the Court. Thus, in *Palko v. Conn.*, supra, the Court held that due process did not bar a state appeal from a defense acquittal based upon an erroneous construction of the law, but its opinion also indicated that other forms of double jeopardy might well violate the Fourteenth Amendment.

Criticism of the fundamental rights interpretation. While it won majority support for many years, the fundamental rights interpretation was criticized over those years by several dissenting justices. They contended that the fundamental rights interpretation promoted a largely ad hoc, personal application of the Fourteenth Amendment. They argued that its general standards (e. g., "fundamental fairness") granted a largely "unconfined power" to the judiciary that was contrary to the basic premise of a written constitution. *Duncan v. La.*, supra (Black, J., con.). In response to these contentions, the justices in the majority frequently stated that application of the fundamental rights interpretation was not basically subjective, but rested upon a pervasive consensus of society that could be determined independently of a justice's personal views. They also stressed that, in any event, the fundamental rights interpretation was consistent with the history and language of the Fourteenth Amendment, as viewed in light of the traditional interpretation of the Fifth Amendment due process clause. *Adamson v. Cal.*, supra (Frankfurter, J., con.).

The dissenting justices criticizing the fundamental rights interpretation generally took the position that the Fourteenth Amendment should be viewed as "incorporating" the entire Bill of Rights. Some of those justices argued that the due process clause did no more than incorporate each of the Bill of Rights guarantees. See *In re Winship*, 397 U.S. 358 (1970) (Black, J., dis.). Others, however, argued for total incorporation plus inclusion of any unenumerated rights that were essential to "fairness" and "individual liberty." See *Adamson v. Cal.*, supra (Murphy, J., dis.); *Poe v. Ullman*, 367 U.S. 497 (1961) (Douglas, J., dis.). Critics of both total incorporation interpretations contended that these interpretations had support neither in the legislative history nor the language of the Fourteenth Amendment. They argued that Congress would have clearly stated that the Bill of Rights was applicable to the states if that had been its intent. They also rejected the contention that total incorporation avoided much of the subjectivity inherent in the fundamental rights approach. Even under the narrower incorporationist interpretation, they argued, the focus of judicial inquiry would simply be shifted from the flexible concept of "fundamental rights" to the equally flexible terms of the specific Amendments, such as "probable cause," "unreasonable search," and "speedy and public trial." The critics also contended that the full application of the Bill of Rights would impose an undue burden on the states and "deprive [them] of opportunity for reforms in legal process designed for extending the area of freedom." *Adamson v. Cal.*, supra (Frankfurter, J., con.). Although the total incorporation approach never commanded majority support, the debate over total incorporation versus fundamental rights did have a substantial influence on the development of the selective incorporation doctrine, which became a dominant force in the 1960's.

The shift to selective incorporation. The fundamental rights approach lost majority support during the early 1960's, although the *Palko* decision, discussed supra, was not overruled until 1970. In 1961, Mr. Justice Brennan, in a dissenting opinion, advanced what is commonly described as the "selective incorporation" view of the Fourteenth Amendment. *Cohen v. Hurley*, 366 U.S. 117 (1961) (Brennan, J., dis.). This view combines aspects of both the "fundamental rights" and "total incorporation" interpretations of the Fourteenth Amendment. Selective incorporation accepts the basic premise of the fundamental rights interpretation that the Fourteenth Amendment encompasses all rights, substantive and procedural, that are "of the very essence of the scheme of ordered liberty." *Cohen v. Hurley*, supra (Brennan, J., dis.). It recognizes that not all rights enumerated in the Bill of Rights are necessarily

[11]

fundamental, and that other rights may be fundamental even though not within the specific guarantees of the Bill of Rights. It rejects the fundamental rights interpretation, however, insofar as that
view stresses the "totality of circumstances" in the
particular case. Evaluating the fundamental nature
of a right in terms of the "factual circumstances
surrounding each individual case" is viewed as "ex-
tremely subjective and excessively discretionary."
Limiting a decision to only one aspect of the particular right also is rejected as presenting the same
difficulty. *Pointer v. Texas,* supra (Goldberg, J.,
con.). Accordingly, in determining whether an enumerated right is fundamental, the selective incorporation doctrine requires that the Court look at the
total right guaranteed by the particular Bill of Rights
provision, not merely at a single aspect of that right
nor the application of that aspect in the particular
case. If it is decided that a particular right is
fundamental, that right will be incorporated into the
Fourteenth Amendment "whole and intact." The
enumerated right will then be enforced against the
states in every case according to the same standards
applied to the federal government. With respect to
those guarantees within the Bill of Rights held to
be fundamental, there is, as Justice Douglas put
it, "coextensive coverage" under the Fourteenth
Amendment and the Bill of Rights. See *Johnson v.
La.,* 406 U.S. 356 (1972).

The selective incorporation doctrine did not gain immediate acceptance by the Court. It was sharply criticized as an artificial compromise between the fundamental rights and total incorporation doctrines. *Duncan v. La.*, supra (Harlan, J., dis.). By 1963, however, it had the support of at least three justices. In addition, two Justices, Black and Douglas, while remaining supporters of total incorporation, accepted selective incorporation as a lesser evil than the fundamental rights interpretation. As a result, the post-1963 decisions consistently followed the selective incorporation standard. Because of the particular composition of the majority, opinions for the Court generally did not refer to the selective incorporation doctrine as such, but those opinions made clear that a selective incorporation standard was being applied. See, e. g., *Benton v. Md.*, 395 U.S. 784, 795 (1969). ("Once it is decided that a Bill of Rights guarantee is fundamental * * *, the same constitutional standards apply against both the State and Federal Governments.") Very frequently, the results reached in applying this standard were also supported by the remaining justices, who favored the traditional fundamental rights analysis. Indeed, at least one of the justices in this group appeared to follow the view that a Bill of Rights guarantee held to be within the Fourteenth Amendment ordinarily would take on the same dimension as applied to the federal government, and contrary rulings, like *Palko* or *Powell*, only would be justified by a special showing of the unique needs of the states in the areas involved. See *Benton v. Md.*, 395 U.S. at 808, n. 12 (collecting the opinions of Stewart, J.).

The adoption of the selective incorporation position during the early 1960's was accompanied by a movement towards a broader view of the nature of a "fundamental procedural right." Consistent with selective incorporation, the Court's assessment was directed at the significance of the right when viewed as a whole, rather than concentrating solely on the particular aspect presented in the case at hand. In addition, the right was viewed with reference to its operation within the "common law system of [criminal procedure] * * * that has been developing * * * in this country, rather than its theoretical justification as a necessary element of a 'fair and equitable procedure.'" *Duncan v. La.,* supra. Finally, greater emphasis was placed upon the very presence of a right within the Bill of Rights as strong evidence of its fundamental nature.

Applying this approach, the Supreme Court during the 1960's held fundamental (and therefore applicable to the states under the same standards applied to federal government) the following Bill of Rights guarantees: the freedom from unreasonable searches and seizures and the right to have excluded from criminal trials any evidence obtained in violation thereof, *Mapp v. Ohio*, 367 U.S. 643 (1961), and *Ker v. Cal.*, 374 U.S. 23 (1963); the privilege against self-incrimination, *Malloy v. Hogan*,

378 U.S. 1 (1964); the guarantee against double jeopardy, *Benton v. Md.*, 395 U.S. 784 (1969); the right to the assistance of counsel, *Gideon v. Wainwright*, 372 U.S. 335 (1963); the right to a speedy trial, *Klopfer v. N. C.*, 386 U.S. 213 (1967); the right to jury trial, *Duncan v. La.*, supra; the right to confront opposing witnesses, *Pointer v. Texas*, supra; the right to compulsory process for obtaining witnesses, *Washington v. Texas*, 388 U.S. 14 (1967); and the prohibition against cruel and unusual punishment, *Robinson v. Cal.*, 370 U.S. 660 (1962). Moreover, in light of these rulings, two earlier cases are now viewed as incorporating within the Fourteenth Amendment the Sixth Amendment rights to a public trial and to notice of the nature and cause of the accusation. See *In re Oliver*, 333 U.S. 257 (1948) (cited in *Duncan* as incorporating the right to public trial); *Cole v. Ark.*, 333 U.S. 196 (1948). The only remaining guarantees addressed specifically to criminal procedure are the Eighth Amendment prohibition against excessive bail and the Fifth Amendment requirement of prosecution of infamous crimes by grand jury indictment. The Supreme Court has not ruled directly on the bail clause, but the court's characterization of that clause in *Schlib v. Kuebel*, 404 U.S. 357 (1971), suggests that it would be incorporated within the Fourteenth Amendment if the issue were squarely presented. Prosecution by grand jury indictment, on the other hand, was found not to be fundamental, and therefore not required

of the states, in *Hurtado v. Cal.*, supra; that decision continues to be followed as valid precedent and appears unlikely to be overruled. See *Gerstein v. Pugh*, 420 U.S. 103 (1975).

Future developments. As new justices have come to the Court, they generally have accepted the selective incorporation rulings even though they might not have supported selective incorporation as a matter of first impression. There have been some exceptions, however. In *Apodaca v. Or.,* 406 U.S. 404 (1972) (con.), Justice Powell noted his preference for a fundamental rights approach, and argued that not every feature of the Sixth Amendment right to a jury trial should apply to the states. Consider also *Crist v. Bretz*, 437 U.S. 28 (1978) (Powell, J., dis., joined by Burger, C. J. and Rehnquist, J., criticizing the Court's "jot-for-jot" Fourteenth Amendment incorporation of the federal standard as to the attachment of jeopardy under the double jeopardy clause). Notwithstanding such occasional complaints, however, the Court as a whole appears likely to continue to construe the Fourteenth Amendment as applying to the states the same constitutional standards (except for the Fifth Amendment's indictment requirement) as are applied to federal prosecutions under the Bill of Rights guarantees. If a majority of the justices conclude that a previous constitutional interpretation applied to the federal courts may go beyond the requirements of fundamental fairness, they are more likely to reexamine that interpretation than to reargue the relationship between the Fourteenth Amendment and the Bill of Rights. The decisions interpreting the Sixth Amendment right to jury trial, discussed below, are illustrative.

In holding that the Fourteenth Amendment fully absorbed the jury trial right, the majority in *Duncan v. La.*, supra, noted the state's contention that incorporation would disrupt long established state practices by requiring adherence to past interpretations of the Sixth Amendment that were developed solely in terms of federal court practice. The majority responded, in part, that those past interpretations were "always subject to reconsideration" in light of new developments. Subsequently, in *Williams v. Fla.*, 399 U.S. 78 (1970), the Court reconsidered the scope of the Sixth Amendment, ruled that it did not require a twelve-person jury as utilized in the federal courts, and consequently upheld the state's use of a six person jury in a non-capital felony case.

A similar approach was taken in *Apodaca v. Or.*, supra, although there a division over incorporationist theory did influence the result. In *Apodaca*, four justices, including three appointed after *Duncan*, found that the Sixth Amendment did not require unanimous jury verdicts and therefore a state's acceptance of 10–2 verdicts did not violate the Fourteenth Amendment. Four justices, relying in part upon past Sixth Amendment decisions, held that unanimity was constitutionally required. Only Justice Powell challenged the premise that the same constitutional standards should apply to federal and state cases. Applying a fundamental rights analysis, he concluded that unanimity should not be required of the states, but should be required of the federal government under the prior Sixth Amendment rulings. He therefore contributed the fifth vote to uphold the state practice in *Apodaca* (although he would have joined the other four justices in a federal case).

It should be noted that the reexamination route followed in *Williams* and *Apodaca* does not necessarily require alteration of federal court practice even though the Court rejects a restrictive constitutional standard previously applied to federal courts. Although the Constitution no longer requires adherence to the more restrictive standard, the Supreme Court can continue to apply that standard to the federal courts pursuant to its supervisory power over those courts. Thus, the Federal Rules of Criminal Procedure continue to require twelve person juries and unanimous verdicts. See Fed.R.Crim. P. 23, 31.

3. EXPANSION OF INDIVIDUAL PROVISIONS

Introduction. The decisions of the past twenty years not only made most of the Bill of Rights guarantees applicable to the states via the Fourteenth Amendment, but they also substantially expanded the scope of those guarantees as applied to both federal and state procedure. Several constitutional guarantees were applied to previously unregulated areas of criminal procedure. Other guarantees were more fully defined to apply more comprehensive and detailed restrictions in areas that had long been subject to constitutional regulation.

Of course, the vast majority of the post-1960 decisions did not involve dramatic new applications of constitutional limitations. Only a small group of decisions fell within that category. Most of the new rulings moved only a slight step beyond previous limitations. Moreover, not all of the cases adopted even minor extensions of prior limitations. In a number of cases, the Court refused to impose new limitations, and, in a few instances, it overturned previously established limitations. The general trend of the decisions, however, was to further "constitutionalize" criminal procedure, and the decisions contributing to this trend may well have produced more significant new developments in criminal procedure than all of the decisions of the previous century.

The sections that follow present an overview of the current constitutional limitations imposed upon the different phases of the criminal justice process, with primary emphasis upon the Supreme Court decisions of the last twenty years. The reader should keep in mind that these sections describe only the general thrust of the current limitations and a far more complete analysis of specific rulings and the rationales advanced in both majority and dissenting opinions is needed to fully appreciate the scope of the limitations applied in a particular area.

4. POLICE INVESTIGATION

The general trend. Probably the most highly publicized group of Supreme Court decisions of the past twenty years have been those dealing with basic police investigatory practices, such as interrogation, physical searches, electronic eavesdropping, eye-witness identification procedures, etc. Several of these investigatory procedures had already been subjected to considerable constitutional regulation prior to the 1960's. In the area of searches, a series of decisions based upon the Fourth Amendment and dating back to 1914 had established an extensive body of constitutional rules regulating federal officers. The practice of police interrogation had also been examined in a significant number of cases. The Court's post-1960 decisions revised and substantially expanded the limitations applicable to such previously regulated practices. In addition, those decisions imposed restraints upon practices, such as lineup identification and wiretapping, that had largely been untouched by the earlier constitutional rulings. Most of the more significant new limitations were imposed during the 1960's. Indeed, in the 1970's, the Court arguably retreated from the implications of some of those limitations. However, several other decisions of the 1970's also added to the constitutional regulation of investigatory practices, most notably arrests and searches.

With the limitations of the post-1960 decisions added to the considerable body of prior law, the area of police investigation has become one of two phases of the criminal process (the other being the trial itself) that are most extensively regulated by constitutional limitations. The total body of Supreme Court and lower court precedents is immense. It includes, of course, not only rulings holding various police practices unconstitutional, but also numerous rulings finding other practices to be constitutionally acceptable. Because of its size and its importance, the body of rulings dealing with investigatory practices is reviewed at greater length in Chapters 2–5. We will take note here, however, of the basic remedy—the exclusion of unconstitutionally obtained evidence—that has served as the foundation for the development of much of the constitutional regulation of the police practices area.

The exclusionary rule. The one major element common to the constitutional regulation of all aspects of police investigatory practices is the so-called "exclusionary rule." This rule provides for the exclusion from a criminal prosecution of evidence obtained in violation of the Constitution. Today, the question of the constitutionality of a particular police practice is ordinarily presented to the courts via a motion to exclude evidence pursuant to this rule.

The exclusionary rule was not always recognized, however, as an appropriate remedy for all constitutional violations. It has traditionally been applied to violations of the Fifth Amendment privilege against self-incrimination, since that provision specifically prohibits the use of "compelled" testimony in a criminal case. *Boyd v. U. S.,* 116 U.S. 616 (1886). The Supreme Court readily supported also the application of the exclusionary rule where unconstitutional police practices produced inherently unreliable evidence (e. g., a confession obtained by torture). The Court had difficulty, however, with the application of the rule to exclude relevant and trustworthy evidence obtained in violation of a constitutional guarantee that did not refer, even indirectly, to the admissibility of evidence. This problem was considered initially in ruling on the admissibility of evidence obtained in violation of the Fourth Amendment prohibition against unreasonable searches and seizures.

The Court held in *Weeks v. U. S.,* 232 U.S. 383 (1914), that any evidence obtained by federal officers in violation of the Fourth Amendment would be barred from a federal prosecution. Subsequently, in *Wolf v. Colo.,* 338 U.S. 25 (1949), the Court ruled that, although Fourteenth Amendment due process encompassed the "security of one's privacy * * * which is at the core of the Fourth Amendment," it did not require that state courts exclude all evidence obtained in violation of the Fourth (and Fourteenth)

Amendment. The Court created a narrow exception to *Wolf* in *Rochin v. Cal.,* 342 U.S. 165 (1952), holding that the Fourteenth Amendment did require exclusion of evidence obtained by police activities that were so flagrantly abusive of individual privacy as "to shock   *   *   *   the conscience" of a "civilized society." *Wolf* continued to state the general rule, however, until the early 1960's. The Court then held both that the Fourteenth Amendment fully incorporated the Fourth Amendment guarantee (see p. 14), and that the exclusionary rule was an essential element of that guarantee. The latter point was made in *Mapp v. Ohio,* 367 U.S. 643 (1961), which overruled *Wolf.* The *Mapp* court rejected the "factual grounds upon which *Wolf* was based"; it noted that other remedies against unreasonable searches (e. g., tort suits) had proven ineffective, the trend in the state courts was now toward adoption of the exclusionary rule (over one half of the states had adopted the rule as a matter of state law), and various inconsistencies in the prior application of the rule had been removed. The Court concluded that the exclusionary rule, by removing the incentive to disregard the Fourth Amendment, constituted "the only effectively available way   *   *   *   to compel respect for the constitutional guarantee." It discounted Justice Cardozo's argument that the rule permitted the "criminal   *   *   *   to go free because the constable had blundered," noting that "another consideration, the imperative of judicial integrity," must prevail. "Nothing," it noted, "can destroy a government more quickly than its failure to observe its own laws."

The *Mapp* rationale was subsequently extended to require exclusion of evidence obtained through other unconstitutional practices. *Wong Sun v. U. S.,* 371 U.S. 471 (1963), excluded an oral statement of a defendant made in direct response to an unconstitutional entry and arrest. Evidence obtained in violation of defendant's Sixth Amendment right to counsel was also held constitutionally inadmissible. *Massiah v. U. S.,* 377 U.S. 201 (1964) (confession) (see § 26); *U. S. v. Wade,* 388 U.S. 218 (1967) (lineup identification) (see § 31). Additionally, in *Miranda v. Ariz.,* 384 U.S. 436 (1966), the Fifth Amendment privilege against self-incrimination was applied to custodial interrogation, thereby extending the Fifth Amendment's exclusionary requirement to statements unconstitutionally obtained from such interrogation without regard to whether those statements were inherently untrustworthy (see § 27).

Although the exclusionary rule is now well established in Supreme Court precedent, its application to reliable evidence, other than that obtained in violation of the Fifth Amendment, has remained a very controversial subject. In particular, several justices have questioned the comparative costs and gains resulting from the exclusion of evidence obtained through illegal searches. They note that courts are allowed to accept illegally obtained evidence in various contexts (see §§ 35, 36) and do not thereby condone the illegalities in the acquisition of the evidence. They accordingly take the position, supported by language in several recent majority opinions, that the "imperative of judicial integrity," alluded to in *Mapp,* plays a very "limited role" in the justification of the exclusionary rule. *Stone v. Powell,* 428 U.S. 465 (1976). They see the deterrence rationale of *Mapp* as the primary justification for excluding illegally seized evidence, and they question whether the exclusionary rule is a cost-efficient deterrent. Chief Justice Burger has concluded that it is not, and he has suggested that overruling *Mapp* might well be necessary to encourage legislatures to provide more appropriate statutory remedies for persons injured by illegal searches (e. g., "direct sanctions on errant police officers or on the public treasury by way of tort actions"); *Stone v. Powell,* supra (con.). Justice White has suggested that *Mapp* be modified so that unconstitutionally seized evidence not be excluded where the officer who seized the evidence was "acting in the good faith belief that his conduct comported with existing laws" and had "reasonable grounds for [that] belief." *Stone v. Powell,* supra (dis.). Three other members of the Court have also expressed an interest in adopting such a modification, and *Mich. v. DeFillippio,* described at p. 121 infra, may constitute the initial step in that direction. See *Stone v.*

Powell, supra (Burger, J., con.);   *Brown v. Ill.,* 422
U.S. 590 (1975) (Powell and Rehnquist, JJ., con.);
Brewer v. Williams, 430 U.S. 387 (1977) (Burger, C.
J., dis., and Powell, J., con.).

5. PRETRIAL PROCEEDINGS

Many pretrial proceedings have far more practical
significance than the trial itself. Nevertheless, tak-
en as a group, pretrial procedures are subject to far
less extensive constitutional regulation than either
trials or police investigations. Much of the constitutional regulation that does exist is the product of
decisions of the last decade, during which the Court
has shown an increased interest in the operation of
pretrial proceedings. The Court's decisions have
varied considerably, however, in their treatment of
different pretrial determinations. They have reaffirmed that constitutional limits are largely inapplicable to certain determinations, suggested the possible application of new limits to others, and actually
applied significant new restrictions to still others.

Bail. The Eighth Amendment provides that "excessive bail shall not be required," but the standards
for determining what constitutes "excessive bail"
have not been fully developed by the Supreme
Court. Indeed, only one major decision deals directly with that issue. In *Stack v. Boyle,* 342 U.S. 1
(1951), the Court stated that bail set "at a figure
higher than an amount reasonably calculated" to pro-

vide assurance that the accused would be present at trial was "excessive under the Eighth Amendment." The specific ruling of *Stack,* however, was rather narrow; the court below had violated "statutory and constitutional standards" in fixing bail of petitioners (indicted for conspiring to advocate overthrow of the government) "in a sum much higher than that usually imposed for offenses with like penalties" without any "factual showing to justify such action."

The *Stack* opinion, in noting that "traditional standards" require consideration of individual factors in setting bail, raises serious doubts as to the constitutionality of the practice, followed in many courts, of imposing a standard bail based solely on the seriousness of the crime charged. See *Ackies v. Purdy,* 322 F.Supp. 38 (S.D.Fla.1970). *Stack's* emphasis on potential flight as the key determinant in setting bail also raises doubts as to reliance upon the accused's potential dangerousness in determining conditions of pretrial release. This issue is often hidden by the magistrate's failure to state the basis for his bail decision, but is directly presented by so-called "preventive detention" legislation. See *Blunt v. U. S.,* 322 A.2d 579 (D.C.App.1974). Finally the discussion of bail in *Stack* raises doubts as to whether a court can automatically require financial security (e. g., a bond) where a defendant cannot provide that security due to a lack of funds. One court has suggested that a magistrate must consider other "less drastic alternatives" (e. g., personal recognizance, or third party supervision) and determine that they will not reasonably assure the defendant's appearance before imposing a financial requirement which the defendant cannot meet. *Pugh v. Rainwater,* 557 F.2d 1189 (5th Cir. 1977). So far, none of these issues have been resolved by the Court (possibly because a challenge to bail does not easily reach the level of Supreme Court review before the trial is completed and the challenge becomes moot).

The prosecutor's decision to charge. The American prosecutor has broad discretion in determining whether to initiate formal charges. Of course, the prosecutor may not proceed without probable cause, and most jurisdictions do provide for some independent reviewing mechanism to ensure that probable cause exists. But where the evidence is sufficient, there usually is no requirement that the prosecutor bring charges or that charges be brought at the highest level. The prosecutor may decide not to proceed, notwithstanding a strong case, for a variety of reasons ranging from limited prosecutorial resources to a judgment that a conviction would do "more harm than good." He may decide to proceed on less than the highest charge supported by the evidence for similar reasons. The Supreme Court has consistently recognized the broad range of the prosecutor's discretion in both refusing to charge and selecting the charge. It has refused, for example, to strike down a statutory scheme that allows a prosecutor to choose between two offenses, carrying substantially different punishments, but prohibiting exactly the same conduct. *U. S. v. Batchelder,* 442 U.S. 114 (1979). On the other hand, the Court frequently has noted that the prosecutor's discretion is subject to the limits imposed by the equal protection clause of the Fourteenth Amendment. Several opinions have indicated, for example, that it is a constitutional defense to a criminal charge that the prosecutor selected the defendant for prosecution, while refusing to prosecute others who committed the same crime, if the prosecutor's decision was based on grounds barred by the equal protection guarantee. See *Oyler v. Boles,* 368 U.S. 448 (1962). As to what grounds would be barred by that guarantee, the Court has stated only that "selective enforcement" cannot be "based upon an unjustifiable standard such as race, religion, or other arbitrary classifications." Id.

Review of the prosecutor's decision. The Fifth Amendment requires that all prosecutions for infamous crimes be commenced by grand jury indictment. Thus, a prosecutor's decision to charge a person with an infamous crime (encompassing all federal offenses carrying a term of imprisonment in excess of one year) will not be given effect unless the grand jury finds the evidence is sufficient and itself issues the charge in the form of an indictment. A major function of the grand jury, the Court has said, is "to stand between the accuser and the accused * * * to determine whether a charge is founded upon reason or was dictated by an intimidating power or by malice and personal ill will." *Wood v. Ga.,* 370 U.S. 375, 390 (1962). Whether the grand jury provides effective "screening" or acts more as a "rubber stamp of the prosecutor" is a matter of considerable dispute. The Court nevertheless has refused to review the evidence before a grand jury to ensure that the grand jury properly performed its screening function in issuing an indictment. *Costello v. U. S.,* 350 U.S. 359 (1956).

As we noted previously, the requirement of prosecution by grand jury indictment is not incorporated within the Fourteenth Amendment's due process clause and therefore does not apply to the states. *Hurtado v. Cal.* (p. 16). In *Hurtado,* the Court upheld state prosecution via an information (a formal charge issued by the prosecutor) following use of an alternative screening procedure—a preliminary hearing, conducted by a magistrate, at which the prosecution had to justify its information by establishing probable cause to believe the defendant committed the offense charged. The Supreme Court has held, however, that prosecution by information also is acceptable constitutionally without a preliminary hearing or any similar reviewing procedure. *Lem Woon v. Or.,* 229 U.S. 586 (1913). Due process does not require that there be an independent determination by a magistrate or grand jury that there is sufficient evidence to justify prosecution. (However, where a person is arrested without a warrant and subjected to "extended restraint on liberty following his arrest," the Fourth Amendment requires a prompt ex parte probable cause determination by a magistrate. *Gerstein v. Pugh*, p. 133).

Despite the absence of a constitutional mandate, almost all states provide for the screening of felony cases by preliminary hearing or grand jury review, and many states use both procedures. Either process, once provided, must meet constitutional standards of due process and equal protection. Thus, the Court has held that the grand jury cannot be selected on a racially discriminatory basis. *Cassell v. Texas,* 339 U.S. 282 (1950). See also *Coleman v. Ala.* (p. 360) requiring appointed counsel at a preliminary hearing).

Joinder of offenses. Where a defendant allegedly has violated several criminal statutes, local law commonly determines whether the prosecutor may or must bring those charges in a single prosecution or in separate prosecutions. Most often, local law grants the prosecutor the option to bring either separate prosecutions or a single prosecution when the several charges arose from the same criminal episode. However, in such cases, the Fifth Amendment's double jeopardy prohibition is likely to have a substantial influence on the prosecutor's exercise of his discretion. While the double jeopardy clause does not directly mandate that different charges be joined in the same prosecution, it has that effect when it prohibits the prosecutor from subsequently presenting those charges that are not joined in the initial prosecution. Indeed, two separate double jeopardy doctrines can have that effect since both bar successive prosecutions under some circumstances.

Initially, successive prosecutions may be barred by the Fifth Amendment's basic prohibition against repeated jeopardy for the "same offense." A particular course of conduct may violate two distinct state criminal provisions, but those provisions may nevertheless be considered part of the "same offense" under the double jeopardy clause. The test to be applied "to determine whether there are two offenses or only one" is that set forth in *Blockburger v. U. S.*, 284 U.S. 299 (1932). Very simply, it is "whether each [criminal] provision requires proof of an additional fact which the other does not." An obvious illustration of separate provisions that are part of the same offense are the higher and lower degrees of the same crime (e. g., first degree and second degree homicide). However, the two provisions need not be part of a formal degree classification system in order to constitute one offense under the *"Blockburger* test." In *Brown v. Ohio*, 432 U.S. 161 (1977), for example, the Court found theft of a vehicle and joyriding in that vehicle were part of the same offense since, as defined by Ohio law, theft was simply joyriding with an additional element (an intent to permanently deprive the owner of the property). On the other hand, by carefully defining the elements of each offense, the state can, consistent with *Blockburger,* divide a single course of action relating to a single subject into a series of separate offenses. See, e. g., *Gore v. U. S.,* 357 U.S. 386 (1956) (sale of narcotics could constitute separate offenses of sale without a prescription, sale in an unstamped package, and sale with knowledge of illegal importation, because each crime required an element not included in the others).

If separate statutory violations produced by a single course of conduct are part of the same offense under *Blockburger*, the double jeopardy bar ordinarily will force the prosecutor to choose between charging both violations in a single prosecution or relinquishing the charge not brought in that prosecution. Unless there is a waiver by a defense request for separate trials or opposition to consolidation, see *Jeffers v. U. S.,* 432 U.S. 137 (1977), a separate prosecution on the second charge will be barred without regard to whether that charge is higher or lower than the charge originally brought. Thus, in *Brown v. Ohio,* supra, after defendant was prosecuted and convicted of joyriding, he could not be prosecuted for the higher offense of theft of a vehicle. Similarly, in *Harris v. Okla.,* 433 U.S. 682 (1972), after defendant was convicted of felony murder for a murder committed in the course of an armed robbery, he could not be prosecuted for the lesser, predicate felony of armed robbery. Though a single prosecution in such cases would permit the presentation of both charges, it should be noted that state law traditionally will bar cumulative sentences; the maximum sentence will be limited to that available for the highest offense on which a conviction is obtained. Indeed, several Supreme Court opinions suggest, in dictum, that this traditional limitation is constitutionally required since the double jeopardy clause bars not only multiple prosecutions, but also "multiple punishments" for the "same offense." *Simpson v. U. S.,* 435 U.S. 6 (1978). In *Whalen v. U. S.,* —— U.S. —— (1980), however, the four justices who reached that issue argued that the state could, if it chose, authorize cumulative punishments for violations of separate statutes that are part of the "same offense" under the *Blockburger* test. The justices maintained that the double jeopardy definition of the "same offense" differed as to multiple prosecutions and multiple punishments, and in the latter context, the legislature could define offenses so as to recognize the need for multiple punishments for compounded violations (e. g., rape and felony murder based on the rape) even though those violations could not be charged in seperate prosecutions.

A second double jeopardy doctrine—the collateral estoppel doctrine—primarily affects joinder of violations that are separate offenses under *Blockburger,* but arise out of the same criminal episode. Here again, the Constitution does not require joinder, but may bar prosecution for the offense not included in the first prosecution. The collateral estoppel doctrine was recognized as an aspect of double jeopardy in *Ashe v. Swenson*, 397 U.S. 436 (1970). The doctrine bars prosecution on a second offense where the defendant was previously acquitted on a factually related offense and that acquittal was based on a factual element that is also an essential element of the second offense. Thus, in *Ashe*, a defendant charged with robbing the initial victim in a single, multi-victim robbery, and acquitted by the jury on the ground that he had not been present at the robbery, could not subsequently be prosecuted on a charge of robbing the next victim. As the Court noted, the effect of the collateral estoppel doctrine is to prevent the prosecutor from "treat[ing] the first trial as no more than a dry run for [a] second prosecution" on the related charge. A prosecutor cannot afford to present less than his strongest case on the first charge in anticipation that his evidence can always be strengthened on the second charge. If the first prosecution results in an acquittal, collateral estoppel may well bar a second prosecution on the related charge.

It should be emphasized that where the offenses are separate, as in *Ashe*, separate prosecutions present no problem if the prosecutor obtains convictions on each offense (and therefore avoids the collateral estoppel bar). In *Ciucci v. Ill.*, 356 U.S. 571 (1958), exactly that pattern was presented in a case in which the defendant had killed several people in the same criminal episode. When the conviction for the killing of the first victim did not result in the requested death sentence, the prosecutor returned with separate charges on a second killing, and then on a third, where the death sentence finally was obtained. Relying on a due process analysis in a pre-incorporation opinion, the Court found no constitutional violation. In *Ashe,* Justice Brennan, in a concurring opinion, took a position that would have overruled *Ciucci.* He argued the double jeopardy clause should require the prosecution, "except in most limited circumstances, to join at one trial all the charges against a defendant which grow out of a single criminal act, occurrence, episode or transaction." This position has been criticized on the ground, inter alia, that it goes far beyond the "same offense" language of the double jeopardy clause. *Ashe v. Swenson* (Burger, C. J., dis.). The Supreme Court has had various opportunities to adopt Justice Brennan's "same transaction" rule, but it has consistently refused to do so. See *Brown v. Ohio,* supra. Several states have adopted that rule, however, as required under state double jeopardy provisions. See, e. g., *P. v. White,* 212 N.W.2d 222 (Mich.1973).

Joinder of parties. Where several persons have participated in a single offense or a series of related offenses, state law ordinarily grants the prosecutor discretion to prosecute them jointly or separately. In at least one situation, where the prosecutor desires to use a confession of one of the participants, the prosecutor's exercise of discretion is likely to be influenced by constitutional limitations. *Bruton v. U. S.,* 391 U.S. 123 (1968), held that where the confession of one co-defendant contains references to a second co-defendant, and the confessor refuses to take the stand, the use of that confession in a joint trial violates the second co-defendant's Sixth Amendment right of confrontation even though the jury had been informed that the confession constitutes admissible evidence only against the confessor. While *Bruton* does not bar joinder of accomplices where the prosecution intends to use a confession, it imposes as a significant price the deletion of the confession's prejudicial references to the other accomplice, which often will substantially undercut the effectiveness of the confession as evidence against the confessor. But see *Parker v. Randolph,* 442 U.S. 62 (1979) (*Bruton* did not require reversal where the state used interlocking confessions by each of the joined defendants and proper limiting instructions were given).

While dealing only with the confession issue, *Bruton* suggests a potential constitutional basis for other challenges to joint trials where prejudicial evidence against one co-defendant does not apply to his joined accomplices. *Bruton* expressed considerable doubt as to the capacity of the jury to follow instructions that it disregard the references to the second defendant in the first defendant's confession.

If this concern is extended to the jury's ability to keep separate other types of evidence, the Court may well recognize at least minimal constitutional restraints on joinder, particularly where the prosecution intends to use highly inflammatory evidence applicable only to one co-defendant. Relying on non-constitutional grounds, courts have held that a severance is required where evidence introduced against one joined defendant has no relevance to offenses charged against other defendants. *Kotteakos v. U. S.*, 328 U.S. 750 (1946). Joinder also may be barred by the defendant's Sixth Amendment right to present evidence (see p. 76) where he can show that his alleged accomplice would testify on his behalf at a severed trial, but would exercise his privilege to refuse to testify in a joint trial. *U. S. v. Vigil*, 561 F.2d 1316 (9th Cir. 1977).

Location of the prosecution. In federal cases the prosecutor's discretion regarding the location of the prosecution is limited by Article III, § 2, which requires trial in the state where the offense "shall have been committed," and the Sixth Amendment, which guarantees an impartial jury "of the state and district wherein the crime shall have been committed." In applying these limitations, the Court has relied heavily on Congressional designation of the place or places where a particular offense "is committed," since what acts constitute the commission depends largely on the legislative definition of the offense. Congress, in turn, has provided for quite extensive prosecutorial discretion, which has been accepted without significant constitutional objection. For example, where the use of an agency of interstate commerce (e. g., a common carrier) is an element of the offense, prosecution has been authorized in any state through which the agency passed. *Armour Packing Co. v. U. S.,* 209 U.S. 56 (1908); *U. S. v. Johnson,* 323 U.S. 273 (1944).

The Supreme Court has not had occasion since the selective incorporation of the jury trial guarantee to determine whether that guarantee imposes any special limits on state choice of venue. Serious difficulties are not likely to arise since state law traditionally requires prosecution in that state judicial district (e. g. county) in which the offense was "committed."

Timing of the prosecution. Prosecutorial discretion relating to the timing of the prosecution is limited by the Sixth Amendment requirement that "the accused shall enjoy the right to a speedy trial." The Court has held that denial of this right automatically requires dismissal of the delayed prosecution with prejudice; the impact of the denial is too diffuse to permit trial courts to seek to tailor the remedy (e. g., by reducing defendant's sentence) to the hardship caused in the particular case. *Strunk v. U. S.,* 412 U.S. 434 (1973). Flexibility has been the governing philosophy, however, in

determining whether delay constitutes a denial of
the right.   Thus, the leading speedy trial decision,
Barker v. Wingo, 407 U.S. 514 (1972), rejected what
it described as "inflexible approaches" (e. g., imposing a specific time limitation) in favor of "a
balancing test, in which the conduct of both the
prosecution and the defendant are weighed."   *Barker* listed four factors to be considered in the
individual case: (1) length of delay; (2) the government's justification for the delay; (3) whether and
how the defendant asserted his right to a speedy
trial; and (4) prejudice caused by the delay, such as
lengthened pretrial incarceration, lengthened anxi-
ety, and possible impairment of the presentation of a
defense.   In balancing these factors, the Court
suggested that while a defense demand for a speedy
trial was not essential, the absence of a demand
would work strongly against the defendant who
had counsel. The speedy trial right, it noted, was
unlike most other constitutional rights in that the
"deprivation of the right may work to the accused's
advantage," and it could not be assumed that
defendant wanted a speedy trial, delay being a "not
uncommon defense tactic."   The absence of a defense
demand played a large role in sustaining the delay of
over five years in *Barker* (throughout most of that
period, Barker had not objected to continuances since
he was at large on bail and was hopeful that charges
would be dropped if the ongoing prosecution of his
accomplice eventually resulted in an acquittal).

Most of the speedy trial cases before the Court have involved lengthy delays following defense demands for a prompt trial, and the primary emphasis has been on evaluating the cause for the delay. While each ruling has been tied to the facts of the particular case, the decisions clearly indicate that the state must offer some affirmative justification, not merely the absence of a deliberate attempt to pressure the defendant. Thus, *Smith v. Hooey,* 393 U.S. 374 (1969), and *Dickey v. Fla.,* 398 U.S. 30 (1970), found a constitutional violation where the state failed to make any effort to respond to the demand of a defendant, then serving a federal sentence, for a prompt trial on pending state charges. The state's failure to even request that federal officials make the defendant available could not be justified by its lack of authority to compel such cooperation. Neither could its failure be justified on the ground that the cost of transporting the prisoner would have had to be borne by the state. On the other hand, in *Barker,* supra, the Court had no difficulty in upholding that portion of the delay that was due to the illness of the chief investigating officer, though that delay occurred after defense counsel first began to object to continuances.

The speedy trial guarantee protects the defendant only against undue delay between the initiation of prosecution and trial. *U. S. v. Marion,* 404 U.S. 307 (1971). See also *Dillingham v. U. S.,* 423 U.S. 64

(1975) (prosecution is initiated, for speedy trial purposes, with the filing of formal charges or the arrest and holding of the defendant for the purpose of filing charges). However, undue delay between the completion of the crime and the institution of prosecution can constitute a violation of due process. *U. S. v. Lovasco,* 431 U.S. 783 (1977) . To establish such a due process violation, defense must show initially that the prosecution had sufficient evidence to institute prosecution at an earlier point, and that the delay resulted in actual trial prejudice (e. g., the loss of favorable witnesses). *U. S. v. Lovasco,* 431 U.S. 783 (1977). In addition, the court must find that the reasons for the delay were so unjustifiable as to "deviate from 'fundamental conceptions of justice.'" Id. *Lovasco,* supra, held that that standard was not violated where the delay was due to the prosecutor's desire "to await the results of additional investigation" which might identify other participants in the offense. Due process apparently would be violated if the prosecution delayed solely because it hoped to gain a tactical advantage through the defendant's loss of evidence over the period of the delay. *U. S. v. Marion,* supra.

Defendant's choice of plea. Following the filing of the information or indictment, the defendant is "arraigned"; that is, he is advised of the formal charges against him and is called upon to enter his plea—guilty, nolo contendere (where permitted), or not guilty. The Court has long recognized that the

defendant's choice of plea is often the most crucial
decision he makes, particularly if he enters a plea of
guilty (as occurs in 70–85% of the felony cases reaching the arraignment stage in most jurisdictions). Accordingly, it has stressed the need for ensuring that his
choice represents a free and reasoned response to
the charges, and several constitutional provisions
have been construed to serve that end. Thus, the
Sixth Amendment requirement that the defendant
"be informed of the nature and cause of the
accusation" has been viewed as requiring, at a
minimum, that the indictment or information be
sufficiently specific in describing the charges to
permit the defendant to enter a reasoned plea
thereto. *Russell v. U. S.,* 369 U.S. 749 (1962).
Similarly, the Sixth Amendment right to the
assistance of counsel, including the indigent defendant's right to the services of court-appointed counsel,
has been held to require assistance in determination
of plea as well as at trial. See *White v. Md.* (p. 359)
and *Von Moltke v. Gillies* (p. 373).

Acceptance of a guilty plea. The defendant's
free choice of plea is also protected by the
long-standing constitutional prohibition against acceptance of guilty pleas that are not "voluntary."
This prohibition has been imposed pursuant to the
due process clause and has been likened by the Court
to the prohibition against admission of involuntary
confessions. *Waley v. Johnston,* 316 U.S. 101 (1942).
Application of the voluntariness standard largely

rests on a "totality of circumstances" analysis similar to that employed in determining the voluntariness of confessions (see § 25), although certain factors might be given somewhat different weight as applied to guilty pleas. See, e. g., *N. C. v. Alford*, (p. 45). Since a plea reflects a waiver of various trial rights, voluntariness necessarily includes, in addition to the absence of coercion, awareness of what is being relinquished. *Brady v. U. S.*, (p. 46).

The voluntariness requirement imposes a duty upon the trial judge to ensure that the guilty plea is made knowingly and without coercion. The Court has emphasized that the scope of that duty, like the definition of voluntariness itself, is governed by constitutional standards. However, the leading cases on this point, *Boykin v. Ala.*, 395 U.S. 238 (1969), and *Henderson v. Morgan*, 426 U.S. 637 (1976), are quite limited in their holdings. *Boykin* held only that the judge's duty was not fulfilled where, "so far as the record shows, the judge asked no questions of the [defendant] concerning his plea and [defendant] did not address the court." The guilty plea record, the Court noted, should clearly establish a knowing waiver of the constitutional rights relinquished by pleading guilty, particularly the rights to a jury trial, to confront one's accusers, and to refuse to testify at trial. While many jurisdictions require the trial judge to inform the defendant of these rights and others, see e. g., Fed.R.Crim.P. 11, various courts have held that the "specific articulation of the *Boykin* rights is not a sine qua non of a valid guilty plea." *Wilkins v. Erickson,* 505 F.2d 761 (9th Cir. 1974). The crucial issue is whether the record as a whole affirmatively establishes that the defendant entered his plea understandingly.

Henderson v. Morgan, supra, held that the record did not establish an understanding plea to second degree murder where the elements of that offense were not charged in the indictment, neither the defense lawyers nor the trial court explained to defendant that the offense required an intent to kill, and the defendant's version of the offense, as explained by counsel, stressed that he "meant no harm" to the victim. *Henderson* did not go so far as to require that the judge inform the defendant of the major elements of the offense, although many trial courts follow that practice. See, e. g., Fed. R.Crim.P. 11; *Von Moltke v. Gillies* (p. 373). Neither did it state the judge must determine that there is a factual basis for the plea, although many jurisdictions require that the trial court make such a determination. See Fed.R.Crim.P. 11. *N. C. v. Alford,* 400 U.S. 25 (1970), did suggest that a finding of a factual basis is necessary where the defendant desires to plead guilty, but claims that he is innocent. *Alford* found no constitutional violation in the acceptance of a plea from a defendant who claimed to be innocent where (1) the defendant desired to enter the plea to a lesser offense to avoid the possibility of a substantially harsher penalty (the death sentence) on a higher offense and (2) the trial court had received a summary of the state's case which contained "strong evidence of actual guilt." The defendant's position as to his innocence was not substantially different from that of a defendant who pleads nolo contendere, and the "strong factual basis" indicated that the "plea was being intelligently entered."

Negotiated pleas. Prior to the decision in *Brady v. U. S.*, 397 U.S. 742 (1970), some uncertainty existed as to the voluntariness of a guilty plea that was the product of "plea bargaining"—i. e., a negotiated arrangement under which the defendant pleads guilty in return for certain concessions, such as the reduction of charges or the promise of a more lenient sentence. *Brady* did not itself involve a negotiated plea, but a plea entered by defendant pursuant to a statutory scheme [held unconstitutional in *U. S. v. Jackson* (p. 56)] under which the defendant could avoid a potential death penalty by pleading guilty. However, in discussing the validity of Brady's plea, the Court analogized his plea to a negotiated plea. The Supreme Court had long held that a confession was involuntary if induced by promises of lenient treatment, and it was argued in *Brady* that the same standard should apply to guilty pleas. The *Brady* opinion rejected that contention, noting that the defendant there was represented by counsel and had "full opportunity to assess the

[46]

advantages and disadvantages of a trial as compared with those attending a plea of guilty." The Court noted also that to reject all pleas induced by promises of more lenient treatment would be, in large part, to "forbid guilty pleas altogether." It stressed that the granting of concessions to those pleading guilty was consistent with the administrative as well as rehabilitative goals of the criminal justice system. The state was "extend[ing] a benefit to a defendant who in turn extends a substantial benefit to the state and who demonstrates by his plea that he is ready and willing to admit his crime and to enter the correctional system in a frame of mind which affords hope for success in rehabilitation over a shorter period of time than might otherwise be necessary." Guilty pleas could not be treated as involuntary simply because they were "motivated by the defendant's desire to accept the certainty * * * of a lesser penalty rather than * * * [a trial that might result in] conviction and a higher penalty."

While upholding negotiated pleas in general, *Brady* clearly indicated that such pleas could still be involuntary under particular circumstances. The *Brady* opinion noted, for example, that a plea would not be voluntary if "induced by threats (or promises to discontinue improper harassment), misrepresentation (including unfulfilled or unfulfillable promises), or perhaps by promises that are by their nature improper as having no proper relationship to the prosecutor's business (e. g., bribes)." *Brady v. U. S., supra.* The opinion also suggested that a plea would be subject to attack if the defendant was unaware of the "actual value of any commitment made to him by the court, prosecutor, or his own counsel." Later cases have been concerned primarily with the application of these standards. In *Santobello v. N. Y.,* 404 U.S. 257 (1971), the Court held a negotiated plea invalid where the plea was based on an unfulfilled promise. The prosecutor there had inadvertently failed to keep his promise to make no recommendation concerning defendant's sentence. The Court left open the further issue as to whether an appropriate remedy in such a case might be resentencing with enforcement of the promise as opposed to withdrawal of the plea (the traditional remedy for involuntary pleas).

In *Bordenkircher v. Hayes,* 434 U.S. 357 (1978), the Court dealt with the nature of improper threats that induce a guilty plea. In that case, the prosecutor charged defendant with a crime that carried a sentence of five years imprisonment, but noted at the outset that a recidivist charge, carrying a mandatory sentence of life imprisonment, would be added if the defendant did not plead guilty to the initial charge. The Court held that this was not a situation suggesting a vindictive attempt by the prosecutor to punish the defendant for exercising his right to demand a trial. Rather, it reflected the "give and take" of plea bargaining, with the prosecutor agreeing to forego a legitimate recidivist charge to produce the "mutuality of advantage" of a negotiated plea. The *Bordenkircher* opinion stressed that the defendant, represented by counsel, was "presumptively capable of intelligent choice in response to prosecutor persuasion." Some lower courts have suggested that the same is not true where the trial judge engages in plea negotiation with the defense because of the "unequal positions of the judge and the accused." *U. S. ex rel. Elksnis v. Gilligan,* 256 F.Supp. 244 (S.D.N.Y.1966). Compare *U. S. ex rel. Rosa v. Follette,* 395 F.2d 721 (2d Cir. 1968) (judicial participation "does not in itself render the plea involuntary"). The Supreme Court has not yet reached this issue.

The Court has not further explored the *Brady* suggestion that defendant must appreciate the "actual value" of the concessions granted in return for his guilty plea, but *McMann v. Richardson* (p. 299) suggests that the crucial issue here may be the competency of counsel. *McMann* considered the bearing of a misapprehension as to the strength of the prosecutor's case upon the voluntariness of a plea. If counsel was competent, the Court noted, the plea was not subject to attack even though the misapprehension was due to a subsequent change in the law that counsel could not readily have anticipated. The defendant chose to take "the benefits, if any, of a plea of guilty" rather than risk a trial. In making that decision, he accepted "the inherent risk that good-faith evaluations of a reasonably competent attorney will turn out to be mistaken either as to the facts or as to what a court's judgment might be on given facts."

Pretrial discovery. The Sixth Amendment requires that the defendant "be informed of the nature and cause of the accusation" against him. This requirement has application primarily to the indictment or information, which must identify the offense charged and "sufficiently apprise the defendant of what he must be prepared to meet." *Russell v. U. S.,* 369 U.S. 749 (1962). That standard commonly is met by a concise statement in the indictment or information of the essential facts constituting the offense charged. *U. S. v. Debrow,* 346 U.S. 374 (1953). Pretrial notice of the specific prosecution evidence that will be offered to establish those facts ordinarily comes through pretrial discovery procedures.

While all jurisdictions provide the defense with some pretrial discovery, the scope of that discovery varies widely. Compare, e. g., Fed.R.Crim.P. 16 with Fla.R.Crim.P. 3.220. As currently interpreted, the Constitution grants the states considerable flexibility in determining the appropriate scope of pretrial discovery. The Supreme Court has noted that, "in some circumstances, it may be a denial of due process for a defendant to be refused any discovery of his statements to the police." *Clewis v. Texas,* 386 U.S. 707 (1967). However, in the only two cases involving a state's refusal to afford such discovery, due process objections were rejected on the ground that there was "no showing of prejudice." Id. A constitutional grounding for pretrial discovery also has been suggested in a series of cases, described at p. 69, requiring prosecution disclosure of exculpatory evidence. These cases have dealt primarily with disclosure at trial, but one of the major cases in the group, *Brady v. Md.,* 373 U.S. 83 (1963), involved a pretrial request for disclosure. Moreover, lower courts have noted that certain types of exculpatory material will be of almost no use to the defendant unless disclosed before trial. Where, for example, the prosecutor knows of a witness who would provide testimony favorable to the accused, and the defense is not likely to be aware of that witness, disclosure of the witness' name at trial may be too late to obtain his testimony. *U. S. v. Gleason,* 265 F.Supp. 880 (S.D.N.Y.1967). In such cases, the prosecutor's constitutional obligation to disclose exculpatory material may impose a constitutional requirement of pretrial discovery that extends beyond the requirements of local law. Cf. *U. S. v. Campagnuolo,* 592 F.2d 852 (5th Cir. 1979).

Many jurisdictions make pretrial discovery, to some extent, a "two way street." They require not only that the prosecution grant discovery to the defense, but that the defense grant discovery to the prosecution. *Williams v. Fla.,* 399 U.S. 78 (1970), upheld a limited form of prosecution pretrial discovery as imposed by a state alibi rule. A divided Court held that the Florida requirement that defendant give advance notice of an alibi defense (including the names and addresses of alibi witnesses) did not violate defendant's privilege against self-incrimination. The majority stressed that the Florida rule only required the defendant to disclose evidence that he intended to produce subsequently at trial, and, if he changed his mind, the rule permitted the defendant to abandon the alibi defense without any harm to his case. Although the opinion was limited to alibi discovery, the majority's analysis of the self-incrimination issue arguably could be extended to uphold provisions granting the prosecution pretrial discovery of various other matters (e. g., scientific reports, expert witnesses) that defendant intends eventually to produce at trial. On the other hand, if the state requires pretrial disclosure of the names of general defense witnesses who are likely to furnish the prosecution with evidence useful in proving its case-in-chief, the *Williams* analysis may not apply. Here the discovery requirement would force defendant to give incriminating leads that it might otherwise not have provided (since the witnesses would not be used if the prosecution failed to establish its case-in-chief). See *Allen v. Superior Ct.,* 557 P.2d 65 (Cal.1976) (rejecting such a discovery requirement). Compare *U. S. v. Nobles,* 422 U.S. 225 (1975) (where a defense investigator testified at trial as to statements made

[52]

to him by prosecution witnesses, permitting prosecution inspection of the investigator's report, for possible impeachment use, did not violate defendant's Fifth Amendment rights since no portion of the report reflected information given to the investigator by the defendant).

Where a state provides for prosecution discovery, *Wardius v. Or.*, 412 U.S. 470 (1973), establishes that it also must provide reciprocal defense discovery. *Wardius* held that due process was violated by an alibi-notice provision that required defense disclosure of its alibi witnesses without requiring the prosecution to make reciprocal disclosure of its alibi rebuttal witnesses. The Court noted that, while the "due process clause has little to say regarding the amount of discovery which the parties must be afforded," it "does speak to the balance of forces between the accused and his accuser." The state "may not insist that trials be run as 'a search for truth' so far as defense witnesses are concerned, while maintaining 'poker game secrecy for its own witnesses.'"

6. THE TRIAL STAGE

Almost half of the Bill of Rights guarantees relating to the criminal justice process specifically refer to trial rights. Also, the due process clause, while it has been applied by the Supreme Court at every stage in the process, probably has had more applications at the trial stage than any other. It is not surprising, therefore, that the trial is one of the two steps in the criminal justice process (the other being the police investigation) that is most closely regulated by constitutional limitations. Indeed, although the trial is used far less frequently than many other steps in the process, it is treated constitutionally very much as the centerpiece of the process.

The right to a jury trial. While the Sixth Amendment declares that an accused shall have the right to a jury trial "in all criminal prosecutions," that provision has always been read in light of the common law tradition which did not provide juries for "petty offenses." *D. C. v. Clawans,* 300 U.S. 617 (1937). An offense may not be characterized as "petty" if it carries a penalty of potential imprisonment in excess of six months, *Baldwin v. N. Y.,* 399 U.S. 66 (1970), but an offense with a lesser penalty also may fall outside the petty offense category depending upon its "moral quality" and its relationship to the common law crimes. *D. C. v. Clawans,* supra. In the case of criminal contempts, which ordinarily are not governed by a statutorily prescribed penalty, the contempt falls outside the petty offense category when the penalty actually imposed exceeds six months imprisonment. *Muniz v. Hoffman,* 422 U.S. 454 (1975). See also *Bloom v. Ill.,* 391 U.S. 194 (1967) (although criminal contempts were treated as a separate species at common law, they are "criminal prosecutions" under the jury trial guarantee).

[54]

Of course, a jurisdiction may grant a more expansive right to a jury trial than required by the Sixth Amendment, and many states currently provide for jury trials for most petty offense cases. A jurisdiction also may grant the prosecutor or the court the right to insist upon a jury trial even where the defendant desires a bench trial. See Fed. R.Crim.P. 23. The defendant's Sixth Amendment right to a jury trial does not carry with it a correlative right to insist upon a trial before a judge alone. *Singer v. U. S.,* 380 U.S. 24 (1965).

Although most jurisdictions provide for a 12 person jury in felony cases, that is not a constitutional requirement. *Williams v. Fla.* (p. 17) upheld the use of a six person jury for non-capital felony cases. The key to constitutional acceptance, the Court noted, was that the jury be large enough to fulfill its traditional functions, i. e., "to promote group deliberation, free from outside attempts at intimidation, and to provide a fair possibility for obtaining a representative cross section of the community." In *Ballew v. Ga.,* 435 U.S. 223 (1978), the Court held that a 5-member jury was too small to serve these functions and therefore was not allowable for a non-petty offense. Placing a similar emphasis on the jury's function, the Court has sustained less than unanimous verdicts (at least for state cases, see pp. 17–18) where state law required sufficient votes for conviction to assure adequate deliberations. See *Apodoca v. La.* (p. 17) (upholding 11–1 and 10–2 felony convictions); *Johnson v. La.,* 406 U.S. 356 (1972) (upholding a 9–3 felony conviction); *Burch v. La.,* 441 U.S. 130 (1979) (rejecting a 5–1 vote for non-petty offenses).

The right to a jury trial, like other trial rights, cannot be subjected to a "needless" burden that has a "chilling effect" on the exercise of that right. *U. S. v. Jackson,* 390 U.S. 570 (1968). *Jackson* held that a federal statute imposed such a burden in providing that the death penalty could be imposed upon a defendant tried before a jury, but not a defendant who had a bench trial or pleaded guilty. While the government had a legitimate interest in having the death sentence imposed only on recommendation of the jury, it could readily fulfill that interest (e. g., by having jury sentencing following bench trials or guilty pleas) without imposing a greater risk on those who selected jury trials. Compare *Corbitt v. N. J.,* 439 U.S. 212 (1978) (*Jackson* did not apply to a statute imposing a mandatory life term for first degree murder upon a conviction at trial, while offering a potential for a lesser term on a plea of non vult or nolo contendere; the statutory scheme here did not reserve a maximum penalty exclusively for those who insisted on a jury trial, but operated, instead, in much the same fashion as a negotiated plea). In *Ludwig v. Mass.,* 427 U.S. 618 (1976), the Court held that the right to a jury trial was not unconstitutionally burdened by a state "two-tier" trial system under which a defendant was not entitled to a jury in his initial trial before a magistrate's court, but then, if convicted, received a trial de novo with a jury before a higher trial court. The Court emphasized that the particular two-tier system before it permitted the defendant to rapidly reach the trial de novo stage, by "admitting sufficient findings of fact" before the magistrate court, and thus did not require defendant to "pursue, in any real sense, a defense at the lower tier."

Jury selection. The Supreme Court has relied upon both the Fourteenth Amendment's equal protection guarantee and the Sixth Amendment right to an "impartial jury" in holding unconstitutional various discriminatory jury selection practices. Long before the Sixth Amendment guarantee was applied to the states, the Court relied on the equal protection guarantee to reject racial discrimination in jury selection. *Strauder v. W. Va.*, 100 U.S. 303 (1880). A long line of cases since then have dealt with the troublesome problem of establishing proof of discrimination where the jury selection system does not, on its face, authorize exclusion on racial grounds. Under these cases, a prima facie case of discrimination is established by showing that only a small percentage of blacks have been called to jury duty despite a much larger percentage in the community. The burden then shifts to the state to prove that this pattern did not result from discrimination. *Turner v. Fouche*, 396 U.S. 346 (1970).

The Court has refused, however, to require states to abandon relevant selection criteria because they are susceptible to manipulation and have been used in the past to achieve racial discrimination, at least where there is "no suggestion" those criteria were "originally adopted or subsequently carried forward for the purpose of fostering racial discrimination." *Carter v. Jury Comm.,* 396 U.S. 320 (1970) (finding unconstitutional discrimination in the individual case, but refusing to hold invalid a statute limiting jury service to persons "esteemed in the community for their integrity, good character, and sound judgment").

Relying on the Sixth Amendment, the Court has gone beyond racial discrimination to hold that a jury's representative function requires that it be selected from a "fair cross-section of the community." *Taylor v. La.,* 419 U.S. 522 (1975). Since this fair cross-section requirement is not tied to the premise that a particular group would be sympathetic toward a particular type of defendant, a defendant may raise the requirement even though not a member of the excluded class of jurors. *Taylor v. La.,* supra (male may object to exclusion of women). The exact scope of the fair cross-section requirement remains somewhat uncertain. *Taylor* held that it was violated by a state practice of excluding females unless they volunteered for jury service. See also *Duren v. Mo.,* 439 U.S. 357 (1979) (*Taylor* applied to a state granting an automatic

exemption to women when all but a small portion of
the women claimed the exemption). *Witherspoon v.
Ill.,* 391 U.S. 510 (1968), a capital case, distinguished
between the jury's sentencing function and its guilt
adjudication function in assessing the constitutionality
of the exclusion of a particular group of jurors. In
that case, the state granted the jury broad discretion
as to imposing capital punishment, but then automatically excluded all prospective jurors who had
"conscientious or religious scruples" against the death
penalty, even though they might be willing to
consider its imposition in the particular case. The
Court held that this exclusion, by producing a jury
composed only of those who were "uncommonly
willing to condemn a man to die," denied defendant
an impartial jury on the sentencing issue. See also
Adams v. Texas, —— U.S. —— (1980) (same exclusion
also invalid where jury had narrower discretion, but
still had authority to evaluate aggravating and
mitigating circumstances relating to capital punishment). On the other hand, the *Witherspoon* Court
also held that the defendant had not been denied a
representative jury on the issue of guilt since there
had been no concrete showing that the excluded
jurors differed from the general populace in their
approach to that issue. In *Hamling v. U. S.,* 418 U.S.
87 (1974), the Court rejected a cross-section objection
on a somewhat different ground. The Court there
ruled that, even if "the young" should be "an
identifiable group entitled to a group-based protec-

tion under * * * prior decisions," the defendant had not been denied a representative jury simply because the jury selection list was compiled every four years and therefore excluded young persons who had become eligible during the interim period. The cross-section requirement, the Court noted, does not deny the government sufficient "play in the joints of the jury selection process" to accommodate "the practical problems of judicial administration."

Once a jury venire is selected from a fair cross-section of the community, the individual jurors must be screened to ensure the jury's impartiality. This screening process ordinarily involves a voir dire of the prospective jurors and the exercise of challenges for cause and peremptory challenges. The constitutional regulation of these procedures is quite limited, and seems to be directed primarily at racial bias. In *Ham v. S. C.,* 409 U.S. 524 (1973), for example, the Court held that a bearded civil rights worker, convicted of marijuana possession, had no constitutional right to insist that the trial judge allow voir dire questions concerning defendant's wearing of a beard. The Court acknowledged that it was possible that one or more potential jurors may have been prejudiced against bearded persons, but it stressed that the state must be allowed to give trial courts "broad discretion" in conducting the voir dire. *Ham* also ruled, however, that possible racial prejudice presented a special problem because, inter alia, a principal purpose of the Fourteenth Amendment was to bar racial discrimination. Thus, in the context of that case, where the defendant also was black and claimed that he had been "framed because of his civil rights activities," due process was violated by the trial court's refusal to allow voir dire questions concerning racial prejudice. Compare *Ristaino v. Ross,* 424 U.S. 589 (1976) (due process did not require racial prejudice questions simply because there was a black defendant and a white victim in a robbery case; those circumstances did not suggest a "significant likelihood that racial prejudice might infect [the] trial"). In *Swain v. Ala.,* 380 U.S. 202 (1965), even possible racial discrimination was held not to violate due process in the use of peremptory challenges. The Court there refused to hold unconstitutional the prosecutor's use of peremptory challenges to strike all prospective black jurors in a case involving a black defendant. The majority stressed that the "essential nature of the peremptory challenge is that it is one exercised without a reason stated, without inquiry, and without being subject to the court's control." It did leave open, however, the possibility that the systematic use of peremptory challenges to exclude blacks from all juries would violate the Fourteenth Amendment.

Trial publicity. Where a case has received considerable newspaper or television publicity, the selection of an impartial jury requires extra care. The Court has never insisted that prospective jurors be totally unaware of all adverse publicity.

Such a standard, it has noted, would be impossible "in those days of swift, widespread, and diverse methods of communications." On the other hand, the jurors must not have been so influenced by the publicity that they cannot put aside any "preconceived notions" and "render a verdict based on the evidence presented in court." *Irvin v. Dowd,* 366 U.S. 717 (1961). The Court's rulings on the impact of prejudicial publicity have tended to be based on the facts of the particular case. *Irvin,* supra, found that extensive and highly prejudicial pretrial publicity had resulted in the selection of a tainted jury. The Court stressed, in particular, the voir dire examination at which several jurors had acknowledged that they were firmly convinced of defendant's guilt. *Rideau v. La.,* 373 U.S. 723 (1963), went a step beyond *Irvin* and reversed a conviction without requiring a particularized showing of juror prejudice. The Court found that "it was a denial of due process * * * to refuse a request for a change in venue" when the entire community has been "exposed repeatedly and in depth" to the "spectacle" of defendant confessing to the crime in a police interview broadcast on local television. *Murphy v. Fla.,* 421 U.S. 794 (1975), on the other hand, held that defendant had not been denied a fair trial even though several jurors had learned from news accounts of his prior crimes. Only about one fourth of the potential jurors examined had to be excused because of firmly set opinions; the voir dire statements of the jurors who were seated revealed no hostility that would cause one to doubt their assurances of impartiality; and the community atmosphere was not "inflammatory."

Estes v. Texas, 381 U.S. 532 (1965), and *Sheppard v. Maxwell*, 384 U.S. 333 (1966), extended the analysis of the pretrial publicity cases to media coverage during the trial. In *Estes,* a divided Court (5–4) held that the Fourteenth Amendment prohibited a state from televising courtroom proceedings over the objection of the defendant. Relying on *Rideau*, the majority found that the likely prejudicial impact of televising on the jury justified reversal of defendant's conviction without showing specific instances of "isolatable prejudice." Indeed, four members of the majority expressed the view that public television of a trial was inherently prejudicial, but the fifth justice limited his concurrence to "criminal trial[s] of great notoriety" such as that involved in *Estes.* In *Sheppard* a more substantial majority relied upon several factors in concluding that massive, highly prejudicial publicity had contributed to a denial of due process. Those factors included the trial judge's failure to provide privacy for the jury, to insulate witnesses from newsmen, and to control various activities of newsmen that contributed substantially to the "carnival atmosphere" of the trial.

In *Sheppard*, the Court suggested that various measures might be taken to limit prejudicial publicity, including a court order directing the prosecutor and

[63]

defense counsel not to make potentially prejudicial statements to the press. Cf. A.B.A. Code of Professional Responsibility, D.R. 7–107 (prohibiting pretrial extra-judicial statements by the prosecutor and defense counsel concerning such matters as defendant's prior record and counsel's opinion as to the "merits of the case"). In *Gannet Co. v. DePasquale,* 443 U.S. 368 (1979), a divided (5–4) Court held that the trial judge also could close a pretrial hearing on the admissibility of the defendant's confession where the defendant requested the closed hearing to avoid a further "buildup of adverse publicity." The Court held that the Sixth Amendment right to a public trial was a personal right of the accused, and did not create a constitutional right of the general public to attend the suppression hearing. Assuming arguendo that the press had a First Amendment right of access—a position urged by Justice Powell, who provided the 5th vote for the majority—the trial court had given appropriate deference to the First Amendment right in concluding that "under the circumstances of this case, that right was outweighed by the defendant's right to a fair trial." Cf. *Richmond Newspapers v. Va.* (p. 67).

If a trial court holds an open suppression hearing, whether or not constitutionally required to do so, *Nebraska Press Ass'n v. Stuart,* 427 U.S. 539 (1976), bars the issuance of a "gag order" prohibiting the press from reporting what occurred at that hearing.

Nebraska Press also rejected a gag order prohibiting pretrial publication of information gained from other sources. Such an order, the Court noted, was subject to the heavy First Amendment presumption against prior restraints, and could not be justified in light of the numerous other measures (e. g., change of venue) that might be taken to ensure that defendant receives a fair trial notwithstanding adverse publicity.

The right to an impartial judge. Just as the Sixth Amendment requires an impartial jury, due process requires an impartial judge, particularly in cases involving a bench trial. *Ward v. Village of Monroeville*, 409 U.S. 57 (1972). However, a judge ordinarily is subject to a due process challenge only if he has a financial interest or some other "personal involvement" in the case. It is not objectionable, for example, that the trial judge presided at a pretrial proceeding and therefore has already considered some of the evidence in the case. *Withrow v. Larkin*, 421 U.S. 35 (1975). It is objectionable, however, that the judge's salary will depend upon the fines he assesses. *Tumey v. Ohio*, 273 U.S. 510 (1927). Similarly, where a contempt charge is based upon defendant's highly personal attack against the trial judge, that judge is constitutionally precluded from presiding at a subsequent non-summary contempt proceeding. *Mayberry v. Pa.*, 400 U.S. 455 (1971). In neither case is it necessary to establish that the judge is in fact prejudiced. The guiding standard on personal involvement, the Court has emphasized, must be the "likelihood or appearance of bias" rather than "proof of actual bias." *Taylor v. Hayes,* 418 U.S. 488 (1974).

The right to a public trial. A trial court's authority to exclude the public from a criminal trial is limited by two constitutional guarantees—the Sixth Amendment right of the accused to a public trial and the First Amendment right of the public and press to attend criminal trials. So far, the Supreme Court has not found it necessary to explore the precise confines of either guarantee. The leading decision on the defendant's Sixth Amendment right is *In re Oliver,* 333 U.S. 257 (1948). *Oliver* involved an unusual closed proceeding—a summary contempt proceeding held before a secret "one-man grand jury"—and the exclusion of the public was only one of several factors cited in holding the proceeding unconstitutional. The Court did stress the "inherent dangers" of a closed proceeding and suggested that total exclusion of spectators (including exclusion of defendant's relatives and friends) would be difficult to justify. Lower court cases since *Oliver* have dealt primarily with defense objections to the exclusion of the general populace from a portion of a criminal trial. Very often relatives of the accused and members of the press have remained in the courtroom during these "closed proceedings." The lower courts usually have upheld such restrictions on public attendance where justificed by a "substantial interest." See

U. S. ex rel. Latimore v. Sielaff, 561 F.2d 691 (7th Cir. 1977) (upholding exclusion of general populace during testimony of young rape victim); *U. S. ex rel. Lloyd v. Vincent,* 520 F.2d 1272 (2d Cir. 1975) (upholding exclusion of all spectators during testimony of undercover narcotics agent). Compare *U. S. v. Kobli,* 172 F.2d 919 (3d Cir. 1949) (general populace could not be excluded from an entire sex offense trial).

Where the defendant requests that the trial be closed and thereby waives his Sixth Amendment right to a public trial, the trial court must balance against that request the constitutional right of the public and press to attend a criminal trial. Relying primarily on the strong historical tradition of public access to trials, *Richmond Newspapers v. Virginia,* —— U.S. —— (1980), held that the right of the public and press to attend trials was implicit in the speech and press guarantees of the First Amendment. The trial judge there had closed the entire trial, upon an unopposed request of the defense, so as to prevent "leaks" to jurors and witnesses of information that was not properly before them. There was no suggestion on the record, however, that such leaks could not have been prevented by alternative remedies, such as sequestering the witnesses and jurors. In holding that the closure order was unconstitutional, the Supreme Court decided only that "a criminal trial itself may [not] be closed to the public, * * * without any demonstration that

[67]

closure is required to protect the defendant's superior right to a fair trial, or that some other overriding consideration requires closure." The several opinions of the justices in the (7–1) majority offered little guidance as to those circumstances that might provide an overriding interest that would justify closure, although it was stressed that the public's right of access was "not absolute." The Court also left open the extent to which the First Amendment right of access might apply to pretrial proceedings, though five justices have indicated that the public has at least a limited constitutional interest in attending those proceedings. See *Gannet Co. v. DePasquale* (p. 64). As *Gannet* illustrates, however, the public's right of access may more readily be overridden in the pretrial proceeding, where alternative means are not likely to be as satisfactory in preventing subsequent prejudice at trial.

The presentation of the prosecution's case. The prosecution is subject to various constitutional limitations in presenting its case. As we shall see shortly, the Constitution restricts the type of evidence the prosecutor may use and sets the standard of proof he must meet. But apart from these limitations, the prosecutor also is subject to several due process requirements relating to his role as the representative of the state, "whose interest in a criminal prosecution is not that it shall win a case, but that justice shall be done." *Berger v. U. S.*, 295 U.S. 78 (1935). First, the prosecutor has an obligation to correct the perjured testimony of a prosecution witness when he knows, or should know from information available to his office, that the testimony is perjured. See, e. g., *Alcorta v. Texas,* 355 U.S. 28 (1963) (where defendant claimed that he killed his wife in a jealous rage, due process was violated by the prosecutor's failure to correct a key witness' testimony suggesting that he had only a casual relationship with the wife, the witness having previously informed the prosecutor of several instances of sexual intercourse); *Giglio v. U. S.,* 405 U.S. 150 (1972) (due process violated when the prosecutor, not realizing that promises had been made by his predecessor, failed to correct a witness' statement that no promises had been made in return for his testimony).

Second, when the defense has requested disclosure of specific evidence and that evidence is "material either to guilt or to punishment" and is "favorable to the accused," due process is violated "irrespective of the good faith or bad faith of the prosecutor" if he fails to make the disclosure. See, e. g., *Brady v. Md.,* 373 U.S. 83 (1963) (failure to disclose requested statement of a co-defendant, material to sentencing, which supported defendant's claim that the co-defendant had actually strangled the victim). In applying this due process requirement, the Court treats the suppressed evidence as "material" to guilt or punishment if its disclosure might have produced a different result. This liberal standard of materiality is justified on the ground that the defense request gives the prosecutor ample notice of the need to consider the possible exculpatory impact of the requested evidence. *U. S. v. Agurs*, infra. Third, where there is no defense request or the request is general (e. g., for "anything exculpatory"), due process is violated by a failure to disclose evidence "obviously of such substantial value to the defense that elementary fairness requires it to be disclosed even without a specific request." *U. S. v. Agurs*, 427 U.S. 97 (1976). In applying this due process requirement, the Court uses a much narrower standard of "materiality"—whether "the omitted evidence creates a reasonable doubt that did not otherwise exist." If the prosecution's case is so weak and the non-disclosed evidence so critical as to meet this test, the prosecution should have been aware of its importance even without the assistance of a defense request for its disclosure.

Finally, in his statements to the jury, particularly in his closing argument, the prosecutor is subject to due process prohibitions against prejudicial and inflammatory remarks. *Donnelly v. DeChristoforo*, 416 U.S. 637 (1974). A constitutional violation will only by found, however, if the improper remarks infected the entire trial with unfairness, as judged in relation to cautionary instructions of the trial court, the general tenor of the trial, and the remainder of the prosecutor's comments. Id. See also *Frazier v. Cupp*, 394 U.S. 731 (1969).

The right of confrontation. The Sixth Amendment right of the defendant "to be confronted with the witnesses against him" plays several roles in the criminal justice process. Initially, it guarantees to the defendant the right to be present at his trial. *Ill. v. Allen*, 397 U.S. 337 (1970). Moreover, the state may not impose an unnecessary burden on that right, such as forcing the defendant, over his objection, to appear in prison garb. *Estelle v. Williams*, 425 U.S. 501 (1976). On the other hand, defendant's right to be present may be lost by consent (e. g., where the defendant absents himself during the trial), *Taylor v. U. S.*, 414 U.S. 17 (1973), and by misconduct (e. g., where the defendant is disruptive), *Ill. v. Allen*, supra. As the Court noted in *Allen*, the right will not be applied in such an absolute fashion as to permit the defendant to undermine the administration of the trial. Thus, where the defendant had continued in his disruptive behavior despite due warning, the trial court acted appropriately in banishing him rather than resorting to less desirable remedies (e. g., binding and gagging him) simply to ensure his physical presence in the courtroom. *Ill. v. Allen*, supra.

The confrontation clause also ensures that defendant is given sufficient leeway in cross-examining prosecution witnesses. While states ordinarily permit sufficiently broad cross-examination, a few state limitations have been held unconstitutional. *Smith v. Ill.*, 390 U.S. 129 (1968), found a constitutional violation when defendant was not allowed to ask the principal prosecution witness, a police informer, either his correct name or address. *Davis v. Alaska*, 415 U.S. 308 (1974), found that the trial judge committed constitutional error in denying defense the opportunity to raise a key witness' juvenile delinquent probationary status. The Court noted that the state has a legitimate interest in protecting the anonymity of juvenile offenders, but that interest could not be utilized to bar cross-examination as to a factor obviously relevant to the witness' possible motivation for testifying. Consider also *Chambers v. Miss.* (p. 77).

The confrontation clause also limits the prosecution's ability to use in evidence statements of persons who do not testify at trial and therefore cannot be cross-examined. Such statements, when offered for their truth, ordinarily constitute hearsay, but they may be admissible under local rules of evidence if they fall within a recognized hearsay exception. The Court has stressed, however, that the crucial question under the confrontation clause is not compliance with common law hearsay rules, but fulfillment of the "mission of the confrontation clause to advance the accuracy of the truth determining process * * * by assuring that the trier of fact has a satisfactory basis for evaluating the truth of a prior statement." *Cal. v. Green*, 399 U.S. 149 (1970). Applying this functional analysis, the Court has concluded that "the confrontation clause operates in two separate ways to restrict the range of admissible hearsay," *Ohio v. Roberts,* —— U.S. —— (1980).

First, the Sixth Amendment imposes a "rule of necessity" as to the non-production of the declarant of a hearsay statement. If the witness whose statement the prosecutor intends to use is available to testify, that witness ordinarily must be produced at trial so he can be cross-examined. Moreover, it will be assumed that the hearsay declarant is available, with the prosecution bearing the burden of establishing that he is, in fact, unavailable. See *Barber v. Page,* 390 U.S. 719 (1968) (the declarant's imprisonment in a federal prison did not establish his unavailability where the state had made no effort to secure his appearance through the cooperation of federal prison authorities); *Mancusi v. Stubbs,* 408 U.S. 204 (1972) (declarant's permanent transfer to a foreign country did establish unavailability when there was no established means for compelling his appearance); *Ohio v. Roberts,* supra (prosecution must show a "good-faith effort" to locate missing declarant). Though generally applicable, the rule of necessity is not an absolute rule. Under exceptional circumstances, "the utility of trial confrontation [may be] so remote that it [does] not require the prosecution to produce a seemingly available witness." Id. See *Dutton v. Evans,* 400 U.S. 74 (1970) (prosecution could use hearsay comment of apparently available co-conspirator where the comment was not "crucial," defense fully challenged a fellow prisoner's recollection of the comment, and surrounding circumstances provided particularly strong indicia of the reliability of the comment).

The second confrontation clause limitation on the use of hearsay applies to statements of declarants shown to be unavailable. Here, a hearsay statement may be used if the statement was made under circumstances providing sufficient "indicia of reliability" so that admission without current confrontation will nevertheless "comport with the substance of the constitutional protection." *Ohio v. Roberts,* supra. Applying this standard, the Court has held admissible prior trial testimony of a currently unavailable witness. *Mancusi v. Stubbs,* supra. The fact that the statement was made under oath and subject to cross-examination at a prior trial provides sufficient indicia of reliability to justify admission where current cross-examination is impossible due to the witness' unavailability. *Cal. v. Green,* supra, similarly held that the prior preliminary hearing testimony of an unavailable witness could be admitted where defense counsel's cross-examination at that hearing "was not significantly limited in any way." See also *Ohio v. Roberts,* supra (prior preliminary hearing testimony admissible, though witness had been called by defense at that hearing, when defense counsel's extensive questioning of the obviously hostile witness was the equivalent of cross-examination); *Pointer v. Texas,* 380 U.S. 400 (1965) (confrontation clause barred use or preliminary hearing testimony where defendant lacked counsel at the hearing and therefore did not have an adequate opportunity for cross-examination). Both *Cal. v. Green* and *Ohio v. Roberts* rejected the contention that preliminary hearing testimony should be distinguished from prior trial testimony because defense counsel has less incentive to cross-examine at a preliminary hearing. They left open, however, whether such testimony can be admitted where defense counsel did not actually engage in extensive cross-examination at the hearing, but was given an adequate opportunity for cross-examination.

Perhaps the most unique application of the confrontation clause has been to the out-of-court presentation of information to the jury. We have already seen, in the cases involving prejudicial pretrial publicity (p. 61), that adverse information obtained by the jurors outside of the trial process can require their disqualification. Here, however, the analysis starts with those presenting the information, who are treated as witnesses not subject to confrontation. Thus, in *Parker v. Gladden*, 385 U.S. 363 (1966), where a bailiff expressed his personal opinion as to defendant's guilt and told the jurors that the Supreme Court would rectify an improper guilty verdict, the Court held that defendant had been denied the right of confrontation since the bailiff had become, in effect, a secret witness. Compare *Turner v. La.,* 379 U.S. 466 (1965), where the Court relied solely on the impartial jury rationale in reversing a conviction when two deputy sheriffs, who were key prosecution witnesses, were placed in charge of the jury and fraternized with them throughout the trial.

The right to compulsory process. The Court has decided only one major case relying directly upon the defendant's Sixth Amendment right to "have compulsory process for obtaining witnesses in his favor." *Washington v. Texas,* 388 U.S. 14 (1967), held that the defendant's right to compulsory process was violated by a state statute prohibiting one co-participant in an alleged offense from testifying on behalf of the other participant (although allowing him to testify against the other participant). The statute presented in *Washington* was unique, but two closely related due process decisions could lead to future compulsory process rulings having a far more significant impact upon trial practice. In *Webb v. Texas,* 409 U.S. 95 (1972), the Court held that due process was violated where the trial judge used such "unnecessarily strong terms" in warning a key defense witness about the consequences of perjury that he "effectively drove the witness off the stand." The *Webb* decision quoted extensively from *Washington,* and it may provide the foundation for a Sixth Amendment prohibition against various state practices that unnecessarily discourage witnesses from testifying for the defense. *U. S. v. Thomas,* 488 F.2d 334 (6th Cir. 1973) (involving prosecutor threats).

Chambers v. Miss., 410 U.S. 284 (1973), found a due process violation in the combined impact of two state court rulings that sharply restricted the defendant from bringing before the jury evidence that another person (McDonald) had confessed to committing the crime for which defendant was charged. The trial court had refused on hearsay grounds to admit the testimony of third persons who had heard McDonald confess, and when defendant called McDonald as his own witness, the trial court refused to permit defense cross-examination on the ground that a party vouches for the credibility of his own witnesses. While relying on due process, the Court's opinion suggested that the first ruling might well have violated the compulsory process clause. It indicated that reliance on the hearsay rule did not automatically justify cutting off defendant's opportunity to introduce crucial testimony, particularly where the state relied on a questionable distinction in refusing to apply a hearsay exception. The opinion similarly suggested that the second ruling might have violated the confrontation clause by unduly restricting the defendant's right to cross-examine an obviously "adverse witness." (Under the circumstances of *Chambers,* the defendant's impeachment of his own witness arguably might be encompassed as well by his right to present evidence). So far, the Sixth Amendment implications of *Chambers* have not been developed by the lower courts. To a large extent, they have viewed *Chambers* as limited by the special cir-

cumstances of that case. *Lipinsky v. N. Y.,* 557
F.2d 289 (2d Cir. 1977).

Self-incrimination. The Fifth Amendment privilege against self-incrimination permits the defendant to refuse to take the stand at trial. Most
of the Supreme Court cases concerning this right
have dealt with incidental aspects of its administration. *Griffin v. Cal.,* 380 U.S. 609 (1965), rejecting the traditional practice of many states, held
that the privilege barred any adverse comment by
court or prosecutor on the defendant's failure to
take the stand. The privilege would be undermined,
the Court noted, if the jury was, in effect, invited to
draw an adverse conclusion from the defendant's
failure to testify. Consistent with *Griffin,* the trial
court may give a "protective instruction" advising
the jury that defendant's silence must be disregarded, and *Lakeside v. Or.,* 435 U.S. 333 (1978),
held that such an instruction may be given even over
the objection of defense counsel. In *Brooks v.
Tenn.,* 406 U.S. 605 (1972), the Court, as in *Griffin,*
found that a state practice imposed an unconstitutional burden on the defendant's exercise of his
right not to testify. *Brooks* held invalid a state law
requiring a "defendant desiring to testify" to do so
"before any other testimony for the defense is
heard." The effect of the statute was to force the
defendant to make his choice as to whether to
testify before he had heard the testimony of his
witnesses. The Court acknowledged that the state

has a legitimate interest in ensuring that a defendant not color his testimony to conform to the prior testimony of defense witnesses, but "pressuring the defendant to take the stand, by [otherwise] foreclosing later testimony [was] not a constitutionally permissible means of insuring his honesty."

Proof beyond a reasonable doubt. The prosecution's obligation to establish the defendant's guilt by "proof beyond a reasonable doubt" is a universally accepted principle of our criminal justice process. Indeed, until the applicability of the reasonable doubt standard to juvenile proceedings was questioned in *In re Winship*, 397 U.S. 358 (1970), the Court had found no need to determine whether that standard had a constitutional basis. In holding that the reasonable doubt standard applied to juvenile proceedings, the *Winship* opinion initially noted that the standard did have a constitutional foundation in criminal cases, being an essential element of due process. *Winship* opened the door to the challenge of various elements of the trial process as allegedly inconsistent with the reasonable doubt standard. Several cases, for example, have considered the constitutionality of jury instructions that might be viewed as inconsistent with the reasonable doubt standard. In evaluating such claims, the Court has stressed that the particular language challenged must be viewed in the context of the overall charge. *Cupp v. Naughten*, 414 U.S. 141 (1973). Thus, while a charge on the presumption of innocence provides "significant additional guidance" to the jury in applying the reasonable doubt standard, the Court has found, considering the total instruction (and other aspects of the case), that the failure to give that charge violated due process in one case but not in another. Compare *Ky. v. Whorton,* 441 U.S. 786 (1979); *Taylor v. Ky.,* 436 U.S. 478 (1978). The reasonable doubt standard also has served as the constitutional basis for challenges to a trial or appellate court's review of the sufficiency of the evidence (where the standard is whether "there was sufficient evidence to justify a rational trier of the facts to find guilt beyond a reasonable doubt"). *Jackson v. Va.,* 443 U.S. 307 (1979).

7. POST–TRIAL PROCEDURES

Sentencing. The Supreme Court consistently has held that the sentencing process, while not "immune" from the restrictions of due process, is subject to considerably less extensive procedural requirements than the trial process. That conclusion has been based, in part, on the historical separation of the trial and sentencing stages, as reflected in many constitutional guarantees that clearly refer only to the trial. It also has been justified on the ground that fulfillment of the basic objectives of sentencing, particularly the emphasis on relating punishment to the individual as well as the crime, often requires more flexible procedures than those applied to the determination of guilt. Thus, in

Williams v. Okla., 358 U.S. 576 (1959), the Court held that a sentencing judge could "consider responsible unsworn or 'out-of-court' information relative to the circumstances of the crime and to the convicted person's life and characteristics." And, in *Williams v. N. Y.,* 337 U.S. 241 (1949), it held that the defendant had no constitutional right to an adversary sentencing proceeding in which he could cross-examine persons who had supplied information to the court. Consider also *U. S. v. Grayson,* 438 U.S. 41 (1978) (in considering "the defendant's whole person and personality," the sentencing judge may give consideration to defendant's untruthfulness in his trial testimony, notwithstanding defendant's complaint that he has never been indicted, tried, or convicted for the alleged perjury).

While recognizing that sentencing is different, the Court has not automatically assumed that basic procedural rights are inconsistent with sentencing objectives. It has analyzed separately the role of each right and the particular context in which it is raised. Under this approach, several procedural guarantees have been held applicable to the sentencing stage. Thus, *Mempa v. Rhay* (p. 363) established that the indigent defendant's Sixth Amendment right to appointed counsel applies to the sentence-setting proceeding, even where the trial court delayed setting the prison sentence until after defendant violated his initial sentence of probation. *Gagnon v. Scarpelli* (p. 364) further held that, while a probation revocation proceeding is not itself part of the "criminal prosecution" governed by the Sixth Amendment, due process requires the appointment of counsel when the issues presented at that proceeding indicate that counsel's assistance will be needed to obtain a fair hearing. *Morrissey v. Brewer,* 408 U.S. 471 (1972), similarly held that, while a parole revocation proceeding "is not part of a criminal prosecution and thus the full panoply of rights due a defendant * * * does not apply," due process still requires a hearing at which the parolee is given ample notice, is allowed to present evidence on his own behalf, and is allowed cross-examination of adverse witnesses (unless an exception is justified by "good cause"). In *Gardner v. Fla.,* 430 U.S. 349 (1977), the Court, noting the "severity" and "finality" of capital punishment, distinguished *Williams v. N. Y.,* supra, and held that due process was violated by reliance upon an undisclosed presentence report in imposing capital punishment.

Appeals. The Supreme Court held in *McKane v. Durston,* 153 U.S. 684 (1894), that a state was not constitutionally required to provide appellate review of criminal convictions. See also *Ross v. Moffit* (p. 345). All states now provide for appellate review, however, and the Court has held that, once established, appellate review cannot be restricted or burdened on arbitrary grounds. Thus, *Griffin v. Ill.* (p. 343) held that the availability of review cannot be conditioned on the convicted defendant's financial status; where a state requires a trial transcript for review, it must provide that transcript for the indigent. Indeed, *Douglas v. Cal.* (p. 343) held that the state also must provide the indigent appellant with appointed counsel on a first appeal that is granted as a matter of right. Compare *Ross v. Moffit* (p. 345) (appointed counsel not necessary on application for discretionary review).

N. C. v. Pearce, 395 U.S. 711 (1969), granted further protection to the appellate process in barring potential vindictiveness against those who use the process. *Pearce* involved defendants who had appealed their initial convictions, obtained reversals, were retried and convicted on the same charges, and then sentenced to more severe sentences than on the first conviction. *Pearce* held that due process prohibited the imposition of a more severe sentence for the purpose of discouraging defendants from exercising their statutory right to appeal. Moreover, to facilitate attack on such improper motivation, the Court required that: (1) "whenever a judge imposes a more severe sentence upon a defendant after a new trial, the reasons for his doing so must affirmatively appear" on the record, and (2) "those reasons must be based upon objective information concerning identifiable conduct on the part of the defendant occurring after the time of the original sentencing proceeding." These "prophylactic requirements" constitute a dramatic departure from traditional sentencing practice which does not require any statement justifying the sentence or restrict consideration to defendant's behavior during a specific period. In *Chaffin v. Stynchcombe*, 412 U.S. 17 (1973), the *Pearce* requirements were held inapplicable to jury sentencing since the jury "is unlikely to be sensitive to the institutional interests that might occasion higher sentences by a judge desirous of discouraging what he regards as meritless appeals." The *Pearce* analogy was held applicable, however, to bar the prosecutor's initiation of a higher charge after defendant sought a trial de novo on appeal from a misdemeanor conviction. *Blackledge v. Perry*, 417 U.S. 21 (1974). Compare *Colten v. Ky.*, 407 U.S. 104 (1972) (*Pearce* requirements do not apply to a higher sentence for conviction on the same charge following a trial de novo; the possibility of vindictiveness is not inherent in the two tier system, as the trial de novo is automatically available without challenging the validity of the first trial).

Retrials. The double jeopardy clause of the Fifth Amendment provides that no person shall be "twice put in jeopardy" for the "same offense." We have already considered what constitutes a prosecution for the "same offence" for Fifth Amendment purposes. See p. 32. Whether a person is placed in "jeopardy" depends upon the stage reached in the prosecution. Jeopardy attaches in jury trials once the jury is "empaneled and sworn," and it attaches in bench trials when "the first witness is sworn." *Crist v. Bretz*, 437 U.S. 28 (1978). Once one trial has reached the point where jeopardy attached, any retrial for same offense presents potential constitutional difficulties. The prohibition against twice putting a person in jeopardy is not absolute, however, and not every retrial for the same offense is constitutionally prohibited.

The double jeopardy prohibition is most flexible as applied to retrials following a mistrial (i. e., a court order dismissing the jury before a verdict is reached). A trial judge granting a mistrial ordinarily contemplates that a new trial will be permitted, but there are situations in which those double jeopardy concerns applicable even before a verdict has been reached—the "minimization of harassing exposure to the harrowing experiences of a criminal trial, and the valued right [of the defendant] to continue with the chosen jury," *Crist v. Bretz,* supra—will bar a new trial. If the mistrial was ordered at the request of the defense, a new trial ordinarily will not be barred unless the defense acted in response to prosecutorial or judicial overreaching that was designed to provoke the mistrial. *U. S. v. Dinitz,* 424 U.S. 600 (1976). Where the mistrial was ordered over defense objection (or without giving the defense an opportunity to object), a retrial will be barred unless the "declaration of the mistrial was dictated by 'manifest necessity' or the 'ends of public justice.' " *Ill. v. Somerville,* 410 U.S. 458 (1973). If the mistrial was due to an uncontrollable event (e. g., the illness of a juror or a jury

[85]

that could not agree on a verdict), it ordinarily will meet this "manifest necessity" standard and a retrial will be permitted. Where the mistrial was due to some error by counsel or the trial judge, the Court will look to several factors in applying the "manifest necessity" standard. These include: (1) if the error was by the prosecutor, whether it was the type of error that might be intentionally manipulated to gain a new trial at which the prosecution could strengthen its case, *Downum v. U. S.*, 372 U.S. 734 (1963); (2) whether the trial court could have utilized alternative remedies for the error that would have permitted the trial to continue to an impartial verdict that could be sustained on appeal, compare *U. S. v. Jorn*, 400 U.S. 470 (1971) with *Ill. v. Somerville*, supra; (3) whether the trial judge's rejection of alternatives to a mistrial involved the assessment of factors (e. g., jury reaction to a prejudicial remark) that are not particularly "amenable to appellate scrutiny." *Ariz. v. Washington*, 434 U.S. 497 (1978).

Along with the mistrial, a trial court also may keep a case from reaching a verdict by dismissing the prosecution on grounds that do not contemplate a retrial. When such a dismissal is issued after jeopardy has attached, the primary concern is whether it amounts, in effect, to an acquittal. If the court's ruling is based on its conclusion that the evidence is insufficient to establish the offense charged, it is treated like a jury verdict of acquittal and further proceedings are not allowed. See *Sanabria v. U. S.,* 437 U.S. 54 (1979). If the dismissal is based on other grounds, not involving a resolution of the factual elements of the offense, then the state can provide for a prosecution appeal and a retrial if the prosecution is successful in overturning the dismissal. Thus *U. S. v. Scott,* 437 U.S. 82 (1978), upheld a government appeal from a mid-trial dismissal that had been issued on the theory that preindictment delay had resulted in a denial of due process.

As suggested above, if the trial reaches a verdict and the jury acquits, reprosecution is barred. The state cannot gain reversal of that acquittal even if the acquittal probably was based on some error in the instructions or the admission of evidence. As the Court noted in *Scott,* supra, "to permit a second trial after an acquittal, however mistaken the acquittal may have been, would present an unacceptably high risk that the Government, with its vastly superior resources, might wear down the defendant so that 'even though innocent he may be found guilty.' "

Where the trial ends in a verdict of guilty, reprosecution also is barred unless the defendant successfully challenges that verdict. If he chooses, the defendant may accept the guilty verdict and thereby prevent the government from subjecting him to the "embarrassment, expense, and ordeal" of another trial. *U. S. v. Wilson,* 420 U.S. 332 (1975).

If the defendant appeals the guilty verdict, and
gains a reversal, he then may be retried, unless
the reversal was grounded on the insufficiency of
the evidence to support the verdict. *Burks v.
U. S.,* 437 U.S. 1 (1978). The double jeopardy principle allowing retrials following appellate reversals is
often described as the "*Ball* principle," after *U. S.
v. Ball,* 163 U.S. 662 (1896). It is justified as
serving "defendant's rights as well as society
interests" since a contrary position would obviously
discourage appellate courts from granting reversals.
U. S. v. Tateo, 377 U.S. 463 (1964). The *Ball*
principle does not apply to a reversal based on the
insufficiency of the prosecution's evidence since that
ruling is equivalent to a directed verdict of acquittal
at trial. *Burks v. U. S.,* supra. Similarly, when
defendant is charged with a higher offense, but is
convicted on a lesser charge, the jury's refusal to
convict on the higher charge is the equivalent of an
acquittal; if the defendant appeals the conviction
and obtains a reversal, the *Ball* principle permits a
retrial only on the lower charge. Where a
conviction is challenged successfully at the trial
level, the successful defense challenge permits
further proceedings in much the same way as a
successful defense appeal permits further proceedings under the *Ball* principle. Here the prosecution
may appeal the trial court's decision overturning the
guilty verdict. As noted in *U. S. v. Wilson,* supra,
such a government appeal does not raise double
jeopardy difficulties since a reversal on appeal will

not require a retrial, but only a reinstatement of the original conviction.

Finally, is should be noted that the double jeopardy clause only bars reprosecution by the same sovereign. Thus, if the defendant is tried for bank robbery at the federal level, even if acquitted, he may be prosecuted by the state for the same activity under state law. *Bartkus v. Ill.*, 359 U.S. 121 (1959). See also *Abbate v. U. S.*, 359 U.S. 187 (1959) (federal prosecution following state prosecution). Of course, a jurisdiction may relinquish its authority to take advantage of this "dual sovereignty" doctrine, as many states have done. Moreover, the doctrine does not apply to separate prosecutions under state laws and local ordinances. Since local units of government receive their ordinance authority from the states, they are not considered separate sovereignties. *Waller v. Fla.*, 397 U.S. 387 (1970).

8. RETROACTIVITY

A number of the decisions noted in the previous sections adopted what was admittedly "new constitutional doctrine" rather than just an extension of previous precedent. See *Desist v. U. S.*, 394 U.S. 244 (1969). Many of the decisions so characterized have not been given full retroactive effect (i. e., applied on appeal and in habeas corpus proceedings to all prior convictions). For example, the rulings in *Mapp v. Ohio* (p. 23) (applying the exclusionary rule to illegally seized evidence), *Griffin v. Cal.* (p.

78) (prohibiting adverse prosecutorial comment on the defendant's failure to testify) and *Duncan v. La.* (p. 15) (requiring the states to provide jury trials for non-petty offenses) were limited largely to prospective application. See *Mich. v. Payne,* 412 U.S. 47 (1973). The same is true of many of the cases discussed in later chapters. See, e. g., *Coleman* (p. 360); *Miranda* (p. 228); *Wade* (p. 266); and *Katz* (p. 101).

In determining whether a new ruling should be given retroactive effect, the Court has relied primarily upon three considerations: "(a) the purpose to be served by the new standards, (b) the extent of the reliance by law enforcement authorities on the old standards, and (c) the effect on the administration of justice of a retroactive application of the new standards." *Stovall v. Denno,* 388 U.S. 293 (1967). The Court has noted, however, that the "foremost" factor is the first. Decisions have sought to distinguish between new rulings that are designed to "avoid unfairness at the trial by enhancing the reliability of the fact-finding process" and those designed to serve other, independent interests, such as individual privacy. Rulings in the latter category have been held not to require retroactive application. Thus, the Court ruled that *Mapp* could be limited to prospective application because, inter alia, the deterrent function of the exclusionary rule would not be enhanced by retroactive application. "[T]he misconduct of the police prior to *Mapp* had already occurred and [would] not be corrected by releasing the prisoners involved." *Linkletter v. Walker*, 381 U.S. 618 (1965).

Where the new ruling clearly is designed to enhance the reliability of the guilt determination process, it generally has been given retroactive effect. There have been a few instances, however, in which rulings at least partially serving that function, e. g., *Wade* and *Gilbert* (providing counsel at lineups), have been applied only prospectively. Emphasis here has been on the second and third considerations noted above—reliance of law enforcement officials on prior standards and the administrative burden of retroactive application. In examining the reliance factor, the Court has looked particularly to the clarity of prior law—i. e., whether, under prior precedent, the state's practice was clearly constitutional or subject to significant doubt. In examining the administrative burden, the Court has sought to evaluate the procedural difficulties presented in applying the particular ruling to cases decided long before that ruling. *Desist v. U. S.*, supra. It also has given considerable weight to the application in such cases of prior rulings that served to ensure the reliability of the fact-finding process (although not so effectively as the new rulings). *Stovall v. Denno*, supra.

9. BASIC THEMES

The Supreme Court has decided hundreds of cases involving questions of constitutional-criminal procedure over the past twenty years. Each of those cases undoubtedly was decided, in large part, on the basis of distinctive considerations relating to the particular issue presented by the individual case. The Court's opinions also reflect, however, certain general themes that have contributed, at least as helpful guideposts, to the decisions in substantial groups of cases presenting diverse issues. While perhaps a dozen such themes might be extracted from the Court's opinions, we will concentrate on a handful that have particular relevance to the material covered in later chapters. We start with three themes that received consistent majority support over the past twenty years.

First, the Court's opinions have emphasized that criminal procedure involves important aspects of individual liberty and therefore is not to be viewed as a specialized field of law having an impact only on the immediate participants in the process. As Chief Justice Warren put it: "No general respect for, nor adherence to, the law as a whole can well be expected without judicial recognition of the paramount need for prompt, eminently fair and sober criminal law procedures. The methods we employ in the enforcement of our criminal law have aptly been called the measures by which the quality of our civilization may be judged." *Coppedge v. U. S.*, 369 U.S. 438 (1962).

Closely related to this theme has been the emphasis on achieving equality in the administration of the

[92]

criminal law. The Court has recognized the unequal impact of criminal procedure on the poor and racial minorities and has sought to eliminate at least the official aspects of such inequality. Although only a few decisions have been based squarely on the equal protection clause, others, like *Gideon* (p. 342) and *Miranda* (p. 228), had strong equal protection overtones.

A third, generally accepted theme relates to the appropriate function of federal-state relations in framing constitutional standards for criminal procedure. Prior to the 1960's, the Court had frequently noted that "the very essence of our federalism [requires] that the states should have the widest latitude in the administration of their own system of criminal justice." *Hoag v. N. J.*, 356 U.S. 464 (1958). It was suggested that differences in the types of crimes investigated, in the nature of the communities immediately concerned, and in the organization of law enforcement agencies required that more flexible constitutional standards be applied to the state than the federal government. Since the early 1960's, a majority of the Court has consistently rejected this position. It has emphasized that, while states may properly serve as laboratories to try novel social and economic systems, they should not be allowed the same discretion "when fundamental rights" are involved. Moreover, several justices have maintained that a uniform constitutional standard, though more restrictive, actually improves federal-state relations by (1) encouraging cooperation between federal and state police agencies through elimination of suspicion that their working arrangements "were designed to take advantage of the more flexible standards applicable to state prosecutions," and (2) eliminating the friction between state and federal courts that flows from the application of more flexible, largely unpredictable standards to the states that make it more difficult for state courts to anticipate federal rulings and therefore result in more reversals of state rulings. See *Pointer v. Texas* (p. 5) (Goldberg, J., con.); *Mapp v. Ohio* (p. 23).

Several other important themes have been influential at times, but have not received consistent acceptance over the past twenty years. The reception of these themes has shifted with the composition of the Court and with the context in which they were presented. They have been emphasized in some majority opinions and discounted in others. Falling in this category are three themes that relate respectively to the weight to be given to history, the priority to be given to different procedural rights, and the appropriate scope of constitutional rulings.

Various rulings throughout the last twenty years have reflected the view that the historical acceptance of a procedural practice, particularly its acceptance at the time of the adoption of the Constitution, creates a strong, almost insurmountable presumption of constitutionality. See, e. g., *Baldwin v.*

[94]

N. Y. (p. 54); *U. S. v. Watson* (p. 133). Of course, the historical precedents do not always point in a single direction, but when they do, justices supporting this view adhere to Justice Frankfurter's position, advanced with reference to the self-incrimination privilege, that "a page of history is worth a volume of logic." *Ullmann v. U. S.*, 350 U.S. 422 (1956) (con.). Other justices have given far less weight to history. They have been much more willing to point to "changed circumstances," or a better understanding of the function of a constitutional guarantee, and to conclude that a particular practice is unconstitutional notwithstanding its historical acceptance. See, e. g., *Bloom v. Ill.* (p. 54); *Taylor v. La.* (p. 58). (Since the modern police department and prosecutor's office are largely post-1789 developments, it often is not difficult to find "changed circumstances" that may be used to discount historical precedents).

Another general theme that has divided the Court concerns the priority to be given to different procedural rights, particularly in devising remedies for violations of those rights. Some justices have stressed that in reviewing convictions and providing collateral relief, the Court should give primary weight to preventing the possible conviction of an innocent person. They therefore would treat some rights differently than others, depending on whether the particular right had a potential bearing on the accuracy of the determination of defendant's factual guilt.   Where a right has no such bearing, because it is not concerned with the reliability of the fact-finding process, these justices would find less need for providing especially expansive procedural avenues for challenging alleged violations of that right. Supporters of this view, for example, would not permit a collateral attack to a conviction based on the admission of illegally seized evidence (unrelated to reliability) but would permit such a challenge based on jury bias (clearly related to reliability). See *Schneckloth v. Bustamonte* (p. 399) (Powell, J., con.).   Other justices argue that all constitutional guarantees should be treated alike, and extensive relief should be available for any constitutional violation.   See *Stone v. Powell* (p. 400) (Brennan, J., dis.).   Each position has managed to capture majority support at times, although the more recent decisions arguably have favored placing primary emphasis on claims relating to the accuracy of the fact-finding process.   See *Stone v. Powell* (p. 400); *Harris v. N. Y.* (p. 303).   But note *Rose v. Mitchell* (p. 402).

Many of the most highly publicized rulings of the 1960's appeared to reflect still another general theme on which the Court has divided—that the Supreme Court opinions should not only decide the particular case before the Court, but often should also set forth specific constitutional requirements that go beyond the facts of the particular case and deal with a practice in general.   The opinions in

Miranda (p. 228), *Wade* (p. 266) and *Fay* (p. 399), for example, arguably fit this mold. In each, the Court set forth a detailed set of standards applicable to a very general fact situation. Indeed in several of these cases, the standards imposed arguably went beyond the particular constitutional violation in order to provide a prophylactic safeguard against potential violations. See, e. g., *Miranda, Wade*, and *N. C. v. Pearce* (p. 83). On the other hand, there were other cases of the 1960's in which broad rulings were proposed but failed to gain majority support. See, e. g., *Estes v. Texas* (p. 63); *Terry v. Ohio* (p. 157). Moreover, support for broad rulings diminished substantially during the 1970's, when the Court's rulings often were tied to a variety of factors requiring a case-by-case analysis. See, e. g., *Barker v. Wingo* (p. 40); *Schneckloth v. Bustamonte* (p. 172); *Manson v. Brathwaite* (p. 278). But compare *Morrissey v. Brewer* (p. 82), a 1970's decision setting forth extensive constitutional requirements for all parole and probation revocation hearings. See also *Argersinger v. Hamlin* (p. 351).

It has not always been clear why broad rulings were adopted in some cases and not in others, even when the composition of the Court did not differ. Some justices have suggested that the broad rulings were adopted only when they were needed to ensure the effective day-by-day implementation of constitutional rights. See, e. g., the various opinions in *Miranda* and *Pearce.* Limited rulings based upon a series of variable factors were viewed as too easily evaded and therefore largely ineffective. There is some indication, however, that, at least in certain areas, several justices also viewed the establishment of specific standards to ensure day-by-day implementation of constitutional rights as largely a legislative task, which the Court should take upon itself only where the legislature has not acted. Thus, the *Miranda* and *Wade* opinions both noted that the affirmative safeguards required there were not absolute constitutional necessities, and both expressly invited legislative formulation of alternative schemes that would provide equally adequate safeguards. It also is noteworthy that both decisions dealt with police investigatory practices. Some justices have indicated that they will be less reluctant to impose broad rulings on the trial process, where the issues presented are raised in a relatively uniform and familiar context and fall within the traditional expertise of the courts. *In re Gault,* 387 U.S. 1, 70 (1967) (Harlan, J., con.).

The future implementation of the basic themes outlined above will depend in large measure on the particular composition of the Court, but the very presence of the decisions of the past twenty years ensures that these themes will continue to occupy the Court's attention over the next several years.

CHAPTER 2

ARREST, SEARCH AND SEIZURE

10. INTRODUCTION

The Fourth Amendment. The Fourth Amendment to the U. S. Constitution reads: "The right of the people to be secure in their persons, houses, papers, and effects, against unreasonable searches and seizures, shall not be violated, and no Warrants shall issue, but upon probable cause, supported by Oath or affirmation, and particularly describing the place to be searched, and the persons or things to be seized." The Amendment is applicable to the states through the due process clause of the Fourteenth Amendment (see § 2), and thus evidence obtained in violation of the Amendment is subject to exclusion in the state courts, *Mapp v. Ohio,* 367 U.S. 643 (1961), as well as the federal courts, *Weeks v. U. S.,* 232 U.S. 383 (1914). The same standards of reasonableness and probable cause govern both federal and state activities. *Ker v. Cal.,* 374 U.S. 23 (1963); *Aguilar v. Texas,* 378 U.S. 108 (1964).

Seizure of the person. Because of the exclusionary sanction, the Fourth Amendment is more commonly thought of as a limitation on the power of police to search for and seize evidence, instrumentalities, and fruits of crime. However, an illegal arrest or other unreasonable seizure of the person is itself a violation of the Fourth and Fourteenth Amendments, *Terry v. Ohio,* 392 U.S. 1 (1968); *Henry v. U. S.,* 361 U.S. 98 (1959), although it is no defense to a state or federal criminal prosecution that the defendant was illegally arrested or forcibly brought within the jurisdiction of the court, *Frisbie v. Collins,* 342 U.S. 519 (1952), except perhaps when the circumstances are particularly shocking. *U. S. v. Toscanino,* 500 F.2d 267 (2d Cir. 1974).

Whether an arrest or other seizure of the person conforms to the requirements of the Constitution is nonetheless frequently a matter of practical importance. The police are authorized to conduct a limited search without warrant incident to a lawful arrest (see § 14B), and thus the admissibility of physical evidence acquired in this way depends upon the validity of the arrest. The same is true of certain other evidentiary "fruits" obtained subsequent to and as a consequence of the arrest (see § 34).

The major issues. Several Fourth Amendment issues of current significance are surveyed in this Chapter. Consideration is first given to the areas and interests protected by the Amendment (see § 11), for they determine what constitutes a "search" and thus what activities are subject to the requirements of the Amendment. The most pervasive requirement of the Amendment is that of "probable cause," needed for lawful arrests and searches both with and without warrant, and special attention is therefore given to the meaning and significance of this quantum-of-evidence standard (see § 12). Other constitutional requirements for obtaining physical evidence by search warrant (see § 13), without a warrant (see § 14), and with consent (see § 18) are separately considered. Finally, to illustrate the flexibility of the Fourth Amendment limitations, this Chapter also covers some unique practices for which separate rules have been developed because of the limited intrusion or special need attending their use: brief detentions for purposes of investigation (see § 15); grand jury subpoenas (see § 16); and inspections and regulatory searches (see § 17).

11. PROTECTED AREAS AND INTERESTS

Property interests vs. privacy interests. What is a search under the Fourth Amendment? The traditional approach was to speak of intrusion into certain "constitutionally protected areas," in that the Fourth Amendment protects the "right of the people to be secure in their persons, houses, papers, and effects, against unreasonable searches and seizures." This property approach was rejected in *Katz v. U. S.,* 389 U.S. 347 (1967), in favor of a privacy approach. In concluding that a nontrespassory eavesdropping into a public telephone booth constituted a search, the Court declined to characterize the booth as a "constitutionally protected area": "For the Fourth Amendment protects people, not places. What a person knowingly exposes to the public, even in his own home or office, is not a subject of Fourth Amendment protection * * *. But what he seeks to preserve as private, even in an area accessible to the public, may be constitutionally protected."

The majority opinion in *Katz* does not elaborate upon the privacy approach, except for the helpful observation that defendant's activities were protected because the government intrusion "violated the privacy upon which he justifiably relied." Justice Harlan, concurring, suggested a "two-fold requirement: first, that a person have exhibited an actual (subjective) expectation of privacy; and, second, that the expectation be one that society is prepared to recognize as 'reasonable.'" [But later, dissenting in *U. S. v. White,* 401 U.S. 745 (1971), he cautioned against undue emphasis upon actual expectations, which "are in large part reflections" of what the law permits.] He also noted, quite correctly, that in asking what protection the Fourth Amendment affords people (i. e., where an expectation of privacy is reasonable), it is generally necessary to answer with reference to a place, so that many of the earlier property-based decisions are not disturbed by *Katz.*

[102]

Plain view, smell and hearing. It is not a search under *Katz* for an officer, lawfully present at a certain location, to detect something by one of his natural senses. *U. S. v. Fisch,* 474 F.2d 1071 (9th Cir. 1973) (no search to hear "by the naked ear" conversation in adjoining motel room). The result is ordinarily the same when common means of enhancing the senses, such as a flashlight, *Marshall v. U. S.,* 422 F.2d 185 (5th Cir. 1970), or binoculars, *P. v. Ciochon,* 319 N.E.2d 332 (Ill.App.1974), are used. But the use of such devices in particular circumstances may be so highly intrusive as to justify the conclusion that a search has occurred, *U. S. v. Kim,* 415 F.Supp. 2152 (D.Haw.1976) (high-powered telescope used to determine from distance of quarter mile contents of papers being read in high-rise apartment). Also, it is a search to utilize more sophisticated means, such as an x-ray machine, *U. S. v. Albarado,* 495 F.2d 799 (2d Cir. 1974), or magnetometer, *U. S. v. Epperson,* 454 F.2d 769 (4th Cir. 1972).

Residential premises. Even entry and examination of residential premises is not a search if those premises have been abandoned. *Abel v. U. S.,* 362 U.S. 217 (1960). Consistent with *Katz,* the proper test for abandonment in this context "is not whether all formal property rights have been relinquished, but whether the complaining party retains a reasonable expectation of privacy in the articles alleged to be abandoned." *U. S. v. Wilson,* 472 F.2d

901 (9th Cir. 1973). As for premises not abandoned, it is a search for an officer to make an uninvited entry into even the hallway of a single-family dwelling, but the result is otherwise if the entry is into the common hallway of an apartment building. *S. v. Crider,* 341 A.2d 1 (Me.1975). In the latter instance, some courts reach a contrary result if the building is sufficiently secured so that even common areas are not accessible to the general public. *U. S. v. Carriger,* 541 F.2d 545 (6th Cir. 1976).

Looking in or listening at a residence is no search if the officer uses his natural senses and is positioned on nearby public property, *P. v. Wright,* 242 N.E.2d 180 (Ill.1968), on the adjacent property of a neighbor, *C. v. Busfield,* 363 A.2d 1227 (Pa. Super.1976), or on part of the curtilage of the premises being observed which is the "normal means of access to and egress from the house." *Lorenzana v. Sup. Ct.,* 511 P.2d 33 (Cal.1973). As for entry of or looking into or listening at related structures, such as barns or garages, the pre-*Katz* result was that this is no search if the structure was outside the curtilage, but now the question is whether the place—either in or out of the curtilage—is one as to which the owner has a reasonable expectation of privacy. *P. v. Weisenberger,* 516 P.2d 1128 (Colo. 1973).

As for entry of adjoining lands, the modern approach again is not merely to ask if the curtilage has been breached, but rather whether the conduct intrudes upon a justified expectation of privacy. Illustrative is *Wattenburg v. U. S.*, 388 F.2d 853 (9th Cir. 1968), where the court ruled inadmissible evidence obtained from the search of a stockpile of trees located on the grounds of defendant's motel, but indicated that this was not merely because the trees were located within the curtilage, but rather because the meticulous inspection of the trees intruded upon defendant's privacy. Mere looking into these lands from adjacent property will seldom constitute a search, but the *Katz* test will sometimes be met even here if the viewing can be accomplished only by most extraordinary efforts unlikely to be utilized by "any curious passerby." *U. S. v. McMillon,* 350 F.Supp. 593 (D.D.C.1972).

Other premises and places. Before *Katz,* the protections of the Fourth Amendment were "not extended to the open fields," *Hester v. U. S.*, 265 U.S. 57 (1924), typically viewed as all lands not falling within the curtilage. *Care v. U. S.*, 231 F.2d 22 (10th Cir. 1956). After *Katz,* some courts still view a straightforward application of *Hester* as proper, but the better view is that while "open fields are not areas in which one traditionally might reasonably expect privacy," *U. S. v. Freie,* 545 F.2d 1217 (9th Cir. 1976), in a few instances police intrusion into a so-called open field should be considered a search because of the extreme degree of police scrutiny involved or the extraordinary means taken by the owner to preserve as private what occurred in the field.

Though the Fourth Amendment mentions only "houses," offices, stores and other commercial premises are also protected. *See v. City of Seattle,* 387 U.S. 541 (1967). Whether a particular investigative practice directed at such a place is a search often involves considerations similar to those discussed above as to residences, though it is no search for an officer to enter where and when there is an "implied invitation for customers to come in." *Wilson v. C.,* 475 S.W.2d 895 (Ky.App.1971). Even if certain business premises are generally open to the public, surveillance into private areas therein, such as fitting rooms and rest rooms, constitutes a search. *S. v. Bryant,* 177 N.W.2d 800 (Minn.1970).

In the pre-*Katz* case of *Lanza v. N. Y.,* 370 U.S. 139 (1962), the protections of the Fourth Amendment were deemed inapplicable to a jail, where "official surveillance has traditionally been the order of the day." Without expressly rejecting that view, the Court has more recently said that at best prisoners have a "reasonable expectation of privacy * * * of a diminished scope." *Bell v. Wolfish,* 441 U.S. 520 (1979).

Vehicles. It is no search for the police, from a lawful vantage point, to examine the exterior of a vehicle, *Cardwell v. Lewis,* 417 U.S. 583 (1974), or to see the contents by looking through the windows, *Cook v. C.,* 216 S.E.2d 48 (Va.1975). Entry of the car is a search under *Katz*, unless of course the vehicle had been abandoned in such a way that the user no longer had "a reasonable expectation that the automobile would be free from governmental intrusion." *S. v. Achter*, 512 S.W.2d 894 (Mo. App.1974).

Effects. It has long been accepted that the protections of the Fourth Amendment do not extend to effects which have been abandoned. *Hester v. U. S.*, supra (containers thrown into field); *Abel v. U. S.*, supra (items left in waste basket upon hotel checkout). After *Katz*, the question is not whether the object has been abandoned in the property sense, but rather "whether the defendant has, in discarding the property, relinquished his reasonable expectation of privacy" as to it. *City of St. Paul v. Vaughn*, 237 N.W.2d 365 (Minn.1975). Taking this approach, it has correctly been held that examination of the contents of a garbage can is a search, for the expectation is that the garbage will be hauled away and then lose "its identity and meaning by becoming part of a larger conglomeration of trash elsewhere." *P. v. Edwards*, 458 P.2d 713 (Cal.1969).

In *Warden v. Hayden*, 387 U.S. 294 (1967), the Court discarded the so-called "mere evidence" rule, whereunder objects of evidential value only could not be seized pursuant to a warrant, *Gouled v. U. S.*, 255 U.S. 298 (1921), or incident to arrest, *U. S. v. Lefkowitz*, 285 U.S. 452 (1932). This rejection of the distinction between "mere evidence" and instrumentalities, fruits of crime, and contraband was based upon the conclusions that (1) nothing in the language of the Fourth Amendment supports the distinction; (2) privacy is disturbed no more by a search for evidentiary material than other property; (3) the Fourth Amendment protects privacy rather than property, so that the defendant's or the government's property interest in the items seized is not relevant; and (4) the distinction had spawned numerous exceptions and great confusion.

The Court in *Hayden* was careful to emphasize that "the items of clothing involved in this case are not 'testimonial' or 'communicative' in nature, and their introduction therefore did not compel respondent to become a witness against himself in violation of the Fifth Amendment." This led some courts to conclude that the result would be otherwise if private papers were seized, but that position was rejected in *Andresen v. Md.,* 427 U.S. 463 (1976). The Court there held that though the Fifth Amendment privilege against self-incrimination protects a person from having to produce testimonial documents in response to a subpoena, the privilege against self-incrimination affords no protection against a search warrant, as when a warrant is utilized the person in possession has not been compelled to make the record or to authenticate it by production.

The fact that "mere evidence" is being sought, or that it is being sought from a "third party," does not limit the manner of seizure. In *Zurcher v.*

Stanford Daily, 436 U.S. 547 (1978), the respondent, a college newspaper, argued that, because it had not been a participant in the crime being investigated, the prosecutor had violated the Fourth and First Amendments by seeking evidence allegedly in its possession (photographs) through a warrant-authorized search of its offices rather than through a subpoena duces tecum. Rejecting this claim, the Court noted that nothing in the Fourth Amendment suggests third parties are entitled to greater protection against searches than suspects; indeed, a contrary rule would be unworkable in that search warrants are often obtained when the identity of all those involved in the crime under investigation is not known. The First Amendment also did not require use of a subpoena duces tecum instead of a warrant, but only that the Fourth Amendment requirements be applied with "particular exactitude."

Surveillance of relationships and movements. The courts have upheld a number of surveillance practices on the questionable ground that no justified expectation of privacy was infringed because what was discovered had been revealed in a limited way to a limited group for a limited purpose. In *Smith v. Md.,* 442 U.S. 735 (1979), for example, police use of a pen register to record the numbers called on a phone was held to be no search, as the defendant had conveyed such information to the telephone company equipment when dialing. By an equally narrow view of the *Katz* expectation of privacy test, it has been held that use of a mail cover, recording information on the outside of incoming mail, is no search. *U. S. v. Choate,* 576 F.2d 165 (9th Cir. 1978). The Court similarly has said that a bank depositor "takes the risk, in revealing his affairs to [his bank]," that the information will be conveyed by the bank to police, and thus has no Fourth Amendment protection against such transfer. *U. S. v. Miller,* 425 U.S. 435 (1976). As for use of an electronic tracking device or "beeper" to keep track of a vehicle's movements, some courts say this is no search because the movements occur in public, *U. S. v. Hufford,* 539 F.2d 32 (9th Cir. 1976), while others reach the contrary result by reasoning that the "beeper" permits surveillance of much greater intensity and length than would be possible by direct observation. *U. S. v. Moore,* 562 F.2d 106 (1st Cir. 1977).

12.   "PROBABLE CAUSE" AND RELATED PROBLEMS

When and why "probable cause" in issue. The Fourth Amendment provides that "no Warrants shall issue, but upon probable cause," and thus it is apparent that a valid arrest warrant or search warrant may only be issued upon an affidavit or complaint which sets forth facts establishing probable cause. Those arrests and searches which may be made without a warrant must not be "unreasonable" under the Fourth Amendment, and because the requirements in such cases "surely cannot be less stringent" than when a warrant is obtained, *Wong Sun v. U. S.,* 371 U.S. 471 (1963), probable cause is also required in such circumstances. *Draper v. U. S.,* 358 U.S. 307 (1959).

When the police act without a warrant, they initially make the probable cause decision themselves, although it will be subject to after-the-fact review by a judicial officer upon a motion to suppress evidence found because of the arrest or search. When the police act with a warrant, the probable cause decision is made by a magistrate in the first instance, but his decision may likewise be challenged in an adversary setting upon a motion to suppress.

Although there are many circumstances in which arrests and searches may be made without a warrant (see § 14), the Supreme Court has expressed a strong preference for arrest warrants, *Beck v. Ohio,* 379 U.S. 89 (1964), and search warrants, *U. S. v. Ventresca,* 380 U.S. 102 (1965), on the ground that interposing an orderly procedure whereby a neutral and detached magistrate makes the decision is better than allowing those engaged in the competitive enterprise of ferreting out crime to make hurried decisions which would be reviewable by a magistrate only after the fact and by hindsight judgment. This preference has even resulted in a subtle difference between the probable cause required when there is no warrant and that required when there is; "in a doubtful or marginal case a search under a warrant may be sustainable where without one it would fall." *U. S. v. Ventresca,* supra.

Although there is reason to question whether before-the-fact review when warrants are sought is always as cautious as presumed by the Supreme Court, the warrant process at least has the advantage of providing a before-the-fact record of the facts upon which probable cause is based. If the police have acted without a warrant, the probable cause determination must be made primarily upon the basis of the officer's testimony on the motion to suppress, and thus there is some risk that the facts brought out at that time may not be limited to those upon which the officer acted. But when the police have acted with a warrant, the factual justification is under the prevailing practice set out in a complaint or affidavit, and at the motion to suppress hearing the issue is whether those pre-recorded facts show probable cause. Thus, a defective complaint or affidavit may not be saved by police testimony that they actually had additional facts, *Whiteley v. Warden,* 401 U.S. 560 (1971), although where not barred by statute it is possible to receive testimony that additional facts were orally presented to the magistrate at the time of the warrant application. *Frazier v. Roberts,* 441 F.2d 1224 (8th Cir. 1971).

Even an affidavit sufficient on its face may be challenged upon a later motion to suppress. If the defendant makes a substantial preliminary showing

that a false statement was included therein by an
affiant who either knew the statement was false or
acted with reckless disregard for the truth, and it
appears that the allegedly false statement was material (i. e., necessary to the earlier probable cause
finding), the Fourth Amendment requires that a
hearing be held at defendant's request. If the
defendant then proves the allegation of perjury or
reckless disregard by a preponderance of the evidence, the affidavit must then be judged with the
false material excised. *Franks v. Del.*, 438 U.S. 154
(1978). The Court in *Franks* did not require invalida-
tion because of a material false statement negligent-
ly made, as a few courts had previously done,
Theodor v. Sup. Ct., 501 P.2d 234 (Cal.1972), or
because of an immaterial but deliberately false statement, as many courts had previously done, *U. S. v.
Carmichael*, 489 F.2d 983 (7th Cir. 1973).

Probable cause for arrest does not necessarily
constitute probable cause for a search warrant, nor
does probable cause for a search warrant necessarily
provide grounds for arrest; each requires the same
quantum of evidence, but as to somewhat different
facts and circumstances. For a search warrant, two
conclusions must be supported by substantial evidence: (1) that the items sought are connected with
criminal activity; and (2) that the items will be
found in the place to be searched. By comparison,
for arrest there must be probable cause (1) that an
offense has been committed; and (2) that the person
to be arrested committed it. Thus, a showing of the

probable guilt of the person whose premises are to
be searched is no substitute for a showing that items
connected with the crime are likely to be found
there, and an affidavit for a search warrant need
not identify any particular person as the offender,
U. S. v. McNally, 473 F.2d 934 (3d Cir. 1973).

Information which may be considered.   Probative evidence may be considered in determining
whether there is probable cause, without regard to
whether such evidence would be admissible at trial.
Thus, it is proper to consider hearsay, *Draper v.
U. S.,* supra, and a prior police record, *Brinegar v.
U. S.,* 338 U.S. 160 (1949).   As the Court explained
in *Brinegar,* those rules of evidence at trial which
exclude probative evidence because of "possible mis-
understanding or misuse by the jury" have no place
at the probable cause determination: "In dealing
with probable cause * * *, as the very name
implies, we deal with probabilities.   These are not
technical; they are the factual and practical considerations of everyday life on which reasonable and
prudent men, not legal technicians, act.   The standard of proof is accordingly correlative to what must
be proved."

Information from informants.   Those probable
cause cases which have reached the Supreme Court
have dealt almost exclusively with the troublesome
question of when probable cause may be established
solely upon the basis of information from an informant or upon such information plus some corroborat-

ing facts. If probable cause is to be based solely upon the informant's information, then the warrant application, or the testimony at the suppression hearing if there was no warrant, *Beck v. Ohio,* supra, must reveal (1) underlying circumstances showing reason to believe that the informant is a credible person, and (2) underlying circumstances showing the basis of the conclusions reached by the informant. *Aguilar v. Texas,* 378 U.S. 108 (1964). Thus, for example, a search warrant affidavit which merely states that a credible informant reported that narcotics are concealed in certain premises (as in *Aguilar*) is defective in two respects. First, there should have been a disclosure of why the informant is believed to be a credible person, such as that he provided information on past occasions which investigation proved to be correct, *McCray v. Ill.,* 386 U.S. 300 (1967), or that his statement constituted an admission against his own penal interest, *U. S. v. Harris,* 403 U.S. 573 (1971). But, this alone is not enough, for even a credible person may reach unjustified conclusions on the basis of circumstantial evidence or information from unreliable sources. That is, even if it were established that the informant was a credible person, it would still be unclear whether he asserted that there were narcotics in the house because (a) he saw them there, (b) he assumed they were there because of defendant's suspicious conduct, or (c) he was told by someone that they were there. Probable cause cannot be determined without deciding which is the case, for while an informant's direct observation of criminal conduct would suffice, *McCray v. Ill.,* supra, is cannot be decided whether the suspicious conduct is adequate unless the precise nature of that conduct is revealed to the judge, *U. S. v. Ventresca,* supra, while hearsay-upon-hearsay can hardly be adequate unless it is determined that the ultimate source of the information was also credible and in a position to know of what he speaks.

If the underlying circumstances concerning the informant's credibility are shown, but the source of his information is not disclosed, it must then be considered whether the informant's tip is "in sufficient detail that the magistrate may know that he is relying on something more substantial than a casual rumor circulating in the underworld or an accusation based merely on an individual's general reputation." *Spinelli v. U. S.,* 393 U.S. 410 (1969). The Court in *Spinelli* said that the detail provided in *Draper v. U. S.,* supra, "provides a suitable benchmark." There, when an informant who had given reliable information in the past indicated that one Draper was peddling narcotics and that he would return from Chicago by train on one of two days with narcotics, and also described Draper and his clothing and said he would be carrying a tan zipper bag and that he habitually walked fast, there was at that moment probable cause for arrest. The officers knew from their past experience that the informant was credible, but they did not know the

[116]

exact source of his information; yet there was probable cause, for, as the Court later explained in *Spinelli,* the agents had been given so many details that they could "reasonably infer that the informant had gained his information in a reliable way." That is, the informant had given enough details to justify the conclusion that his source was reliable—either direct observation, admissions by the defendant, fair conclusions drawn from circumstantial evidence, or information given by another who was reliable and in a position to know.

This self-verifying detail analysis must be distinguished from the question whether it is significant that there has been partial corroboration of the informant's tale. The Supreme Court has used corroboration or assumed that it could be used to show the informant's basis of knowledge, *Draper v. U. S.,* supra; to show the informer's veracity, *U. S. v. Harris,* supra; or to show both, *Spinelli v. U. S.,* supra. Although lower court cases utilizing corroboration in all of these ways are to be found, it has been cogently argued that corroboration is another permissible way to show the informer's veracity (in that "present good performance shows him to be probably 'credible' just as surely as does past good performance"), but cannot be utilized to show basis of knowledge because "partial verification of an unattributed tale does not, by its very nature, pinpoint the source, [or] certify the validity of the possible conclusions interwoven therein." *Stanley v.*

S., 313 A.2d 847 (Md.App.1974).   So the argument
goes, while great detail (even if totally uncorroborat-
ed) shows that a reliable informant has a solid basis
for his knowledge, mere corroboration of certain
assertions by an informant (especially if they go to
innocent acts) does *not* likewise establish that basis
of knowledge.   Thus, in *Spinelli,* where an informant said defendant was accepting wagers at certain
telephone numbers and agents saw defendant go to
an apartment where those telephones were known to
be located, this did not justify the inference the
informant had come by his information in a reliable
way instead of "from an off-hand remark heard at a
neighborhood bar."   By comparison, in some cases
an informer's story will prompt a surveillance by
which police see actions so highly suggestive of
criminal conduct that the observation itself will
amount to probable cause, in which case it is
unimportant whether the credibility of the informant or the basis of his knowledge is ever
established.   *Adams v. Williams,* 407 U.S. 143 (1972).

When probable cause is based in whole or in part
upon information from an informant, his identity
need not always be disclosed at the suppression
hearing.   Disclosure is not required when the officer
has testified in full and has been cross-examined as
to what the informant told him and as to why the
information was believed trustworthy.   *McCray v.
Ill.,* supra.   Although disclosure may be compelled if
there is good reason to doubt the officer's credibili-

ty, *P. v. Leyva,* 341 N.E.2d 546 (N.Y.1975), many courts protect more broadly against perjury and at the same time honor the informer privilege by requiring disclosure only in camera when the defendant has fairly put into issue the existence of the informant or the correctness of the officer's report of the informer's tale or prior performance. *P. v. Darden,* 313 N.E.2d 49 (N.Y.1974).

Information from other sources. The reliability of informants used to uncover narcotics and gambling offenses has been a matter of special concern because they are often engaged in criminal conduct themselves. Thus, when the facts are provided by a police officer, *U. S. v. Ventresca,* supra, a crime victim, *S. v. Haron,* 220 N.W.2d 829 (S.D.1974), an eyewitness, *U. S. v. Rollins,* 522 F.2d 160 (2d Cir. 1975), a cooperative citizen, *Jaben v. U. S.,* 381 U.S. 214 (1965), or an informant not from the criminal milieu, *S. v. Kurland,* 325 A.2d 714 (N.J.1974), there is no need for establishing credibility. It is still necessary to show why the person giving the information has a basis for his knowledge, although the number of details which need be disclosed varies depending upon the circumstances. See *Jaben v. U. S.,* supra, pointing out that tax evasion is not a crime which one might directly observe and that therefore there need not be disclosure of the details of the investigation into defendant's income. A warrantless arrest based upon the conclusory statements or directive of another policeman (i. e., that a certain person should be arrested) is not per se illegal, but will be upheld only upon a subsequent showing that the instigating official possessed facts constituting probable cause. *Whiteley v. Warden,* 401 U.S. 560 (1971).

Degree of probability. When information is provided by sources other than informers, it usually goes to past, completed crimes rather than to future or continuing criminal conduct, and any doubts which exist are not likely to be based upon whether the source is reliable or knows what he claims to know, but rather upon whether the information is complete enough to justify the conclusion that certain evidence is to be found in a certain place or that a certain individual is the offender. It is these cases which most directly raise the issue of what probabilities are required to establish probable cause, and in particular whether there must be a more than 50% probability of the ultimate facts needed to justify arrest or search.

On the issue of whether a crime has occurred, courts usually employ a more-probable-than-not test, so that an arrest or search may not be "based on events as consistent with innocent as with criminal activity." *P. v. Martin,* 511 P.2d 1161 (Cal.1973). The notion is that to permit arrest or search because of equivocal conduct would unduly threaten our sense of privacy. But, in an arrest case must there also be a more than 50% probability that the particular person arrested is the perpetrator? Some-

[120]

times it is said that a sufficient description for arrest must "have that conclusive quality which would necessarily draw attention to a particular individual," *C. v. Richards,* 327 A.2d 63 (Pa.1974), and sometimes that it is only necessary that the description not be "equally applicable to large numbers of people," *C. v. Jackson,* 331 A.2d 189 (Pa.1975). It may well be that which of these approaches should be used depends upon the function to be served by the arrest in the particular case. It is noteworthy that the Supreme Court has been more demanding when the arrest was viewed as apprehension of a person to be charged, *Mallory v. U. S.,* 354 U.S. 449 (1957), or as a basis for nocturnal entry of private premises, *Wong Sun v. U. S.,* supra, than when (as in *Draper v. U. S.,* supra), the arrest merely justified an on-the-street search which could be expected immediately to prove or disprove the suspicion. The underlying notion that the amount of evidence required to satisfy the probable cause test varies depending upon the contemplated degree of intrusion, has been explicitly recognized in other contexts (see §§ 15, 17).

Unconstitutional statute. What if the officer has information providing probable cause to believe that the suspect has violated a criminal statute, but the statute itself is later held unconstitutional? In *Mich. v. DeFillippo,* 443 U.S. 31 (1979), the defendant was arrested pursuant to a local ordinance, later held unconstitutional, making it a violation for a person lawfully stopped to refuse to produce evidence of his identity. Upholding the admission of drugs seized in a search incident to that arrest, the Court noted that a "prudent officer" could not be required "to anticipate that a court would later hold the ordinance unconstitutional." It distinguished decisions rejecting searches pursuant to statute that authorized those searches without complying with Fourth Amendment requirements. The unconstitutional ordinance in *DeFillippo,* it noted, was "relevant to the validity of the search and the arrest only as it pertains to 'facts and circumstances'" that did establish probable cause to believe that the defendant had committed an offense.

13. SEARCH WARRANTS

A. ISSUANCE

Who may issue. Where a state attorney general, as authorized by state law, issued a search warrant in the context of an investigation of which he had taken personal charge, this procedure violated the Fourth Amendment, as he "was not the neutral and detached magistrate required by the Constitution." *Coolidge v. N. H.,* 403 U.S. 443 (1971). But it is not necessary "that all warrant authority must reside exclusively in a lawyer or judge"; an issuing magistrate need only be "neutral and detached" and "capable of determining whether probable cause exists," and thus a clerk of court could be authorized to issue arrest warrants for municipal ordinance violations. *Shadwick v. City of Tampa,* 407 U.S. 345 (1972). It does not necessarily follow that a clerk could be permitted to issue search warrants, as to which the probable cause issues are often much more complex. Even a judicial officer may not issue a warrant if he has such a personal interest in the matter that his impartiality is in doubt, as where a magistrate receives a fee only when he responds affirmatively to warrant requests. *Connally v. Ga.,* 429 U.S. 245 (1977).

Passage of time since facts gathered. If information showing probable cause that a crime was committed is gathered, and assuming no other evidence to the contrary is later uncovered, this probable cause will still be present weeks, months, or years later. The same is not true, however, as to information showing probable cause to believe that certain items are to be found at a particular place. As time passes, the chances increase that the goods have since been removed from that location. For this reason, an affidavit in support of a search warrant must contain a statement as to the time when the facts relied upon occurred. *C. v. Simmons,* 301 A.2d 819 (Pa.1973). This statement of time must be reasonably definite, but declarations that the observations were made "recently" or "within" or "during" a named period have been

[123]

approved. *Rugendorf v. U. S.*, 376 U.S. 528 (1964); *Huff v. C.*, 194 S.E.2d 690 (Va.1973).

Just how long a time period may elapse without probable cause vanishing "must be determined by the circumstances of each case." *Sgro v. U. S.*, 287 U.S. 206 (1932). Generally, a longer time will be allowed as to an ongoing criminal enterprise as compared to a one-shot criminal episode. Compare *P. v. Dolgin*, 114 N.E.2d 389 (Ill.1953), holding 49 days not too long re search for forged tax stamps being used in an elaborate and extensive counterfeiting scheme, with *P. v. Siemieniec*, 118 N.W.2d 430 (Mich.1962), holding 4 days too long as to a one-time illegal sale of liquor. It is also generally true that more time will be tolerated when the search is for items which have continuing utility and are not strongly incriminating. Thus, the passage of 3 months from a bank robbery is not too long as to search for clothing worn by the robber, but is too long as to search for the bank's money bag. *U. S. v. Steeves*, 525 F.2d 33 (8th Cir. 1975). Likewise relevant is the extent to which the criminal would have had access to the place to be searched during the time which has elapsed. *P. v. Wilson*, 74 Cal.Rptr. 131 (Cal.1968).

Particular description of place or person to be searched. The Fourth Amendment provides that no warrants shall issue except those "particularly describing the place to be searched." This means the description must be such that the executing officer can "with reasonable effort ascertain and identify the place intended." *Steele v. U. S.,* 267 U.S. 498 (1925).

In describing premises to be searched, more care is generally required in urban areas than in rural areas. Farm property, for example, might merely be described in a general way and identified by section, township and range number. *P. v. Lavendowski,* 160 N.E. 582 (Ill.1928). In a city, however, a building must be identified by street and number or by an equally specific description. *Steele v. U. S.,* supra. Minor errors in description, such as an incorrect street number, will not invalidate a warrant if it is still apparent what building or what part of a building is to be searched. *U. S. v. Darensbourg,* 520 F.2d 985 (5th Cir. 1975). In multiple-occupancy structures, the particular unit to be searched must be identified by occupant, room number, or apartment number, *S. v. Gordon,* 559 P.2d 312 (Kan.1977), unless the multi-unit character of the property was not known to the officers applying for or executing the warrant and was not externally apparent. *U. S. v. Santore,* 290 F.2d 51 (2d Cir. 1959).

Similarly, if a search warrant is obtained for search of an automobile, the description must direct the executing officer to one specific vehicle, either by license number, *Hines v. S.,* 275 P.2d 355 (Okla.Crim.1954), or by the make of the car and the name of the operator, *Hatley v. S.,* 113 P.2d 396

(Okla.1941). As to misdescription, the question again is whether the officer could select the proper vehicle, and thus a license number is sufficient notwithstanding a mistake as to the color and model year of the car. *Bowling v. S.,* 408 S.W.2d 660 (Tenn.1966).

A valid warrant for the search of a certain person must indicate the person's name, if known, *Garrett v. S.,* 270 P.2d 1101 (Okla.Crim.1954). If his name is not known, an otherwise complete description, listing such facts as the individual's aliases, approximate age, height and weight, race, and clothing, is adequate. *Dow v. S.,* 113 A.2d 423 (Md.1955).

Particular description of things to be seized. The Fourth Amendment also provides that no search warrants shall issue except those "particularly describing the * * * things to be seized." "The requirement that warrants shall particularly describe the things to be seized makes general searches under them impossible * * *. As to what is to be taken, nothing is left to the discretion of the officer executing the warrant." *Marron v. U. S.,* 275 U.S. 192 (1927).

The degree of particularity required varies somewhat depending upon the nature of the materials to be seized. Greater leeway is permitted in describing contraband (property the possession of which is a crime), and thus during Prohibition a description merely of "cases of whiskey" would suffice. *Steele v. U. S.,* supra. By comparison, innocuous property must be described more specifically so that executing officers will not be confused between the items sought and other property of a similar nature which might well be found on the premises. *In re 1969 Plymouth Roadrunner,* 455 S.W.2d 466 (Mo.1970). The particularity requirement requires even closer scrutiny of warrants for documents because of the potential they carry for very serious intrusions into privacy. *Andresen v. Md.,* 427 U.S. 463 (1976).

Because of First Amendment considerations, this constitutional requirement "is to be accorded the most scrupulous exactitude when the 'things' are books, and the basis for their seizure is the ideas they contain." *Stanford v. Texas,* 379 U.S. 476 (1965). Also, in obscenity cases a search warrant may not authorize the seizure of great quantities of the same publication before the owner has had an opportunity to litigate the question of obscenity, for this would be an unconstitutional prior restraint. *A Quantity of Copies of Books v. Kansas,* 378 U.S. 205 (1964). For the same reason, seizure of even a single copy of a film may not continue if it would prevent further showing of that picture by the exhibitor. *Heller v. N. Y.,* 413 U.S. 483 (1973).

B. EXECUTION

Time of execution. Even where statutes or court rules purport to authorize execution within a fixed period of time, e. g., 10 days, the better view is that execution even within that time is permissible only if "the probable cause recited in the affidavit continues until the time of execution, giving consideration to the intervening knowledge of the officers and the passage of time," *U. S. v. Nepstead,* 424 F.2d 259 (9th Cir. 1970). Three members of the Court have suggested that a search warrant may be executed at night only upon a special showing of a need to do so, as provided by law in several jurisdictions, because of the "Fourth Amendment doctrine that increasingly severe standards of probable cause are necessary to justify increasingly intrusive searches." *Gooding v. U. S.,* 416 U.S. 430 (1974). A search warrant may be executed in the absence of the occupant, *U. S. v. Gervato,* 474 F.2d 110 (3d Cir. 1973).

Entry without notice. 18 U.S.C.A. § 3109 provides that an officer may break into premises to execute a search warrant only "if, after notice of his authority and purpose, he is refused admittance," and many states have comparable statutes. The breaking referred to in such statutes includes any unannounced intrusion, even by opening a closed but unlocked door, *Sabbath v. U. S.,* 391 U.S. 585 (1968), but apparently not entry by subterfuge, *S. v. Valentine,* 504 P.2d 84 (Ore.1973). By analogy to the cases dealing with entry for purposes of arrest (see pp. 142–144), it may be concluded that these statutes state the requirements of the Fourth Amendment, subject to exceptions when exigent circumstances are present. *Ker v. Cal.,* 374 U.S. 23 (1963); *Sabbath v. U. S.,* supra.

The exigent circumstances most likely to be present when a search warrant is to be executed is the risk that notice would result in destruction of the evidence sought. However, entry without notice cannot be so justified merely by the type of crime or evidence involved, but instead requires a specific showing of facts and circumstances involved in that particular case indicating there was a risk that the evidence would be destroyed. *P. v. Gastelo,* 432 P.2d 706 (Cal.1967). "Just as the police must have sufficient particular reason to enter at all, so must they have some particular reason to enter in the manner chosen."

Detention and search of persons on the premises to be searched. An individual who merely happens to be present in premises where a search warrant is being executed may not, by virtue of that fact alone, be subjected to a search of his person. This is because such a search "must be supported by probable cause particularized with respect to that person," a requirement which "cannot be undercut or avoided by simply pointing to the fact that coincidentally there exists probable cause * * * to search the premises where the person may happen to be." *Ybarra v. Ill.,* 444 U.S. 85 (1979).

Of course, if probable cause to search that person did exist and was established when the warrant to search the premises was obtained, that warrant could also authorize search of the person. *U. S. v. Baca,* 480 F.2d 199 (10th Cir. 1973). During execu-

[*129*]

tion of a warrant lacking such authorization, a person might be discovered within as to whom there are grounds for arrest, in which case a search of the person could be undertaken incident to arrest and without reliance upon the search warrant. *Marron v. U. S.,* 275 U.S. 192 (1927). Or, if there are not grounds to arrest but yet probable cause that the person has in his possession the items named in the search warrant, this would appear to be an additional basis for the search, for there would not be time to seek an additional warrant. *U. S. v. Miller,* 298 A.2d 34 (D.C.App.1972). In other circumstances, it might be proper to detain briefly for investigation a person who attempts to leave during execution of a warrant naming items which could easily be removed from the premises, *U. S. v. Festa,* 192 F.Supp. 160 (D.Mass.1960), cf. *Terry v. Ohio,* 392 U.S. 1 (1968), but an actual search of such a person may not be undertaken merely because of suspicion that person may have the objects named in the search warrant. *Ybarra v. Ill.,* supra.

A second justification given for search of persons on the premises where a search warrant is being executed is self-protection of the officer. *U. S. v. Peep,* 490 F.2d 903 (8th Cir. 1974). If there is some basis for thinking that the person may be armed, and if only a frisk is undertaken, this would seem proper. Cf. *Terry v. Ohio,* supra (discussed in § 15).

Seizure of items not named in the warrant. Even if, as required, the police look within the described place only where the described items might be located, *Harris v. U. S.,* 331 U.S. 145 (1947), and terminate the search once those items are discovered, *S. v. Starke,* 260 N.W.2d 739 (Wis.1978), they may discover supposed incriminating evidence other than that named in the warrant. As to this situation, the Court stated in *Coolidge v. N. H.,* 403 U.S. 443 (1971): "Where, once an otherwise lawful search is in progress, the police inadvertently come upon a piece of evidence [in plain view], it would often be a needless inconvenience, and sometimes dangerous—to the evidence or to the police themselves—to require them to ignore it until they have obtained a warrant particularly describing it."

The requirement of inadventent discovery, which may not actually have been accepted by a majority of the Court, see *North v. Superior Court,* 502 P.2d 1305 (Cal.1972), was explained on the ground that if the warrant fails to mention a particular object but "the police know its location and intend to seize it," then there is a violation of the Fourth Amendment requirement that warrants particularly describe the things to be seized. It would seem that discovery is anticipated only where there was "pre-existing knowledge of the identity and location of an item sufficiently in advance of the seizure to permit the warrant to be applied for and issued." *U. S. v. Welsch,* 446 F.2d 220 (10th Cir. 1971). Even if the discovery was inadvertent, the item may be seized only if there is probable cause it constitutes the fruits, instrumentalities or evidence of crime, *C. v. Wojcik,* 266 N.E.2d 645 (Mass.1971).

14. WARRANTLESS SEARCHES AND SEIZURES

A. PERSONS

Arrest. The prevailing view, as a matter of state law, is that an arrest warrant is not required in serious cases notwithstanding the practicability of obtaining one before arrest. Arrest without warrant was lawful at common law when the officer had "reasonable grounds to believe" that a felony had been committed and that the person to be arrested had committed it, and this is the prevailing rule today either as a matter of statute or court decision. This "reasonable grounds" test and the "probable cause" requirement of the Fourth Amendment "are substantial equivalents." *Draper v. U. S.,* 358 U.S. 307 (1959). On the other hand, warrants are sometimes required for minor offenses notwithstanding the need for immediate action. The prevailing law is that an officer may arrest without warrant for all misdemeanors committed in his presence, but that he must obtain a warrant even when he has overwhelming evidence of a misdemeanor which occurred out of his presence. This requirement, even when interpreted to mean that the officer must only have reasonable grounds to believe that a misdemeanor occurred in his presence, *Drago v. S.,* 553 S.W.2d 375 (Tex.1977), is sometimes too restrictive, in that there may be a need for immediate arrest even though the officer did not witness the misdemeanor. Some jurisdictions have thus provided by statute for arrest without warrant on "reasonable grounds" for all offenses.

With the exception of the case in which private premises must be entered to make the arrest (see pp. 140–142), there is no constitutional requirement that an arrest warrant be obtained when it is practicable to do so. While the Court has expressed a "preference for the use of arrest warrants when feasible," see *Gerstein v. Pugh,* 420 U.S. 103 (1975), it also has declined "to transform this judicial preference into a constitutional rule," *U. S. v. Watson,* 423 U.S. 411 (1976). Such a rule, it noted in *Watson,* would "encumber criminal prosecutions with endless litigation with respect to the existence of exigent circumstances." On the other hand, *Gerstein v. Pugh,* supra, held that once a warrantless arrest is made, the Fourth Amendment "requires a [prompt] judicial determination of probable cause as a prerequisite to extended restraint on liberty following [the warrantless] arrest." That determination, upon a standard which "is the same as that for arrest," may be made in an ex parte proceeding (i. e., without defense participation) in the same manner as the issuance of a warrant.

[133]

Search incident to arrest. "When an arrest is made, it is reasonable for the arresting officer to search the person arrested in order to remove any weapons that the latter might seek to use in order to resist arrest or effect his escape [and to] seize any evidence on the arrestee's person in order to prevent its concealment or destruction." *Chimel v. Cal.*, 395 U.S. 752 (1969). Given this justification, doubt existed for some time as to whether a search could be undertaken incident to an arrest for a lesser offense, such as a minor traffic violation, where there would be no evidence to search for and a relatively lesser risk that the arrestee would be armed. But in *U. S. v. Robinson*, 414 U.S. 218 (1973), the Court held that a full search of the person incident to a "full custody arrest" (i. e., one made for the purpose of taking the person to the station) may be undertaken without regard to "what a court may later decide was the probability in a particular arrest situation that weapons or evidence would in fact be found upon the person of the suspect," apparently on the ground that it would be unwise to have courts second-guessing such a "quick *ad hoc* judgment" by arresting officers. The limited frisk alternative of *Terry* (see § 15) was deemed insufficient in the case of arrest, as "the danger to an officer is far greater in the case of the extended exposure which follows the taking of a suspect into custody and transporting him to the police station."

What then of the situation in which the arrest is not of the "full custody" type referred to in

Robinson, as where a traffic violator is arrested in the expectation that he will be released at the scene after signing a promise to appear? At least when the offense is not one for which evidence could be found on the person, it appears that only a frisk may be undertaken and that even this step is impermissible unless the *Terry* grounds for frisk are present. *U. S. v. Robinson,* 471 F.2d 1082 (D.C.Cir. 1972). Even absent such grounds, the officer may direct a motorist lawfully seized for a violation to alight from his car during the encounter. *Pa. v. Mimms,* 434 U.S. 106 (1977).

The Supreme Court's ruling in *Robinson* makes more significant the longstanding issue of what items are subject to seizure once discovered. Clearly seizure is not limited to the items sought; "when an article subject to lawful seizure properly comes into an officer's possession in the course of a lawful search it would be entirely without reason to say that he must return it because it was not one of the things it was his business to look for." *Abel v. U. S.,* 362 U.S. 217 (1960). But in *Abel* there was probable cause to seize the item in question, and on this ground *Abel* was distinguished in *S. v. Elkins,* 422 P.2d 250 (Or.1966), where the officer seized an unlabeled bottle of pills from the pocket of a defendant arrested for public intoxication. The court, noting the absence of cases in point, concluded that the seizure was improper because the officer acted only upon suspicion that the pills might be narcotics and not upon "reasonable grounds to

[135]

believe that the article he has discovered is contraband." Compare the situation as to seizure of items not named in a search warrant, § 13B, which likewise raises the question of how much discretion should be left to the searching officer; and consider *Warden v. Hayden,* 387 U.S. 294 (1967), where the court, in rejecting the contention that abolition of the "mere evidence" rule would result in indiscriminate seizures, emphasized that there "must, of course, be a nexus * * * between the item to be seized and criminal behavior," and that "probable cause must be examined in terms of cause to believe that the evidence sought will aid in a particular apprehension or conviction."

Time of search; inventory. It is clear that a search cannot be justified as being "incident" to arrest if the search is conducted without arrest and at a time when a lawful arrest could not be made because sufficient grounds are lacking, *P. v. Edge,* 94 N.E.2d 359 (Ill.1950), or because of physical inability to make an arrest at that time, *Mosco v. U. S.,* 301 F.2d 180 (9th Cir. 1962). But a search of the person qualifies as a search incident to arrest if "the formal arrest followed quickly on the heels" of that search and was sufficiently grounded upon facts other than those uncovered by the search. *Rawlings v. Ky.,* —— U.S. —— (1980). This is a sound position, as a search before arrest when there are grounds to arrest involves no greater invasion of the person's security and privacy, and has the advantage that if

[136]

the search is not productive the individual may not be arrested at all. *P. v. Simon,* 290 P.2d 531 (Cal.1955). If there was no present intent to arrest and arrest does not promptly follow the search, then the search is not properly characterized as "incident" to arrest, but it is still lawful if made upon probable cause and limited to the extent "necessary to preserve highly evanescent evidence [e. g., fingernail scrapings]." *Cupp v. Murphy,* 412 U.S. 291 (1973).

Courts have generally upheld delayed searches of the person arrested (such as those made on the way to or at the station), either on the theory that police control of the person by arrest is so substantial that it of necessity carries with it a continuing right of search, *S. v. Luckett,* 327 So.2d 365 (La.1976), or on the ground that the police are entitled to inventory the property found on a person before placing him in a cell. *P. v. Perel,* 315 N.E.2d 452 (N.Y.1974). A contrary result has sometimes been reached because of a prior failure of the police to permit the defendant to exercise his right of stationhouse release. *Zehrung v. S.,* 573 P.2d 858 (Alaska 1978). In *U. S. v. Edwards,* 415 U.S. 800 (1974), the Court held that "once the defendant is lawfully arrested and is in custody, the effects in his possession at the place of detention that were subject to search at the time and place of his arrest may lawfully be searched and seized without a warrant even though a substantial period of time has elapsed between the

arrest and subsequent administrative processing on
the one hand and the taking of the property for use
as evidence on the other," at least where such
searches are not unreasonable "either because of
their number or their manner of perpetration."
This qualification suggests that neither *Robinson*
nor *Edwards* disturb the holding in *Schmerber v.
Cal.,* 384 U.S. 757 (1966), that, except where delay
would threaten loss of the evidence, a search
warrant is required to intrude into an arrestee's
body.

"Subterfuge" arrests. *Robinson* has been criticized on the ground that it opens the door to
"subterfuge" arrests for minor offenses made to
support searches of persons for evidence of more
serious offenses as to which probable cause is lacking, particularly in light of the fact that *Robinson*
was applied in the companion case of *Gustafson v.
Fla.,* 414 U.S. 260 (1973), to a situation in which the
officer had complete discretion as to whether to
arrest or give a citation and whether to search if an
arrest was made.   Evidence has been suppressed
upon a showing that the desire to seek such evidence
was the motivation behind arrest for such minor
crimes as vagrancy, *Green v. U. S.,* 386 F.2d 953
(10th Cir. 1967), or a traffic violation, *Amador-
Gonzales v. U. S.,* 391 F.2d 308 (5th Cir. 1968).   But
some courts have overlooked strong evidence of such
a "subterfuge."   See *P. v. Watkins,* 166 N.E.2d 433
(Ill.1960) (officers assigned to gambling squad who

suspected defendant possessed gambling paraphernalia arrested him for parking too close to a crosswalk, searched his person and found policy slips); *Anderson v. S.*, 444 P.2d 239 (Okla.Crim.1968) (officer who arrested defendant for making improper right turn and then found marijuana in search was accompanied by federal narcotics agent).

The significance of booking. "Booking" is an administrative step taken after the arrested person is brought to the police station, which involves entry of the person's name, the crime for which the arrest was made, and other relevant facts on the police "blotter," and which may also include photographing, fingerprinting, and the like. Because booking results in a record of some of the circumstances of arrest, the question has arisen whether the entries made are relevant in determining the lawfulness of the arrest. A few courts have taken the position that an entry that the defendant was arrested "on suspicion of" or "for investigation of" a certain offense shows that the arrest was without probable cause, *Staples v. U. S.*, 320 F.2d 817 (5th Cir. 1963), but in practice such entries are often made solely for the purpose of identifying those cases being referred to the detective division. It has been held that if a person was booked for one offense, his arrest may thereafter be upheld on the ground that the police had sufficient evidence of a quite different offense, *Ricehill v. Brewer*, 459 F.2d 537 (8th Cir. 1972). A contrary conclusion, it is argued, would prevent arrest "on a trumped-up charge," *Wainwright v. New Orleans,* 392 U.S. 598 (1968) (dissent of Chief Justice to dismissal of writ of certiorari), and on this basis some courts have declined to inquire into the existence of probable cause for an offense unrelated to that for which the defendant was booked. *U. S. v. Atkinson,* 450 F.2d 835 (5th Cir. 1971).

B.   PREMISES

Entry to arrest. In *Payton v. N. Y.,* —— U.S. —— (1980), the Court held that the Fourth Amendment prohibits the police from making a warrantless nonconsensual entry into a suspect's home to make a routine arrest. The Court reasoned that the "basic principle of Fourth Amendment law" that searches and seizures inside a home without a warrant are presumptively unreasonable, long applied when the objective was to search for an object, "has equal force when the seizure of a person is involved." This is because "any differences in the intrusiveness of entries to search and entries to arrest are merely ones of degree rather than kind," and they "share this fundamental characteristic: the breach of the entrance to an individual's home." As for the argument that a warrant requirement was impractical, the Court, after noting it had been provided with no "evidence that effective law enforcement has suffered in those States that already have such a requirement," declared that "such arguments of policy must give way to a constitutional command that we consider to be unequivocal."

Prior to *Payton,* the Court had held that police may enter premises without a warrant in immediate pursuit of a person to be arrested who sought refuge therein on seeing the police approach, *U. S. v. Santana,* 427 U.S. 38 (1976). Such an entry may also be made in hot pursuit of an offender, as in *Warden v. Hayden,* 387 U.S. 294 (1967), where the police were informed that an armed robbery had taken place and that the suspect had entered a certain house five minutes before they reached it, as delay under these circumstances would endanger the lives of the police and others. Once inside, the Court concluded in *Hayden,* the police were justified in looking everywhere in the house where the suspect might be hiding and also (before his capture) where weapons might be hidden.

Payton casts no doubt on those decisions, for the Court emphasized it was dealing with in-premises arrests for which no exigent circumstances claim had been made. Thus, the Court in *Payton* had no occasion to elaborate upon what would amount to exigent circumstances. The Court did, however, place considerable reliance upon *Dorman v. U. S.,* 435 F.2d 385 (D.C. Cir. 1970), where exigent circumstances were found to be present based upon these factors: (1) a crime of violence was involved; (2) the suspect was reasonably believed to be armed; (3) there was a very clear showing of probable cause; (4) there was a strong reason to believe the suspect was within the premises; (5) there was a likelihood the suspect would escape if not swiftly apprehended; and (6) the entry was made peaceably.

In response to the "suggestion that only a search warrant based on probable cause to believe the suspect is at home at a given time can adequately protect the privacy interests at stake," the Court in *Payton* concluded that an arrest warrant, though affording less protection than a search warrant, would suffice: "If there is sufficient evidence of a citizen's participation in a felony to persuade a judicial officer that his arrest is justified, it is constitutionally reasonable to require him to open his doors to the officers of the law. Thus, for Fourth Amendment purposes, an arrest warrant founded on probable cause implicitly carries with it the limited authority to enter a dwelling in which the suspect lives when there is reason to believe the suspect is within." But the Court in *Payton* emphasized it did not have before it a case involving entry of a third party's premises, and thus the language just quoted does not cast doubt upon the conclusion of some courts that in a third party situation a search warrant is required because an arrest warrant "affords no basis to believe that the suspect is in some stranger's home." *Fisher v. Volz,* 496 F.2d 333 (3d Cir. 1974).

Entry without notice. Many jurisdictions have statutes which expressly provide that an officer may not break into private premises for purposes of arrest unless he has been denied admittance after giving "notice of his office and purpose." However, these statutes have generally been interpreted as codifying the common law rule with its exceptions for "exigent circumstances." These laws apply to actual breaking of doors and windows as well as merely opening an unlocked door, but not to entry by subterfuge. *U. S. v. Beale*, 445 F.2d 977 (5th Cir. 1971). Courts have excused notice and demand when it reasonably appeared that: (1) the occupants were already aware of the presence of the police and their objective, *Matthews v. U. S.*, 335 A.2d 251 (D.C.App.1975); (2) prompt action was required for the protection of a person within, *P. v. Woodward*, 190 N.W. 721 (Mich.1922); (3) unannounced entry was required for protection of the officer, *S. v. Max*, 263 N.W.2d 685 (S.C.1978); (4) unannounced entry was required to prevent the destruction of evidence, *Borum v. U. S.*, 318 A.2d 590 (D.C.App. 1974); (5) by unannounced entry actual commission of the offense could be observed, *P. v. Solario*, 566 P.2d 627 (Cal.1977); or (6) by unannounced entry escape of the person to be arrested could be prevented, *P. v. Maddox,* supra. Such belief must be based upon the facts of the particular case, and cannot be justified by a general assumption that certain classes of persons are more likely than others to resist arrest, attempt escape, or destroy evidence. *P. v. Rosales*, 437 P.2d 489 (Cal.1968).

The Supreme Court has yet to speak clearly to the issue. In *Ker v. Cal.*, 374 U.S. 23 (1963), four members of the Court concluded that entry without notice and demand was proper because the evidence (narcotics) could easily be disposed of and it appeared from the defendant's earlier furtive conduct that he was expecting the police. Another justice concurred on the ground that state searches and seizures should be judged by "concepts of fundamental fairness," while the remaining members of the Court argued that under the Fourth Amendment the only exceptions to the demand-notice requirements were "(1) where the persons within already know of the officers' authority and purpose or (2) where the officers are justified in the belief that persons within are in imminent peril of bodily harm, or (3) where those within, made aware of the presence of someone outside (because, for example, there has been a knock at the door) are then engaged in activity which justifies the officers in the belief that an escape or the destruction of evidence is being attempted."

Search incident to and after arrest. For many years, it could be said that the right to make a warrantless search incident to arrest was one exception which came close to swallowing up the search warrant requirement. Per *Harris v. U. S.*, 331 U.S. 145 (1947), and *U. S. v. Rabinowitz*, 339 U.S. 56 (1950), such searches were permitted of the premises where the arrest occurred, without regard to the practicality of obtaining a search warrant. Under the *Harris-Rabinowitz* rule, the scope of the search extended to the entire premises in which the defendant had a possessory interest, and such searches were usually upheld without any showing of probable cause that the objects sought would be found there. In *Chimel v. Cal.*, 395 U.S. 752 (1969), the Court, noting that in more recent decisions such searches had been justified solely upon the need to prevent the arrested person from obtaining a weapon or destroying evidence, overruled *Harris* and *Rabinowitz* and limited the scope of warrantless searches incident to arrest consistent with that purpose:

"When an arrest is made, it is reasonable for the arresting officer to search the person arrested in order to remove any weapons that the latter might seek to use in order to resist arrest or effect his escape. * * * In addition, it is entirely reasonable for the arresting officer to search for and seize any evidence on the arrestee's person in order to prevent its concealment or destruction. And the area into which an arrestee might reach in order to grab a weapon or evidentiary items must, of course, be governed by a like rule. A gun on a table or in a drawer in front of one who is arrested can be as dangerous to the arresting officer as one concealed in the clothing of the person arrested. There is ample justification, therefore, for a search of the arrestee's person and the area 'within his immediate control'—construing that phrase to mean the area from within which he might gain possession of a weapon or destructible evidence." A broader search of the place of arrest "may be made only under the authority of a search warrant."

Chimel involved a search of an entire house, but the Court made it clear that the new rule would also bar more limited searches, such as the one-room search in *Rabinowitz* and the four-room search in *Harris*. However, some lower courts have applied the *Chimel* "immediate control" test broadly by assuming that defendants maintain control over a considerable area even after they have been arrested. For example, in *U. S. v. Wysocki*, 457 F.2d 1155 (5th Cir. 1972), a search into a box inside a closet was upheld although the arrestee was seated in a chair with one of the two officers immediately behind him.

Chimel is not inconsistent with the notion that if it is necessary for the arrestee to put on clothing or do other things before he is taken to the station, then the police may examine closets and other places to which the arrestee is permitted to move. *Giacalone v. Lucas*, 445 F.2d 1238 (6th Cir. 1971). Similarly, if a "potential accomplice" is also present, he may be frisked for weapons, *P. v. Roach*, 93 Cal.Rptr. 354 (App.1971), and the area within his immediate control may also be searched for weapons and evidence, *U. S. v. Manarite*, 448 F.2d 583 (2d Cir. 1971). Other cases have recognized that subsequent to the arrest the police may sometimes be justified in walking through other parts of the premises, either because other offenders are reasonably believed to be present, *U. S. v. Weber*, 518 F.2d 987 (8th Cir. 1975), or to see if there are others present who might constitute a security risk, *U. S. v. Blake*, 484 F.2d 50 (8th Cir. 1973).

Plain view. As noted in *Coolidge v. N. H.*, supra, "an object which comes into view during a search incident to arrest that is appropriately limited in scope under existing law may be seized without a warrant." Thus, if an object is discovered by the officer from a place where he is lawfully present, that discovery is not illegal, and this is so even if an arrest has been made but the object itself is not within the control of the arrestee under *Chimel. P. v. Block*, 491 P.2d 9 (Cal.1971). But in *Coolidge* it was indicated, though perhaps not by a majority of the Court, see *North v. Superior Court*, 502 P.2d 1305 (Cal.1972), that the item may be seized only if its discovery was "inadvertent," for if the police knew of the identity and location of the object in advance they should have obtained a search warrant for it. This suggests that discovery is anticipated only where there was "pre-existing knowledge of the identity and location of an item sufficiently in advance of the seizure to permit the warrant to be applied for and issued." *U. S. v. Welsch*, 446 F.2d 220 (10th Cir. 1971). Even so limited, the feasibility of the inadvertent discovery test has been questioned by some commentators on the ground that it creates an anomolous situation in which the police will have to show the absence of probable cause.

[147]

Another devise which has been utilized to prevent abuse of the power to enter to arrest is the "timed" arrest doctrine of *McKnight v. U. S.*, 183 F.2d 977 (D.C.Cir. 1950), holding that when the police pass up a convenient opportunity to arrest on the street and "time" the arrest to occur when the defendant is within premises in order to find evidence therein, the evidence found in the premises must be suppressed.

Assuming no problems in the manner in which the plain view is acquired, it does nor necessarily follow that the observed object may be seized. As stated in *Coolidge*, it must be "an incriminating object," which would appear to mean that there must be probable cause that the object is the fruits, instrumentality, or evidence of crime. And that determination must be made by the police without exceeding their authority. See, e. g., *Eiseman v. Superior Court*, 98 Cal.Rptr. 342 (App.1971), holding illegal the seizure of vials observed on a dresser at the time of arrest, as the incriminating nature of their contents was discovered only after the police picked them up and examined them. Compare *P. v. Eddington*, 198 N.W.2d 297 (Mich.1972), holding that the minor intrusion of picking up an object and looking at it is permissible on reasonable suspicion short of probable cause.

Search to prevent loss of evidence. In *Agnello v. U. S.*, 269 U.S. 20 (1925), the Court held that "belief, however well founded, that an article sought is concealed in a dwelling house furnishes no justification for a search of that place without a warrant." But in *Johnson v. U. S.*, 333 U.S. 10 (1948), and *Chapman v. U. S.*, 365 U.S. 610 (1961), reference was made to the possibility of a warrantless dwelling search being upheld upon a showing of a need for immediate action. This issue also took on increased importance because of the *Chimel* decision, and was not directly confronted in *Chimel* because no emergency was present there; the police had sufficient opportunity to obtain a search warrant before they tipped their hand by making an arrest.

But in *Vale v. La.*, 399 U.S. 30 (1970), the circumstances were different; the police had come to arrest the defendant on another matter, observed what reasonably appeared to be a sale of narcotics by the defendant to a person who drove up to his house, arrested the defendant in front of his house, made a cursory inspection of the house to determine if any one else was there, and then (after the defendant's mother and brother entered the house during the inspection) made a warrantless search of the house for the additional narcotics they believed were hidden there. Yet the Court concluded that the state had not met its burden "to show the existence of such an exceptional situation" as to justify a warrantless search, as the goods seized were not actually in the process of destruction or removal from the jurisdiction. The Court also asserted that because the officers had arrest warrants for Vale, "there is thus no reason * * * to suppose that it was impracticable for them to obtain a search warrant as well," but this is a questionable conclusion in view of the fact that here (unlike *Chimel*) the probable cause for search did not exist until the officers on the scene observed the illegal transaction. *Vale*, therefore, cannot easily be squared with the search-of-vehicles cases (see § 14C), but does show that the Court is much more protective of dwellings then vehicles. Also underlying *Vale* may be the notion expressed in *Davis v. U. S.*, 423 F.2d 974 (5th Cir. 1970), that recognition of a general exception to the warrant requirement on the basis of a risk of destruction of evidence by a third party "would result in the evaporation of an arrestee's Fourth Amendment rights" in that "there is almost always a partisan who might destroy or conceal evidence."

Nonetheless, some lower courts have upheld entry and search of premises on probable cause but without a search warrant on the ground that the risk of loss of evidence was sufficient to justify such immediate action. *U. S. v. Doyle*, 456 F.2d 1246 (5th Cir. 1972) (warrantless search of garage for stolen drugs where reason to believe suspects would leave city before search warrant could be obtained); *U. S. v. Rubin*, 474 F.2d 262 (3d Cir. 1973) (warrantless search of house after one defendant, upon arrest nearby, shouted to friends to call home about the arrest). There is also authority that the police may respond to this emergency by impounding the premises and keeping the occupants thereof under surveillance while a search warrant is being obtained, *Ferdin v. Sup. Ct.*, 112 Cal.Rptr. 66 (1974), although the Supreme Court has said it is an "open question" whether persons may be actually detained in such circumstances. *Rawlings v. Ky.*, —— U.S. —— (1980).

In *P. v. Sirhan*, 497 P.2d 1121 (Cal.1972), a warrantless search of defendant's home even without probable cause that evidence would be found was upheld on the ground that prompt action was necessary to discover whether there was a conspiracy to assassinate several political leaders. But the mere fact that a homicide has occurred in certain premises does not of itself establish exigent circumstances justifying a warrantless search. *Mincey v. Ariz.*, 437 U.S. 385 (1978).

C. AUTOMOBILES

Search incident to arrest. Although *Chimel* involved search of premises, the more limited rule of that case is equally applicable to a search of an automobile incident to arrest. *Thompson v. S.*, 488 P.2d 944 (Okla.Crim.1971). Here as well, however, some courts have taken a broad view of what is within the defendant's "immediate control." In *Application of Kiser*, 419 F.2d 1134 (8th Cir. 1969), the court upheld a search under a blanket on the back seat of the car because the arrestee, in the custody of several officers, was "within leaping range."

Search to prevent loss of evidence. In *Carroll v. U. S.,* 267 U.S. 132 (1925), the Court upheld a warrantless search of a vehicle being operated on the highway upon probable cause that it contained contraband, because it could be quickly moved out of the locality. The *Carroll* rule was seldom utilized, for most vehicle searches were justified as incident to the arrest of the driver, and thus it was not until *Chimel* that the precise reach of the *Carroll* rule became a matter of importance. The basic question was whether *Carroll* could be relied upon to justify a warrantless search of the car after arrest of the driver. One court answered in the negative on the ground that "exigencies do not exist when the vehicle and the suspect are both in police custody," *Ramon v. Cupp,* 423 F.2d 248 (9th Cir. 1970), but in *Chambers v. Maroney,* 399 U.S. 42 (1970), the Supreme Court reached a contrary conclusion. In response to the contention that *Carroll* was not applicable on these facts because the car in which the defendant was arrested could simply be held until a search warrant was obtained, the Court in *Chambers* responded: "For constitutional purposes, we see no difference between on the one hand seizing and holding a car before presenting the probable cause issue to a magistrate and on the other hand carrying out an immediate search without a warrant." This would seem somewhat inconsistent with the rationale of *U. S. v. Van-Leeuwen,* 397 U.S. 249 (1970), permitting the lesser intrusion of delaying a mailed package for a day until a search warrant could be obtained.

But *Chambers* does not mean that vehicles are always subject to search without a search warrant. In *Coolidge v. N. H.,* supra, concerning the warrantless seizure and subsequent search of defendant's car following his arrest in his nearby home, the culmination of several weeks of investigation into a murder, the plurality opinion noted that the instant case was distinguishable from *Chambers* in that there the car was discovered being operated shortly after the crime, so that there was no prior opportunity to obtain a search warrant, while in the instant case the police had the grounds for a warrant well in advance and knew where the vehicle might be found. Other bases of distinction mentioned by the *Coolidge* plurality, such as that there the objects being sought "were neither stolen nor contraband nor dangerous" and that neither Coolidge (who was under arrest) nor his wife (who was accompanied by police to another town) could gain access to the car, are less than convincing.

Precisely what constitutes an emergency justifying a warrantless search of a vehicle is a matter which continues to divide the Court, as illustrated by *Cardwell v. Lewis,* 417 U.S. 583 (1974), where, after defendant's arrest at the police station, his car was seized from a nearby parking lot and later subjected to an examination of its exterior. Four members of the Court concluded that there was a need for immediate action because the defendant might otherwise have given the car keys to his wife, and that it made no difference that the police had grounds to obtain a search warrant in advance of the arrest; four others concluded there was no emergency because the police had the car keys in their custody and because, as in *Coolidge,* there was ample opportunity to obtain a warrant before the arrest. (Powell, J., did not reach this issue in his concurring opinion.)   And in *Texas v. White,* 423 U.S. 67 (1975), it was held the police lawfully searched defendant's car at the station following his arrest therein for a recent attempt to pass fraudulent checks; two dissenters argued *Chambers* should not control when "there is no indication that an immediate search [at the arrest scene] would have been either impractical or unsafe."

Taken collectively, these cases appear to mean that while a clear and obvious *prior* opportunity to seek a warrant for a vehicle may not be disregarded (as was the case in *Coolidge*), otherwise a warrantless search of a vehicle may be undertaken even though, strictly speaking, there were no exigent circumstances which made it impossible or even risky to wait until a warrant was obtained.   The Court has more recently acknowledged that warrantless car searches are permissible when the risk of evidence loss is "remote, if not non-existent," and has explained this on the dubious ground that there is a "lesser expectation of privacy in a motor vehicle."

U. S. v. Chadwick, 433 U.S. 1 (1977). There is no comparable lesser expectation as to containers such as luggage, and thus they can be searched without a warrant only upon a genuine showing of exigent circumstances, *U. S. v. Chadwick,* supra, and this is so even if that container is found within a vehicle being subjected to a lawful warrantless search under the *Chambers* rule, *Ark. v. Sanders,* 442 U.S. 753 (1979). It is also so even if the police have lawful possession of the object, as "an officer's authority to possess a package is distinct from his authority to examine it." *Walters v. U. S.,* —— U. S. —— (1980).

Inventory. If the police have lawfully impounded a vehicle (e. g., because it was found illegally parked in such a way as to constitute a traffic hazard), they may, pursuant to an established standard procedure, secure and inventory the vehicle's contents in order to (i) protect the owner's property while it remains in police custody, (ii) protect the police from claims or disputes over lost or stolen property, and (iii) protect the police from potential danger. *So. Dak. v. Opperman,* 428 U.S. 364 (1976). If the driver was stopped on the street while operating the vehicle and then arrested, some courts allow impoundment as a matter of course, *S. v. Shorney,* 524 P.2d 69 (Okla.Crim.1974), but there is a growing body of authority that the police must honor the driver's request that the car instead be lawfully parked there or turned over to a friend, *S. v. Goodrich,* 256 N.W.2d 506 (Minn.1977); some cases even indicate the police must take the initiative and inquire of the driver what disposition he prefers, *S. v. Rome*, 354 So.2d 504 (La.1978). There is also disagreement as to whether, if the car is impounded, the driver must be allowed to decide between inventory and waiver of any claims against the police; compare *P. v. Clark*, 357 N.E.2d 798 (Ill.1976), with *S. v. McDougal*, 228 N.W.2d 671 (Wis.1975). *Opperman* does not settle these matters; there, as the Court stressed, the owner or driver "was not present to make other arrangements."

An inventory is unlawful if it was not undertaken pursuant to standard policy or practice in the department, *S. v. Hudson*, 390 A.2d 509 (Me.1978), or if it appears to have been undertaken solely for some other motive (as shown, for example, by the failure to use inventory forms or to complete the inventory once contraband was discovered), *S. v. McDaniel*, 383 A.2d 1174 (N.J.Super.1978). In terms of scope, the inventory must be limited to areas of the car in which valuables might be found, *U. S. v. Edwards*, 554 F.2d 1331 (5th Cir. 1977), and may not extend to examination of "materials such as letters or checkbooks, that 'touch upon intimate areas of an individual's personal affairs,'" *So. Dak. v. Opperman*, supra (Powell, J., conc.). The view of some courts that the inventory may not extend to containers (such as suitcases) found in the car, *S. v. Gwinn*, 301 A.2d 291 (Del.1973), is supported by the reasoning in *U. S. v. Chadwick*, supra, and *Ark. v. Sanders*, supra.

15.   STOP–AND–FRISK AND OTHER
BRIEF DETENTION

Background.   Police have long followed the
practice of stopping suspicious persons on the street
or other public places for purposes of questioning
them or conducting some other form of investigation, and, incident to many stoppings, of searching
the person for dangerous weapons. Because this
investigative technique, commonly referred to as
stop-and-frisk, is ordinarily employed when there
are not grounds to arrest the suspect and to search
him incident to arrest, it was often questioned
whether the practice could be squared with the
Fourth Amendment. The Supreme Court provided
some answers in *Terry v. Ohio*, 392 U.S. 1 (1968),
and the companion cases of *Sibron v. N. Y.* and
Peters v. N. Y., 392 U.S. 40 (1968).

In *Terry*, where an officer observed three men
who appeared to be "casing" a store for a robbery
and then approached them for questioning and
frisked them, finding weapons on two of them, the
Court held "that where a police officer observes
unusual conduct which leads him reasonably to
conclude in light of his experience that criminal
activity may be afoot and that the persons with
whom he is dealing may be armed and presently
dangerous; where in the course of investigating this
behavior he identifies himself as a policeman and
makes reasonable inquiries; and where nothing in
the initial stages of the encounter serves to dispel his

[157]

reasonable fear for his own or others' safety, he is entitled for the protection of himself and others in the area to conduct a carefully limited search of the outer clothing of such persons in an attempt to discover weapons which might be used to assault him." *Sibron* involved the search of a man observed consorting which narcotic addicts, and there the Court found the officer did not have a reasonable fear for his own safety or that of others; *Peters* was disposed of on the ground that the officer had made a lawful arrest prior to the search which uncovered burglary tools.

The result in *Terry* rests upon three fundamental conclusions the Court reached concerning Fourth Amendment theory.   First of all, the Court concluded that restraining a person on the street is a "seizure" and that exploring the outer surfaces of his clothing is a "search," and thus rejected "the notions that the Fourth Amendment does not come into play at all as a limitation upon police conduct if the officers stop short of something called a 'technical arrest' or a 'fullblown search.'"   Secondly, after noting that the police conduct here was without a warrant and thus subject to the reasonableness rather than the probable cause part of the Fourth Amendment, the Court utilized the balancing test of the *Camara* case (see § 17) to conclude that a frisk could be undertaken upon facts which would not support an arrest and full search.   (Justice Douglas objected in dissent that the Court had in effect said that the police have more power without a warrant than with a warrant, which could have been answered—but was not—by observing that the balancing test applies in determining both the reasonableness of warrantless searches and seizures and, as in *Camara*, the probable cause for those with warrant.) Finally, in response to the defendant's observation that some stops and frisks are employed for harassment and other improper purposes, the Court noted that the exclusionary rule is ineffective when the police have no interest in prosecution and that consequently a flat prohibition of all stops and frisks would not deter those undertaken for improper objectives.

Temporary seizure for investigation. In *Terry*, the Court declined to rule upon "the constitutional propriety of an investigative 'seizure' upon less than probable cause." Yet, it seems that the Court approved such seizures by implication, for (as Justice Harlan observed in his concurring opinion) the conclusion that an officer was entitled to frisk for his own protection must rest upon the assumption that the officer was justified in creating the danger in the first instance by stopping the suspect for investigation. *Terry* was later relied upon in upholding "the officer's forcible stop" in *Adams v. Williams*, 407 U.S. 143 (1972).

It remains unclear what Fourth Amendment evidentiary test is to be applied to temporary seizures, although a clue may be provided by the Court's emphasis in *Terry* upon the situation "where a police officer observes unusual conduct which leads him reasonably to conclude in light of his experience that criminal activity may be afoot." If this language is compared with that usually employed to describe the evidentiary test for arrest, it appears that some difference exists in the degree of probability required. As to the probability required for arrest, it may generally be stated that it must be more probable than not that the person has committed an offense; that is, there must be a more than 50% probability that a crime has been committed, *P. v. Ingle*, 348 P.2d 577 (Cal.1960), and at least some times a more than 50% probability that the person arrested committed it, *Wong Sun v. U. S.*, 371 U.S. 471 (1963) (see pp. 290–291). The language in *Terry* suggests that a substantial possibility that a crime has been or is about to be committed and that the suspect is the person who committed or is planning the offense would suffice for a temporary seizure for investigation. See, e. g., *P. v. Mickelson*, 380 P.2d 658 (Cal.1963), holding that a stopping of a suspect near the scene of a recent robbery because he fitted the general description given by the victim was proper, though arrest would not have been proper because the description might have also fit others in the area.

In *Adams v. Williams*, supra, the Court, 6–3, upheld a stop based upon information the suspect possessed a gun and narcotics, given by a known informant who had provided information in the past. Because the informer could have been prosecuted for making a false complaint if his tip proved false, the tip (though insufficient for arrest) was deemed to have sufficient "indicia of reliability" to justify a stop. The dissenters objected to extending *Terry* so as to permit a stop where the information did not amount to probable cause because of its possible unreliability rather than its incompleteness, and one dissenter added that the power to stop would be subject to abuse if permitted for "mere possessory offenses." But in *Brown v. Texas,* 443 U.S. 47 (1980), where in the afternoon officers saw defendant and another man walk away from each other in an alley in an area with a high incidence of drug traffic, but there was no indication it was unusual for people to be in the alley and the police did not point to any facts supporting their conclusion the situation "looked suspicious," the Court held there were not grounds for a stop.

No grounds are required for the police to engage in a "street encounter" which does not even amount to a Fourth Amendment seizure. A person "has been 'seized' within the meaning of the Fourth Amendment only if, in view of all the circumstances surrounding the incident, a reasonable person would have believed that he was not free to leave," which means that the "subjective intention" of the police officer "is irrelevant except insofar as that may have been conveyed to the" suspect. *U. S. v. Mendenhall,* —— U.S. —— (1980).

A detention for investigation of a somewhat different kind was involved in *U. S. v. VanLeeuwen,*

397 U.S. 249 (1970), where the Court, citing *Terry*, upheld the holding of mailed packages for approximately one day while the police promptly investigated the suspicious circumstances of the mailing and obtained a search warrant for the packages.

Protective search. *Terry* makes it clear that whether it is proper to make a protective search incident to a stopping for investigation is a question separate from the issue of whether it is permissible to stop the suspect. For a protective search, it must reasonably appear that the suspect "may be armed and presently dangerous," which would again appear to require only a substantial possibility, rather than the more than 50% probability which would justify an arrest and full search for carrying a concealed weapon. Although *Terry* also emphasizes that the officer frisked only after he had made some initial inquiries and the responses did not "dispel his reasonable fear," the frisk upheld in *Adams* was not preceded by inquiries.

Terry indicates that a two-step process must ordinarily be followed: the officer must pat down first and then intrude beneath the surface of the suspect's clothing only if he comes upon something which feels like a weapon. In *Adams*, the Court approved the officer's conduct in reaching directly into the suspect's pocket, apparently because the informant had indicated the precise location of the weapon. But in any event, the search is limited by its recognized purpose, that is, "to an intrusion reasonably designed to discover guns, knives, clubs, or other hidden instruments for the assault of the police officer." This means that the search must be limited to those places to which the suspect has immediate access.

Brief detention at the station. It remains unclear whether the *Terry* balancing test may be utilized to support a brief detention for investigation at the station on grounds slightly short of that required for arrest. In *Davis v. Miss.*, 394 U.S. 721 (1969), holding fingerprints inadmissible because obtained after an illegal arrest, the Court noted it was arguable "that because of the unique nature of the fingerprinting process, such detention might, under narrowly defined circumstances, be found to comply with the Fourth Amendment even though there is no probable cause in the traditional sense," in that it "may constitute a much less serious intrusion upon personal security than other types of police searches and detentions." The Court added that a warrant would be required for such a detention, a matter which concurring Justice Harlan preferred to leave open.

Davis suggests that the intended investigative technique is a relevant consideration; the Court emphasized that detention for fingerprinting "involves none of the probing into an individual's private life and thoughts which marks an interrogation or search," cannot "be employed repeatedly to harass any individual," and "is an inherently more reliable and effective crime-solving tool than eyewitness identifications or confessions and is not subject to such abuses as the improper line-up and the 'third degree.' " Consistent with this, it was held in *Dunaway v. N. Y.*, 442 U.S. 200 (1979), that custodial questioning at the station on less than probable cause for a full-fledged arrest was unlawful. But in *Wise v. Murphy*, 275 A.2d 205 (D.C.App.1971), the court stated that a properly conducted lineup would be reliable and that therefore detention to facilitate it would be permissible on less than the grounds needed for arrest. Moreover, statutes authorizing stationhouse detention for other investigative purposes, such as fingerprinting or taking voice or handwriting exemplars, have been upheld. *S. v. Grijalva*, 533 P.2d 533 (Ariz.1975). The status of these provisions is not entirely clear, as *Dunaway* can be read broadly as barring all at-the-station detention on less than full probable cause, or narrowly as dealing only with interrogation and allowing detention for other types of investigation, at least if there is judicial authorization and the suspect is ordinarily given a chance to respond to a summons.

16. GRAND JURY SUBPOENAS

Unlike the detentions for the purpose of collecting evidence considered in *Davis, Dunaway,* and *Wise,* supra, the grand jury subpoena operates largely free of Fourth Amendment restrictions. Insofar as the Constitution is concerned, a subpoena directing a person to testify or produce specific physical evidence before a grand jury need not be supported by a showing of probable cause, reasonable suspicion, or any other factual foundation. *U. S. v. Dionisio,* 410 U.S. 1 (1973) (subpoena requiring production of voice exemplars); *U. S. v. Mara,* 410 U.S. 19 (1973) (subpoena requiring handwriting exemplars). As the Court noted in *Dionisio,* "a subpoena to appear before the grand jury is not a 'seizure' in the Fourth Amendment sense." Unlike an arrest or an "investigative stop," it does not produce an "abrupt" detention, "effected with force or the threat of it," or result "in a record [like an arrest record] involving social stigma." A subpoena, the Court has noted "is served in the same manner as other legal process [and] involves no stigma whatever." *U. S. v. Dionisio,* supra. The Court has acknowledged that the compulsion to appear or produce evidence does require some "personal sacrifice," but that obligation is characterized as simply a "part of the necessary contribution of the individual to the welfare of the public." *Blair v. U. S.,* 250 U.S. 273 (1919). The Court also has stressed, in this connection, that a person subpoenaed retains his privilege against self-incrimination (see § 29) and, where applicable, judicial protection against abuse of the grand jury process. A subpoena issued on the basis of "tips [or] rumors" is not abusive, however, since a grand jury has an obligation to "run down" every "available clue" in conducting its investigation. *U. S. v. Dionisio,* supra.

While the Fourth Amendment does not require a showing of some factual foundation for a subpoena, it does prohibit a subpoena duces tecum too sweeping in its terms "to be regarded as reasonable." *Hale v. Henkel*, 201 U.S. 43 (1906). This prohibition, arguably resting more appropriately on the due process clause, *In re Horowitz*, 482 F.2d 72 (2d Cir. 1972), has application primarily to subpoenas requesting production of numerous documents. In barring overly broad subpoenas duces tecum, courts have sought to ensure that a subpoena (1) commands production only of documents "relevant to the investigation being pursued," (2) specifies the documents to be produced "with reasonable particularity," and (3) includes records "covering only a reasonable period of time." *U. S. v. Gurule*, 437 F.2d 239 (10th Cir. 1970).

17. INSPECTIONS; REGULATORY SEARCHES

The Fourth Amendment has been held to apply to a variety of searches and inspections conducted as part of regulatory schemes. In each case, however, the standards applied have been somewhat different than those applied to searches conducted in the course of criminal investigations.

Inspection of premises. Administrative inspections of residential and commercial premises for fire, health and safety violations may not be undertaken without a search warrant unless the occupant consents to the inspection or the inspection is made in an emergency. The occupant is thus usually free to challenge the inspector's decision to search without the risk of suffering criminal penalties for his refusal. However, a search warrant for such an inspection does not require a showing of probable cause that a particular dwelling contains violations of the code being enforced, but only that reasonable legislative or administrative standards for conducting an area inspection are satisfied with respect to a particular building. This special probable cause test was arrived at "by balancing the need to search against the invasion which the search entails," considering (1) the long history of acceptance of such inspection programs; (2) the public interest in abating all dangerous conditions, even those which are not observable from outside the building; and (3) the fact that the inspections are neither personal in nature nor aimed at discovery of evidence of crime, and thus involve a relatively limited invasion of privacy. *Camara v. Mun. Ct.,* 387 U.S. 523 (1967); *See v. City of Seattle,* 387 U.S. 541 (1967). The *Camara-See* warrant requirement is inapplicable to inspection of businesses with a long tradition of close government supervision, *U. S. v. Biswell,* 406 U.S. 311 (1972) (weapons dealer), but in other instances the inspection, unless consented to, must be pursuant to a warrant based upon a showing that the inspection conforms to an established administrative plan. *Marshall v. Barlow's, Inc.*, 436 U.S. 307 (1978). Entry of premises to fight a fire and thereafter find the cause may be made without a warrant, but subsequent entries must be pursuant to an administrative warrant or, if probable cause of arson exists, a regular criminal warrant on full probable cause. *Mich. v. Tyler*, 436 U.S. 499 (1978).

Border searches. As noted in *Carroll v. U. S.*, 267 U.S. 132 (1925), quoted with approval in *Almeida-Sanchez v. U. S.*, 413 U.S. 266 (1973): "Travellers may be stopped in crossing an international boundary because of national self protection reasonably requiring one entering the country to identify himself as entitled to come in, and his belongings as effects which may be lawfully brought in." Border searches are considered unique, and a person crossing the border may be required to submit to a warrantless search of his person, baggage, and vehicle without the slightest suspicion, just as is true of incoming international mail (at least if correspondence is not read). *U. S. v. Ramsey*, 431 U.S. 606 (1977). However, some evidence short of probable cause must exist to justify more intrusive and embarrassing searches; "a real suspicion" is said to be required for a strip search, and a "clear indication" for examination of body cavities. *Henderson v. U. S.*, 390 F.2d 805 (9th Cir. 1967).

The special rules on border searches also apply to persons who have already travelled some distance into the country, if the circumstances indicate that any contraband which might be found was in the place searched at the time of entry. *Alexander v. U. S.,* 362 F.2d 379 (9th Cir. 1966). But, a border search must occur at the border or "its functional equivalent," and thus a car found near the border but not known to have crossed the border may not be subjected to a warrantless search for illegal aliens, either by a roving patrol or at a fixed checkpoint, in the absence of consent or probable cause. *Almeida-Sanchez v. U. S.,* supra; *U. S. v. Ortiz,* 422 U.S. 891 (1975). Such a vehicle may be stopped briefly to enable questioning of the occupants about their citizenship and immigration status if (a) the stopping occurs at a reasonably located fixed checkpoint, *U. S. v. Martinez-Fuerte,* 428 U.S. 543 (1976), or (b) the officer is aware of specific articulable facts which, together with rational inferences from those facts, reasonably warrant suspicion that the car contains aliens who may be illegally in the country. *U. S. v. Brignoni-Ponce,* 422 U.S. 873 (1975).

Driver's license and vehicle registration checks. Except when there is articulable and reasonable suspicion that a motorist is unlicensed or that a vehicle is not registered, or that either the vehicle or occupant is otherwise subject to seizure for violation of law, the random stopping of an auto and detaining the driver in order to check the license and registration is unreasonable. This does not preclude use of methods for spot checks that involve less intrusion or less discretion, such as stopping all traffic at a roadblock. *Del. v. Prouse,* 440 U.S. 648 (1979).

Airport inspections.   When airport hijacker detection searches were conducted selectively by use of the government's hijacker "profile," they were upheld by reliance on *Terry v. Ohio,* (p. 157). *U. S. v. Lopez,* 328 F.Supp. 1077 (E.D.N.Y.1971).   Now that all passengers and carry-on luggage are checked, the program can be upheld as a form of administrative search under *Camara,* at least so long as prospective passengers retain the right to leave rather than submit to inspection. *U. S. v. Davis,* 482 F.2d 893 (9th Cir. 1973).

Supervision of probationers and parolees.   Probationers and parolees may be subjected to searches without arrest or a search warrant and upon evidence which falls short of the usual probable cause requirement. *Latta v. Fitzharris,* 521 F.2d 246 (9th Cir. 1975); *U. S. v. Consuelo-Gonzalez,* 521 F.2d 259 (9th Cir. 1975).   Although this has sometimes been explained on the ground that probation and parole are acts of grace which are bestowed in exchange for the curtailment of constitutional rights, this is inconsistent with the principle that a state may not attach unconstitutional conditions to the grant of state privileges.   Somewhat more convincing is the argument that what is involved is another type of "administrative search" governed by the balancing test of *Camara,* in that without such close supervision there would be reluctance to grant parole and probation to those who are reasonable risks for such conditional release. *U. S. v. Consuelo-Gonzalez,* supra. If this is so, then the extent to which such special search authority is needed should be set as a condition of release on a case-by-case basis, as indicated by the unique facts of each case, and the condition should not confer this authority on the police.

18.   CONSENT SEARCHES

A.   THE NATURE OF CONSENT

Background.   Where effective consent is given, a search may be conducted without a warrant and without probable cause. At one time, the consent doctrine was assumed to be grounded on the concept of waiver, *Stoner v. Cal.,* 376 U.S. 483 (1964). But in *Schneckloth v. Bustamonte,* infra, the Court concluded that "a [traditional] 'waiver' approach to consent searches would be thoroughly inconsistent with our decisions," and thus held that the issue is whether the person's consent was "voluntary." Although this voluntariness test would appear to focus primarily upon the state of mind of the person allegedly consenting, the Court in *Schneckloth* did not have occasion to consider the notion that because it is the Fourth Amendment prohibition against unreasonable searches which is at issue, the question is whether "the officers, as reasonable men, could conclude that defendant's consent was given." *P. v. Henderson,* 210 N.E.2d 483 (Ill.1965).

Warning of rights. *Schneckloth v. Bustamonte,* 412 U.S. 218 (1973), holds that, while a person's knowledge of his right to refuse is a factor to be taken into account in determining (based on the totality of the circumstances) whether his consent was voluntary, the prosecution is not required to prove that he was so warned or otherwise had such knowledge where the consent was obtained while the person was not in custody. The *Johnson v. Zerbst* (p. 372) test of waiver, "an intentional relinquishment or abandonment of a known right or privilege," was distinguished as applicable only to those constitutional rights which, unlike the Fourth Amendment, are intended to protect a fair trial and the reliability of the truth-determining process; the *Miranda* requirement of Fifth Amendment warnings (see § 27) was distinguished because it only governs interrogation of those in custody.   While this latter distinction suggests that the *Miranda* analogy might be persuasive as to a consent to search given by one in custody, it was held in *U. S. v. Watson,* 423 U.S. 411 (1976), that failure to give Fourth Amendment warnings is not controlling where, as there, the defendant "had been arrested and was in custody, but his consent was given while on a public street, not in the confines of the police station." Most courts view the *Schneckloth* totality of circumstances test as equally applicable to consent obtained from one in custody at the station. *P. v. James,* 561 P.2d 1135 (Cal.1977).

Some courts have taken the position that "a consent to search, given during custodial interrogation must * * * be preceded by a proper *Miranda* warning" because "the request to search is a request that the defendant be a witness against himself which he is privileged to refuse under the Fifth Amendment." *S. v. Williams,* 432 P.2d 679 (Or.1967). The prevailing view, however, is to the contrary, on the ground that a consent to search "is neither testimonial nor communicative in the Fifth Amendment sense." *P. v. Thomas,* 91 Cal.Rptr. 867 (1970). But if the police first obtain statements in violation of *Miranda,* the subsequently obtained consent may be found to be a fruit of the earlier *Miranda* violation. *Pirtle v. S.,* 323 N.E.2d 634 (Ind.1975).

Consent subsequent to a claim of authority. A search may not be justified on the basis of consent when that "consent" was given only after the official conducting the search asserted that he possessed a search warrant, but in fact there was no warrant or an invalid warrant. Such a claim of authority is, in effect, an announcement that the occupant has no right to resist the search, and thus acquiescence under these circumstances cannot be construed as consent. *Bumper v. N. C.,* 391 U.S. 543 (1968). By comparison, the consent is valid if given in response to an officer's declaration that he will *seek* a warrant, as no false or overstated claim of authority has occurred. *P. v. Gurtenstein,* 138 Cal.Rptr. 161 (1977). But if the officer said he would *obtain* a warrant, this invalidates the consent if there were not grounds on which such a warrant could issue. *Flournoy v. S.,* 205 S.E.2d 473 (Ga.1974). Even when there is no assertion of a warrant or threat to obtain one, submission to such declarations as "I am here to search your house" or "I have come to search your house" are almost certain to be viewed as coercive. *Amos v. U. S.,* 255 U.S. 313 (1921).

Other relevant factors. The voluntariness of a consent to search is "to be determined from the totality of all the circumstances," *Schneckloth v. Bustamonte,* supra. Among the other factors to be considered in determining the effectiveness of an alleged consent to search are whether (1) the defendant had "minimal schooling" or was of "low intelligence," *Schneckloth v. Bustamonte,* supra; (2) he was mentally ill, *U. S. v. Elrod,* 441 F.2d 353 (5th Cir. 1971), or intoxicated, *S. v. Kelly,* 376 A.2d 840 (Me.1977); (3) the defendant was under arrest at the time it was given, *U. S. v. Hall,* 565 F.2d 917 (5th Cir. 1978); (4) he was overpowered by arresting officers, handcuffed, or similarly subject to physical restrictions, *P. v. James,* 561 P.2d 1135 (Cal.1977); (5) the keys to the premises searched had already been seized by the police from the defendant, *P. v. Porter,* 236 N.Y.S.2d 162 (Sup.Ct.1962); (6) the defendant employed evasive conduct or attempted to mislead the police, *Castaneda v. Sup. Ct.*, 380 P.2d 641 (Cal.1963); (7) he denied guilt or the presence of any incriminatory objects in his premises, *Higgins v. U. S.*, 209 F.2d 819 (D.C.Cir. 1954); (8) he earlier gave a valid confession, *U. S. v. Boukater*, 409 F.2d 537 (5th Cir. 1969), or otherwise cooperated, as by initiating the search, or at least the investigation leading to the search, *S. v. Kotka*, 152 N.W.2d 445 (Minn.1967); (9) he was hesitant in agreeing to the search, *S. v. Leavitt*, 237 A.2d 309 (R.I.1968); or (10) his request to consult with counsel was refused, *S. v. McClamrock*, 295 So.2d 715 (Fla.App.1974). The presence of some of these factors is not controlling, however, as each case "must stand or fall on its own special facts." *U. S. v. Dornblut*, 261 F.2d 949 (2d Cir. 1959).

Scope of consent. Assuming a valid consent, the police may not exceed the physical bounds of the area as to which consent was granted, such as by looking through private papers after a consent to allow search for narcotics. *U. S. v. Dichiarinte*, 445 F.2d 126 (7th Cir. 1971). There is disagreement as to whether a voluntary consent may be used to justify a second search of the same place after a fruitless first search; compare *P. v. Nawrocki*, 148 N.W.2d 211 (Mich.App.1967), with *S. v. Brochu*, 237 A.2d 418 (Me.1967). At least where, as in *Brochu*, there has been a significant passage of time, the second search involves re-entry of defendant's home, and defendant's status has changed from suspect to accused, the second search cannot be justified on the assumption that defendant's consent is continuing. In any event, a consent may be withdrawn or limited at any time prior to the completion of the search, *Mason v. Pulliam,* 557 F.2d 426 (5th Cir. 1977), though such a revocation does not operate retroactively so as to make invalid a search conducted prior to revocation. *U. S. v. Young,* 471 F.2d 109 (7th Cir. 1972).

Consent by deception. A somewhat related problem concerning the scope of the consent arises when the consent was obtained by deception, as where the suspect gives the policeman a gun on the representation that the officer will aid him in selling it, but the officer then has a ballistics test run on the weapon, as in *C. v. Brown,* 261 A.2d 879 (Pa.1970), or where the suspect gives a blood sample to the police on the representation that it will be tested for alcohol content but it is in fact matched with blood found at the scene of a rape, as in *Graves v. Beto,* 424 F.2d 524 (5th Cir. 1970). The "misplaced trust" cases, upholding the admissibility of voluntary disclosures of criminal conduct to an undercover officer or police agent, *Lewis v. U. S.,* 385 U.S. 206 (1966), *Hoffa v. U. S.,* 385 U.S. 293 (1966), are probably distinguishable. Situations such as *Brown* and *Graves* are more like *Gouled v. U. S.,* 255 U.S. 298 (1921) (where an old acquaintance acting for the police obtained defendant's consent to enter his office, but then conducted an extensive search when defendant

[176]

left the room), in that the officer exceeded the reasonably anticipated scope of the consensual intrusion. That is, in *Lewis* and *Hoffa* the defendant voluntarily revealed his criminal activity to another, but this was not so in *Gouled, Brown,* or *Graves.* See *C. v. Brown,* supra (dissent).

B. THIRD PARTY CONSENT

Background. In the area of consent searches, courts have long recognized that certain third parties may give consent which will permit use of the seized evidence against the defendant. Various theories have been utilized to explain this result. An agency theory was relied upon in *Stoner v. Cal.,* 376 U.S. 483 (1964), where the Court held that Fourth Amendment rights can only be waived by the defendant "either directly or through an agent." But in *Bumper v. N. C.,* supra, the Court seemed to rely upon a property theory in intimating that the grandmother's consent to search of her house for a rifle, had it been voluntary, would have been effective against the grandson who lived there because she "owned both the house and the rifle." In *Frazier v. Cupp,* 394 U.S. 731 (1969), consent by defendant's cousin Rawls to search of a duffel bag jointly used by them was held to be effective against the defendant because he "must be taken to have assumed the risk that Rawls would allow someone else to look inside." Similarly, in *U. S. v. Matlock,* 415 U.S. 164 (1974), the Court indicated that where two or more persons have joint access to or control of premises "it is reasonable to recognize that any of the coinhabitants has the right to permit the inspection in his own right and that the others have assumed the risk that one of their number might permit the common area to be searched." This assumption-of-risk theory is consistent with the justified-expectation-of-privacy approach to the Fourth Amendment in *Katz v. U. S.,* 389 U.S. 347 (1967) (see § 11).

This shift in theoretical basis may affect the result. Under the agency theory it has been held that a wife's consent is ineffective against her husband if she called the police because she was angry at him, *Kelley v. S.,* 197 S.W.2d 545 (Tenn.1946), but the contrary result is correct under the assumption-of-risk theory. *S. v. Madrid,* 574 P.2d 594 (N.M.1978). By like reasoning, under the latter theory *A*'s consent may be upheld as against *B* even though *B* instructed *A* not to consent, *P. v. Reynolds,* 127 Cal.Rptr. 561 (1976), even though the police passed up the opportunity to seek *B*'s consent, *U. S. v. Matlock,* supra, or even though *B*'s consent was earlier sought and refused, *U. S. v. Sumlin,* 567 F.2d 684 (6th Cir. 1977). The most difficult issue is whether *A*'s consent is effective against co-occupant *B* who is then present and objecting. One view is that it is because this risk has been assumed by joint occupancy, *U. S. v. Sumlin,* supra, supportable by the assertion in *Matlock* that each occupant is free "to act in his own or the public interest." The contrary view rests upon the notions that ordinarily a co-occupant would not consent in this situation and that to allow police to proceed on *A*'s consent in such a case would likely produce an "untoward confrontation." *Lawton v. S.,* 320 So.2d 463 (Fla.App.1975).

Relationship of third party to defendant and place searched. Most of the third party consent cases have involved the husband-wife relationship, and the prevailing view is that when a husband and wife jointly own or occupy the premises in question, either may consent to a search of those premises for items which may incriminate the other. *Coolidge v. N. H.,* 403 U.S. 443 (1971). Recent decisions have also upheld consents given by paramours who actually shared the premises on a continuing basis. *U. S. v. Matlock,* supra.

If a child is living at the home of his parents, the head of the household may consent to a search of the child's living quarters. *U. S. v. Wright,* 564 F.2d 785 (8th Cir. 1977). On the other hand, a child may not give effective consent to a full search of the parents' home, *P. v. Jennings,* 298 P.2d 56 (Cal.App.1956), although where it is not unusual or unauthorized for the child to admit visitors into the home, the mere entry of police on the premises with the consent of the child is not improper. *Davis v. U. S.,* 327 F.2d 301 (9th Cir. 1964).

A landlord may not consent to the search of rented premises occupied by a tenant, and this is so even though the landlord may have some limited right of entry for purposes of inspecting or cleaning the premises. *Chapman v. U. S.,* 365 U.S. 610 (1961). A person who rents a hotel room is treated as any other tenant, *Stoner v. Cal.,* supra, although once the time of occupancy has expired and the guest has checked out, a hotel representative may then consent to a search for anything the guest has left behind. *Abel v. U. S.,* 362 U.S. 217 (1960). However, the landlord or his agents (such as a building custodian or superintendent) may consent to a search of hallways, basements, and other area to which all tenants have common access. *U. S. v. Kelly,* 551 F.2d 760 (8th Cir. 1977). A tenant may not consent to search of the part of the premises retained by the landlord, *Weeks v. U. S.,* 232 U.S. 383 (1914), but may consent to search of the premises rented to him for items the landlord may have hidden there. *U. S. v. Green,* 523 F.2d 968 (9th Cir. 1975). A person sharing a house or apartment with another may consent to a search of areas of common usage, *S. v. Thibodeau,* 317 A.2d 172 (Me.1974), and a person in lawful possession of premises may give consent to search of the premises which will be effective against a nonpaying guest or casual visitor, *U. S. v. Buckles,* 495 F.2d 1377 (8th Cir. 1974).

An employer may consent to a search of an employee's work and storage areas on the employer's premises, *U. S. v. Gargiso,* 456 F.2d 584 (2d Cir. 1972), but he may not consent to a search of areas in which the employee is permitted to keep personal items not connected with the employment. *U. S. v. Blok,* 188 F.2d 1019 (D.C.Cir. 1951). Whether an employee can give a valid consent to a search of his employer's premises depends upon the scope of his authority. Generally, the courts have been of the view that a lesser employee, such as a secretary, may not give consent. *P. v. Polito,* 355 N.E.2d 725 (Ill.App.1976). However, if the employee is a manager or other person of considerable authority who is left in complete charge for a substantial period of time, then the prevailing view is that such a person can waive his employer's rights. *S. v. Cook,* 411 P.2d 78 (Or.1966).

Whether a bailee, who does not own the property but has lawful possession of it, can consent to a police search of the property which will be effective against the bailor depends upon whether the nature of the bailment is such that the bailor has assumed the risk. *Frazier v. Cupp,* supra. The risk is assumed when, as in that case, a duffel bag is turned over on the understanding that the bailee may use part of it to store his effects, but not when a locked container is involved and the bailee has no key. *Holzhey v. U. S.,* 223 F.2d 823 (5th Cir. 1955). The extent to which the bailor has surrendered control and the length of the bailment are important; perhaps an attendant in a public garage may consent to the opening of the car door to see items on the floor of the car, *Casey v.*

U. S., 191 F.2d 1 (9th Cir. 1951), but for the bailee to consent to search of the trunk it must appear that the bailee was authorized to open the trunk. *Potman v. S.,* 47 N.W.2d 884 (Wis.1951).

Apparent authority. In *Stoner v. Cal.,* supra, in response to the state's contention that a police search of defendant's hotel room was proper because they reasonably believed that the clerk had authority to consent, the Court emphasized "that the rights protected by the Fourth Amendment are not to be eroded by strained applications of the law of agency or by unrealistic doctrines of 'apparent authority.'" As a consequence, it is unclear what remains of the apparent authority rule, which rests upon the notion that police have not conducted an unreasonable search if they acted upon the consent of a person who reasonably appeared to be in a position to give consent. *P. v. Gorg,* 291 P.2d 469 (Cal.1955). It appears that only reasonable mistakes of law (e. g., whether a hotel clerk can consent to search of a hotel room), as opposed to reasonable mistakes of fact (e. g., whether the person giving consent actually has the property interest in the premises searched which he claims or otherwise appears to have), are insufficient. *U. S. v. Peterson,* 524 F.2d 167 (4th Cir. 1975).

Exclusive control. In third party consent situations, it is necessary to consider the various relationships discussed above as they relate to the particular area or object searched. In *U. S. v.*

Matlock, supra, the Court said the effectiveness of the consent depended upon whether there was "common authority" over the premises, which was said to rest on "mutual use of the property" by one "having joint access or control for most purposes." Consistent with this language is the notion that even if *A* and *B* generally share premises together, they each may still have areas therein of mutually exclusive use. Such is least likely to be true in husband-wife situations, where ordinarily the personal effects of each spouse are not thought to be "off limits" to the other, *S. v. Kennedy,* 452 P.2d 486 (N.M.1969), but the result may well be different in the case of friends sharing an apartment.

CHAPTER 3

WIRETAPPING, ELECTRONIC EAVESDROPPING, AND THE USE OF SECRET AGENTS

19. HISTORICAL BACKGROUND; APPLICATION OF FOURTH AMENDMENT

The Olmstead case. In *Olmstead v. U. S.*, 277 U.S. 438 (1928), the first wiretap case to reach the Supreme Court, the police intercepted communications by placing a tap on defendant's telephone line. In a 5–4 decision, the majority read the Fourth Amendment literally in concluding that the police conduct did not constitute a search and seizure. Two reasons were given: (1) at no time did the police trespass upon defendant's premises, so that no "place" was searched; and (2) only conversations were obtained, so that no "things" were seized.

As indicated herein, both of these grounds have since been rejected, and thus it is not surprising that in recent years the forceful dissents in *Olmstead* have more often been quoted. Justice Brandeis argued that the Amendment did cover wiretapping, and also that the government, as "the omnipresent teacher," should not be upheld in its admitted violation of a state wiretapping law. Justice Holmes,

[184]

dissenting on the latter ground only, characterized wiretapping in violation of state law as "dirty business" and contended that "it is a less evil that some criminals should escape than that the government should play an ignoble part."

Section 605. Congress later enacted the Federal Communications Act of 1934, which provided in § 605: "[N]o person not being authorized by the sender shall intercept any communication and divulge or publish the existence, contents, substance, purport, effect, or meaning of such intercepted communication to any person." On the basis of this language, it was held that a person with standing, i. e., a party to the conversation, *Goldstein v. U. S.,* 316 U.S. 114 (1942), could suppress in a federal prosecution evidence obtained by state or federal officers, *Nardone v. U. S.,* 302 U.S. 379 (1937); *Benanti v. U. S.,* 355 U.S. 96 (1957), by wiretapping interstate or intrastate communications, *Weiss v. U. S.,* 308 U.S. 321 (1939), unless done with the consent of one of the parties to the conversation. *Rathbun v. U. S.,* 355 U.S. 107 (1957). The ruling that wiretap evidence gathered by state officials was admissible in state prosecutions, *Schwartz v. Texas,* 344 U.S. 199 (1952), was finally overruled in *Lee v. Fla.,* 392 U.S. 378 (1968), where the Court emphasized the constitutional extension of the exclusionary rule in *Mapp v. Ohio* (p. 23), and the lack of other effective sanctions for violation of § 605. *Lee* was decided just two days before the Crime Control Act (see § 20) superceded the wiretapping prohibition of § 605.

Non-telephonic electronic eavesdropping. *Goldman v. U. S.*, 316 U.S. 129 (1942), was the "bugging" counterpart of *Olmstead*: because federal officers had merely placed a detectaphone against the outer wall of a private office, the Court held there had been no trespass and thus no Fourth Amendment violation. Similarly, in *On Lee v. U. S.* (p. 199), where incriminating statements were picked up via a "wired for sound" acquaintance of defendant, a 5–4 majority rejected the contention that a trespass by fraud had occurred and thus found no constitutional violation.

That the Constitution does furnish some protection against the electronic seizure of conversations was made plain by *Silverman v. U. S.*, 365 U.S. 505 (1961). There, a unanimous Court held that listening to incriminating conversations within a house by inserting a "spike mike" into a party wall and making contact with a heating duct serving the house occupied by defendants, amounted to an illegal search and seizure. Although the Court asserted it was irrelevant "whether or not there was a technical trespass under the local property law relating to party walls," the opinion did not clearly indicate whether the "intrusion" by the spike into defendants' premises was a critical fact.

Any remaining doubts were dispelled by *Katz v. U. S.*, 389 U.S. 347 (1967). The issue in *Katz* was whether recordings of defendant's end of telephone conversations, obtained by attaching an electronic listening and recording device to the outside of a public telephone booth, had been obtained in violation of the Fourth Amendment. In a 7–1 decision, the Court expressly rejected the "trespass" doctrine of *Olmstead* and *Goldman,* and held that the government action constituted a search and seizure within the meaning of the Fourth Amendment because it "violated the privacy upon which [the defendant] justifiably relied while using the telephone booth." *Katz* thus made it clear that, with the possible exception of the case in which a conversation is overheard or recorded with the consent of a party to the conversation (see § 21), wiretapping and electronic eavesdropping are subject to the limitations of the Fourth Amendment.

20. CONSTITUTIONALITY OF TITLE III OF THE CRIME CONTROL ACT

Under what circumstances, then, may wiretapping and electronic eavesdropping without the prior consent of a party to the conversations be conducted consistent with the Fourth Amendment? Because such surveillance is authorized in limited circumstances by Title III of the Omnibus Crime Control and Safe Streets Act of 1968, 18 U.S.C.A. §§ 2510–2520, the appropriate inquiry is into the constitutionality of that legislation. Though the Supreme Court has never passed upon the Act, guidance on the issues involved may be found in certain decisions of the Court: *Osborn v. U. S.,* 385 U.S. 323 (1966), upholding a judicially authorized use of an undercover agent with a concealed tape recorder; *Berger v. N. Y.,* 388 U.S. 41 (1967), holding the New York eavesdropping law unconstitutional; and *Katz v. U. S.,* 389 U.S. 347 (1967), indicating that the limited eavesdropping undertaken there would have been constitutional if a warrant had first been obtained.

Summary of Title III.   Under the Act, the Attorney General or a specially designated Assistant Attorney General may authorize application to a federal judge for an order permitting interception of wire or oral communications (i. e., wiretapping or electronic eavesdropping) by a federal agency having responsibility for investigation of the offense as to which application is made, when such interception may provide evidence of certain enumerated federal crimes. (Use of a "pen register" to keep a record of telephone numbers dialed is not an interception under the Act, *U. S. v. N. Y. Telephone Co.,* 434 U.S. 159 (1977), and is not a search, *Smith v. Md.,* 442 U.S. 735 (1979).)   A comparable provision permits, when authorized by state law, application by a state or county prosecutor to a state judge when the interception may provide evidence of "murder, kidnapping, gambling, robbery, bribery, extortion, or dealing in narcotic drugs, marijuana or other dangerous drugs, or other crime dangerous to life, limb, or property, and punishable by imprisonment

for more than one year." The judge may only grant
an interception order as provided in § 2518 of the
Act, and evidence obtained in the lawful execution of
such order is admissible in court. Other willful
interception or disclosure of any wire or oral
communication without the prior consent of a party
thereto is made criminal, and evidence so obtained is
inadmissible in any state or federal proceedings, but
suppression is not required merely because of
noncompliance with those requirements in the Act
which do not play a "substantive role" in the
regulatory system. *U. S. v. Donovan,* 429 U.S. 413
(1977).

The Act expressly provides that it does not limit
the constitutional power of the President to take such
measures as he deems necessary "to protect the
Nation against actual or potential attack or other
hostile acts of a foreign power, to obtain foreign
intelligence information deemed essential to the
security of the United States, * * * to protect
national security information against foreign intelligence activities, [or] to protect the United States
against the overthrow of the Government by force or
other unlawful means, or against any other clear and
present danger to the structure or existence of the
Government," and communications intercepted by
authority of the President in the exercise of those
powers may be received in evidence "where such
interception was reasonable." Those powers do not
extend to warrantless tapping in *domestic* security

cases, as Fourth Amendment protections are "the more necessary" for "those suspected of unorthodoxy in their political beliefs." *U. S. v. U. S. District Court,* 407 U.S. 297 (1972).

Under § 2518, an interception order may be issued only if the judge determines on the basis of facts submitted that there is probable cause for belief that an individual is committing, has committed, or is about to commit one of the enumerated offenses; probable cause for belief that particular communications concerning that offense will be obtained through such interception; that normal investigative procedures have been tried and have failed or reasonably appear to be unlikely to succeed if tried or to be too dangerous; and probable cause for belief that the facilities from which, or the place where, the communications are to be intercepted are being used, or are about to be used, in connection with the commission of such offense, or are leased to, listed in the name of, or commonly used by such person. Each interception order must specify the identity of the person, if known, whose communications are to be intercepted; the nature and location of the communications facilities as to which, or the place where, authority to intercept is granted; a particular description of the type of communication sought to be intercepted, and a statement of the particular offense to which it relates; the identity of the agency authorized to intercept the communications and of the person authorizing the application; and the period of time during which such interception is authorized, including a statement as to whether or not the interception shall automatically terminate when the described communication has been first obtained. No order may permit interception "for any period longer than is necessary to achieve the objective of the authorization, nor in any event longer than thirty days." Extensions of an order may be granted for like periods, but only by resort to the procedures required in obtaining the initial order.

Interception without prior judicial authorization is permitted whenever a specifically designated enforcement officer reasonably determines that "(a) an emergency situation exists with respect to conspiratorial activities characteristic of organized crime that requires a wire or oral communication to be intercepted before an order authorizing such interception can with due diligence be obtained, and (b) there are grounds upon which an order could be entered." In such a case, application for an order must be made within 48 hours after the interception commences, and, in the absence of an order, the interception must terminate when the communication sought is obtained or when the application for the order is denied, whichever is earlier.

Within a reasonable time but not later than 90 days after the filing of an application which is denied or the termination of an authorized period of interception, the judge must cause to be served on the persons named in the order or application and other parties to the intercepted communications, an inventory which shall include notice of (1) the fact of the entry of the order or application; (2) the date of the entry and the period of authorized interception, or the denial of the application; and (3) the fact that during the period communications were or were not intercepted. A similar inventory is required as to interceptions terminated without an order having been issued.

Continued surveillance. The most obvious difference between a search for tangible items and the search for wire or oral communications allowed under Title III is the time dimension of the latter kind of search. A search warrant for some physical object permits a single entry and prompt search of the described premises, while Title III permits continuing surveillance up to 30 days, with extensions possible. During the authorized time, all conversations over the tapped line or within the bugged room may be overheard and recorded without regard to their relevance.

As reflected in *Berger,* this striking difference accounts for the major constitutional obstacle to legalized electronic surveillance. In holding a New York law unconstitutional, the Court emphasized that it (1) permitted installation and operation of surveillance equipment for 60 days, "the equivalent of a series of intrusions, searches, and seizures pursuant to a single showing of probable cause"; (2) permitted renewal of the order "without a showing of present probable cause for the continuance of the eavesdrop"; and (3) placed "no termination date on the eavesdrop once the conversation sought is seized." While Title III permits extensions only upon a new showing of probable cause and requires that interception cease once "the objective of the authorization" is achieved, it does permit continued surveillance for up to 30 days upon a single showing of probable cause, and thus goes well beyond the kind of with-warrant electronic surveillance the Supreme Court has approved or indicated would be permitted.

As emphasized in *Berger,* the bugging of a secret agent upheld in *Osborn* was pursuant to an order which "authorized one limited intrusion rather than a series or a continuous surveillance. And, we note that a new order was issued when the officer sought to resume the search and probable cause was shown for the succeeding one. Moreover, the order was executed by the officer with dispatch, not over a prolonged and extended period." And in *Katz* the Court noted that the "surveillance was so narrowly circumscribed that a duly authorized magistrate * * * clearly apprised of the precise intrusion * * * could constitutionally have authorized * * * the very limited search and seizure that the Government asserts in fact took place." The surveillance was limited in that the agents had probable cause to believe defendant was using certain public telephones for gambling purposes about the same time almost every day and thus activated the surveillance equipment attached to the outside of the phone booth only when defendant entered the booth.

[193]

Decisions holding that continued surveillance may also be squared with the Fourth Amendment, e. g., *U. S. v. Cafero*, 473 F.2d 489 (3d Cir. 1973), rely upon the analysis of Justices Harlan and White, dissenting in *Berger*. First, they contend that an electronic surveillance which is continued over a span of time is no more a general search than the typical execution of a search warrant over a described area. As Justice White argued: "Petitioner suggests that the search is inherently overbroad because the eavesdropper will overhear conversations which do not relate to criminal activity. But the same is true of almost all searches of private property which the Fourth Amendment permits. In searching for seizable matters, the police must necessarily see or hear, and comprehend, items which do not relate to the purpose of the search. That this occurs, however, does not render the search invalid, so long as it is authorized by a suitable search warrant and so long as the police, in executing that warrant, limit themselves to searching for items which may constitutionally be seized."

This analogy holds only if it may be concluded that the overhearing or recording of a series of conversations is merely a search, from which certain particularly described conversations will thereafter be seized, as Justice Harlan contended: "Just as some exercise of dominion, beyond mere perception, is necessary for the seizure of tangibles, so some use of the conversation beyond the initial listening process is required for the seizures of the spoken word." A majority of the Court has yet to speak clearly on this point, although in *Katz* there is language characterizing the "electronically listening to and recording" of defendant's words as a "search and seizure."

Lack of notice. The Court in *Berger* also found the New York law "offensive" because it "has no requirement for notice, as do conventional warrants, nor does it overcome this defect by requiring some showing of special facts. On the contrary, it permits uncontested entry without any showing of exigent circumstances. Such a showing of exigency, in order to avoid notice would appear more important in eavesdropping, with its inherent dangers, than that required when conventional procedures of search and seizure are utilized." This criticism goes to the heart of all eavesdropping practices, as the Court noted, in that success depends upon secrecy.

The *Berger* Court did not explore this matter in greater detail, and thus it is not entirely clear whether Title III might be challenged on this basis. In decisions upholding the statute, e. g., *U. S. v. Cafero,* supra, the following arguments have been made: (1) One reason for advance notice, as emphasized by four members of the Court in *Ker v. Cal.,* 374 U.S. 23 (1963), is to guard the entering officer from attack on the mistaken belief he is making a criminal entry, and this danger is not present in most eavesdropping cases—including all which do not require a trespass. (2) Another reason for notice is so that the individual will be aware that a search was conducted, but in the more typical search case this notice may come only after the event by discovery of the warrant and a receipt at the place searched, which is comparable to the Title III requirement of service of an inventory within 90 days. (3) Prior notice is not required when there is reason to believe it would result in destruction of the evidence sought (see p. 129), and while the Court in *Berger* may have been unwilling to uphold all eavesdropping without notice on this ground, this "exigency" is sufficiently established upon a showing that "normal investigative procedures have been tried and have failed or reasonably appear to be unlikely to succeed if tried or to be too dangerous," as required by Title III. An extensive footnote (n. 16) on the subject in *Katz* suggests that the Court finds these arguments compelling.

Other considerations. An exhaustive analysis of Title III would reveal a number of other problems, primarily going to how the Act must be construed in light of the Fourth Amendment. Four of these problems deserve brief mention here. First of all, what meaning is to be given to the "probable cause" requirement in this context? If, as discussed earlier, the Fourth Amendment has some flexibility, so that somewhat less evidence is needed to justify such lesser intrusions as a building inspection, stop-and-frisk, or brief seizure for fingerprinting (see §§ 15, 17), then it may be equally true that more evidence than usual will be required to establish probable cause for the unusual degree of intrusion which results from electronic surveillance. Justice Stewart, concurring in *Berger,* took this approach and thus found the affidavits in that case adequate for a "conventional search or arrest" but insufficient for a 60-day eavesdrop.

Title III requires a particular description of the "type of communication sought to be intercepted, and a statement of the particular offense to which it relates," but it is unclear how this language is to be interpreted. The statute in *Berger* merely required the naming of "the person or persons whose communications * * * are to be overheard or recorded"; the Court held this did not meet the Fourth Amendment requirement that the things to be seized be particularly described and declared that the "need for particularity * * * is especially great in the case of eavesdropping [because it] involves an intrusion on privacy that is broad in scope." Yet, as Justice Harlan noted in dissent, the cases on search for tangible items make it clear that the particularity requirement of the Amendment is a flexible one, depending upon the nature of the described things and whether the description readily permits identification by the executing officer (see p. 126). From this it might be argued that specification of conversations as relating to a certain kind of criminal activity should suffice.

Next, there is the question whether an interception order may be executed by covert entry in the absence of specific judicial authorization for such execution based upon a showing of necessity therefor. In *Dalia v. U. S.*, 441 U.S. 238 (1979), the Court held that neither Title III nor the Fourth Amendment required such specific authorization. The latter holding was based upon the conclusion that nothing in the Amendment suggests "search warrants also must include a specification of the precise manner in which they are to be executed."

Finally, there is the provision in Title III which permits interception without prior judicial approval when there are grounds for an interception order but an emergency exists with respect to conspiratorial activities threatening national security or characteristic of organized crime that require interception before an order could with due diligence be obtained. If strictly construed to ensure that warrantless interceptions are not being upheld after the fact on the basis of what was discovered, this provision is consistent with Fourth Amendment decisions on search for physical evidence without warrant to prevent loss of the evidence (see § 14B). *Katz* condemned the warrantless eavesdropping challenged in that case, but the facts make it clear that there was ample time to secure a warrant.

21. THE USE OF SECRET AGENTS TO OBTAIN INCRIMINATING STATEMENTS

"Wired" agents: On Lee and Lopez. In *On Lee v. U. S.,* 343 U.S. 747 (1952), a wired-for-sound informant entered the laundry of the defendant, an old acquaintance, and engaged him in conversation, resulting in defendant's incriminating statements being transmitted to a narcotics agent outside. At trial, the agent testified as to these statements, but the informer was not called as a witness. A 5–4 majority rejected the claim that the informant committed a trespass by fraud, dismissed as "verging on the frivolous" the contention that the narcotics agent was trespassing by use of the transmitter and receiver, and concluded that in the absence of a trespass there was no Fourth Amendment violation.

Lopez v. U. S., 373 U.S. 427 (1963), concerned an internal revenue agent who, after receiving a bribe offer from the defendant, engaged defendant in subsequent incriminating conversations in the agent's office while equipped with a pocket recorder. The recordings were admitted at trial in support of the agent's testimony. In a 6–3 decision, the Court held no eavesdropping had occurred, in that there had been no invasion of the defendant's premises and the recording revealed only what the defendant willingly disclosed to the agent and what the agent in turn was entitled to disclose to others. The Chief

Justice, concurring specially, asserted that *On Lee* was "wrongly decided" and was distinguishable from *Lopez* because in *On Lee* the eavesdropping deprived the defendant of an opportunity to cross-examine the informer. The three dissenters saw no difference between the two cases, and asserted that the Fourth Amendment should protect a person against the risk that third parties may give independent evidence of conversations engaged in with another.

Without "bugging": Lewis and Hoffa. In *Lewis v. U. S.*, 385 U.S. 206 (1966), a federal narcotics agent misrepresented his identity and expressed a willingness to purchase narcotics, which resulted in his being invited into defendant's home, where an unlawful narcotics sale occurred. Because the agent did not "see, hear, or take anything that was not contemplated and in fact intended by petitioner as a necessary part of his illegal business," but merely entered a home "converted into a commercial center to which outsiders are invited for purposes of transacting unlawful business," the Court found no Fourth Amendment violation. *Gouled v. U. S.*, 255 U.S. 298 (1921), was distinguished in that there a business acquaintance, acting on police order, gained entry to defendant's office as a social visitor and then searched for and seized papers in the defendant's absence.

In *Hoffa v. U. S.*, 385 U.S. 293 (1966), the defendant unsuccessfully challenged on Fourth,

Fifth, and Sixth Amendment grounds the admission of evidence obtained by a Teamsters official who at government instigation visited Hoffa during the latter's earlier trial and overheard conversations between Hoffa and his associates concerning an attempt to bribe jurors. As to the contention that the failure of the informer to disclose his role vitiated the consent to his entry of a constitutionally protected area, Hoffa's hotel suite, the Court noted that Hoffa "was not relying on the security of the hotel room [but rather] upon his misplaced confidence that [the informer] would not reveal his wrongdoing," which is not protected by the Fourth Amendment. The Fifth Amendment claim was summarily dismissed with the observation that "a necessary element of compulsory self-incrimination is some kind of compulsion," absent here because Hoffa's conversations with and in the presence of the informer were "wholly voluntary." As to the Sixth Amendment claim that the informer had intruded upon the confidential attorney-client relationship, the Court concluded that, at least on these facts, such a violation of Sixth Amendment rights in one trial does not render evidence obtained thereby inadmissible in a different trial on other charges. (It was later held in *Weatherford v. Bursey,* 429 U.S. 545 (1977), that if an informer was present at pretrial attorney-client meetings, but he never communicated what he learned thereby, no Sixth Amendment violation has occurred.) Another Sixth Amendment argument, that from the time when there was evidence for arrest Hoffa was entitled to the same protection afforded an arrested person under *Massiah* and *Escobedo* (see § 26), was quickly disposed of on the ground that "there is no constitutional right to be arrested," for otherwise the police would be in the perilous position of having to guess at the precise moment they had probable cause.

The impact of Katz. The thrust of these four cases is that such uses of secret agents, with or without listening or recording devices, are not covered by the Fourth Amendment. It is apparently on this basis that the electronic eavesdropping provisions of Title III expressly exclude from the warrant requirement the interception of communications with the consent of a party to the conversation. However, doubts about the continued vitality of *On Lee, Lopez, Lewis,* and *Hoffa* emerged when the Court in *Katz v. U. S.* (p. 101), rejected the old trespass-into-constitutionally-protected-areas analysis in favor of an expectation-of-privacy approach to Fourth Amendment issues.

The question reached the Court in *United States v. White,* 401 U.S. 745 (1971), where an informer, carrying a concealed transmitter, engaged the defendant in conversations in a restaurant, defendant's home and the informer's car. The informer did not testify at the trial, but the narcotics agents who electronically overheard the conversations did, resulting in defendant's conviction. In a 4-man plurality opinion by White, J., it was concluded (1) that one may not have a "justifiable" expectation that his trusted associates neither are nor will become police agents, and (2) that a different result is not called for when the agent has recorded or transmitted the conversations: "Given the possibility or probability that one of his colleagues is cooperating with the police, it is only speculation to assert that the defendant's utterances would be substantially different or his sense of security any less if he also thought it possible that the suspected colleague is wired for sound." Black, J., concurred on the basis of his *Katz* dissent, which contended the Fourth Amendment did not apply to intangibles.

Brennan, J., concurred in the result in *White* on the ground that *Katz* should not be applied retroactively, but contended that *On Lee* and *Lopez* both should be viewed as overruled by *Katz*, the position apparently taken in each of the three dissenting opinions. None of the dissenters specifically questioned the status of *Lewis* and *Hoffa*, and Harlan, J., in particular, emphasized the difference between the practices involved in those cases and the instant case: "The interest *On Lee* fails to protect is the expectation of the ordinary citizen, who has never engaged in illegal conduct in his life, that he may carry on his private discourse freely, openly, and spontaneously without measuring his every word against the connotations it might carry when instantaneously heard by others unknown to him and unfamiliar with his situation or analyzed in a cold, formal record played days, months, or years after the conversation."

22. DISCLOSURE OF ELECTRONIC SURVEILLANCE RECORDS

If conversations have been overheard or recorded by electronic surveillance in violation of the Fourth Amendment, testimony concerning or recordings of these conversations may be suppressed by a defendant with standing. Under the "fruit of the poisonous tree" doctrine (see § 34), other evidence which was the product of illegal surveillance is also subject to suppression. This has given rise to the issue of what procedures are required to facilitate a determination whether other evidence is in fact the fruit of such a surveillance.

This issue was decided in *Alderman v. U. S., Ivanov v. U. S.,* and *Butenko v. U. S.,* 394 U.S. 165 (1969); *Alderman* involved convictions for conspiring to transmit murderous threats in interstate commerce, while the other cases concerned convictions for transmitting national defense information to the Soviet Union. The defendants sought disclosure of all surveillance records so that they might show that some of the evidence admitted against them grew out of illegally overheard conversations. The government urged that in order to protect innocent third parties participating or referred to in irrelevant conversations overheard by the government, surveillance records should first be subjected to in camera inspection by the trial judge. He would then turn over to defendants and their counsel only those materials "arguably relevant" to defendants' convictions, in the sense that the overheard conversations arguably underlay some item of evidence offered at trial.

The Court, in a 5–3 decision, held that a defendant should receive all surveillance records as to which he has standing (see p. 312). The government's proposal was rejected on the ground that the trial judge often would not be in a position to determine what conversations were relevant: "An apparently innocent phrase, a chance remark, a reference to what appears to be a neutral person or event, the identity of a caller or the individual on the other end of a telephone, or even the manner of speaking or using words may have special significance to one who knows the more intimate facts of an accused's life. And yet that information may be wholly colorless and devoid of meaning to one less well acquainted with all relevant circumstances. Unavoidably, this is a matter of judgment, but in our view the task is too complex, and the margin for error too great, to rely wholly on the in camera judgment of the trial court to identify those records which might have contributed to the Government's case." To protect innocent third parties, the Court added, the trial court could place defendants and counsel under enforceable orders against unwarranted disclosure of the materials they would be entitled to inspect.

Justice Fortas, dissenting in part, argued that the in camera screening procedure should be followed when the trial judge makes written and sealed findings "that disclosure would substantially injure security interests." Justice Harlan, dissenting in part, subscribed to a narrower view that such screening would be appropriate whenever the defendant is charged with spying for a foreign power, in which case protective orders would not deter disclosure to others and the location of listening devices crucial to espionage work would otherwise be needlessly disclosed. In an unsuccessful petition for rehearing, the Attorney General argued against disclosure of records of surveillance activities to gather "foreign intelligence information" on the ground that such activity was practiced by all nations and thus not unreasonable.

In *Giordano v. U. S.,* 394 U.S. 310 (1969), the Court emphasized that the disclosure required in *Alderman* was expressly limited to situations where the surveillance had been determined to be in violation of the Fourth Amendment. Justice Stewart, concurring, suggested that this preliminary determination might sometimes be made in ex parte, in camera proceedings. And in *Taglianetti v. U. S.,* 394 U.S. 316 (1969), the Court rejected defendant's contention that he was entitled to examine additional surveillance records to establish that he might be a party to some other conversations. Distinguishing *Alderman,* the Court concluded that the trial judge could be expected to identify defendant's voice without the defendant's assistance.

By Title VII of the Organized Crime Control Act of 1970, 18 U.S.C.A. § 3504, Congress has attempted to limit the impact of *Alderman* in the federal courts. For one thing, records of an unlawful surveillance which occurred prior to June 19, 1968, (the date that the Omnibus Crime Control and Safe Streets Act of 1968 became law) need not be disclosed "unless such information may be relevant to a pending claim of * * * inadmissibility," which presumably is to be determined by the judge in camera. For another, on the legislative finding that "there is virtually no likelihood" that evidence offered to prove an event would have been obtained by exploitation of an unlawful surveillance occurring more than five years prior to that event, no such claim is to be considered. The constitutionality of these provisions is open to some doubt, considering the fact that the *Alderman* decision was cast in terms of "the scrutiny which the Fourth Amendment exclusionary rule demands."

23. THE USE OF SECRET AGENTS TO "ENCOURAGE" CRIMINAL CONDUCT

Entrapment. Secret agents—sometimes undercover police officers but very often private citizens acting as informants—are frequently utilized to "encourage" others to engage in criminal conduct. Such tactics are for the most part confined to the crimes of prostitution, homosexuality, liquor and narcotic sales, and gambling; normal detection methods are virtually impossible as to these offenses, as they are committed privately with a willing victim who will not complain. The encouragement very frequently involves little more than a feigned offer by the agent to purchase criminal services from the suspect, but on occasion the agent may use considerably more pressure to gain the suspect's agreement to commit an offense.

The Supreme Court has held that techniques of encouragement may not reach the point where they constitute "entrapment"; if they do, the presence of entrapment constitutes a defense to the defendant's otherwise criminal act. The exact definition of entrapment is a matter of dispute, but it clearly includes the situation in which "the criminal design originates with the [police agents] and they implant in the mind of an innocent person the disposition to commit the offense and induce its commission in order that they may prosecute." *Sorrells v. U. S.,* 287 U.S. 435 (1932). So far, the Court has based the defense upon other than constitutional grounds; some of the Justices have relied upon general principles of substantive criminal law and others upon the supervisory power of the Court over the administration of justice in federal courts. *U. S. v. Russell,* 411 U.S. 423 (1973); *Sherman v. U. S.,* 356 U.S. 369 (1958).

Possible constitutional bases. While the entrapment defense is also recognized in the state courts, which for the most part purport to use the *Sorrells-Sherman* test, state convictions are sometimes affirmed notwithstanding evidence of what would constitute entrapment under those decisions, e. g., *P. v. Toler,* 185 N.E.2d 874 (Ill.1962). This has given rise to the question of whether freedom from entrapment is a federal constitutional right for which relief may be granted upon federal habeas corpus, to which the courts have so far responded in the negative. *U. S. ex rel. Toler v. Pate,* 332 F.2d 425 (7th Cir. 1964).

In support of the contention that freedom from entrapment is a right protected under the due process clause, commentators have suggested that: (1) by analogy to the Fourth Amendment protection against unreasonable searches or by application of the penumbral "right of privacy," *Griswold v. Conn.,* 381 U.S. 479 (1965), secret agents may encourage only those individuals as to whom there exists "probable cause" (under the balancing approach, see §§ 15, 17, a lesser quantum of evidence than would be required for arrest); (2) by analogy to the constitutional prohibition on illegally obtained confessions, under which ruses and appeals to sympathy are relevant considerations, *Spano v. N. Y.,* 360 U.S. 315 (1959), secret agents may not overbear a person's will to get him to perpetrate a crime; (3) by analogy to the doctrine that it is cruel and unusual punishment to convict for mere status and without the proof of any act, *Robinson v. Cal.,* 370 U.S. 660 (1962), the acts which serve as the basis for conviction must be attributable to the defendant rather than to the police or their agents; (4) by analogy to the constitutional limitation on abolition of *mens rea, Lambert v. Cal.,* 355 U.S. 225 (1957), the necessary mental element for the crime may not be implanted by entrapment; and (5) by analogy to the constitutional defense of estoppel, which bars conviction for actions undertaken upon official advice that such conduct would not violate the law, *Cox v. La.,* 379 U.S. 559 (1965), secret agents may not induce actions in which the defendant was not predisposed to engage.

In *U. S. v. Russell,* supra, the Supreme Court, while noting that the entrapment defense "is not of a constitutional dimension," acknowledged that there might be "a situation in which the conduct of law enforcement agents is so outrageous that due process principles would absolutely bar the government from invoking judicial processes to obtain a conviction." Due process does not bar conviction of a defendant for sale of narcotics supplied to him by a government agent. *Hampton v. U. S.,* 425 U.S. 484 (1976).

CHAPTER 4

POLICE INTERROGATION AND CONFESSIONS

24. INTRODUCTION

The confession dilemma. No area of constitutional criminal procedure has provoked more debate over the years than that dealing with police interrogation. In large measure, the debate has centered upon the extent of police abuse in seeking confessions and the importance of confessions in obtaining convictions—two matters on which conclusive evidence is lacking.

Because the questioning of suspects has traditionally been undertaken behind station-house doors (for some, a sufficient indication in itself of abuse), there is not sufficient empirical evidence to assert with confidence what always, usually, or often occurs in the course of police interrogation. Attention thus has often turned to celebrated cases of confessions later proved false or to judicial opinions (including many Supreme Court cases, see § 25) revealing outrageous police tactics. Those who assert that police abuses have been widespread contend that these cases are fairly representative, while those of a contrary persuasion claim that these are unusual cases having no relation to day-to-day police work.

There is similar disagreement as to what may be logically presumed from the nature of the police and their task: whether it is proper to presume that policemen usually abide by their sworn duty to comply with the law in enforcing the law; or whether the correct assumption is that the police are so caught up in the difficult task of fighting crime that they believe anything goes.

Hard facts about the need for confessions are also lacking. It may be true, as Justice Frankfurter declared in *Culombe v. Conn.,* 367 U.S. 568 (1961), that "despite modern advances in the technology of crime detection, offenses frequently occur about which things cannot be made to speak," but just how frequently they occur is uncertain. Statistics have been offered to establish that confessions are seldom utilized in serious criminal cases and also to show the contrary. The former are challengeable on the ground that they fail to take account of the over-whelming majority of cases disposed of by pleas of guilty, while the latter are contested because they may only demonstrate that the police often fail to use other investigative techniques.

Assuming other techniques are available, there is still disagreement as to whether interrogation is nonetheless desirable. Some hold to the view, as expressed by Justice Goldberg in *Escobedo v. Ill.,* 378 U.S. 478 (1964), that "a system of criminal law enforcement which comes to depend on the 'confession' will, in the long run, be less reliable and more subject to abuses than a system which depends on extrinsic evidence independently secured through skillful investigation." Others question this assumption and suggest that greater use of certain "extrinsic evidence," such as eyewitness identifications (see ch. 5), would result in even less reliability.

The Supreme Court's response. From 1936 to nearly 30 years later, the Court dealt with confessions admitted in state criminal proceedings in terms of the fundamental fairness required by the Fourteenth Amendment due process clause (see § 2). A so-called "voluntariness" test, which depended upon the "totality of the circumstances," was used to determine whether the Constitution required exclusion of a confession (see § 25). Over the years, it became increasingly apparent that this test was most difficult to administer because it required a finding and appraisal of all relevant facts surrounding each challenged confession.

Essentially the same approach was used by the Court during this period on the infrequent occasions when confessions admitted in federal prosecutions were reviewed. In such instances, it might logically be thought that the Court was then relying upon the due process clause of the Fifth Amendment, although the tendency was to refer to earlier holdings in which the basis of exclusion was the Fifth Amendment privilege against self-incrimination or a common law rule of evidence. *U. S. v. Carignan,* 342 U.S. 36 (1951). Beginning in 1943, a confession obtained by federal officers and offered in a federal prosecution could also be excluded on the ground that it was received during a period of "unnecessary delay" in taking the arrested person before a judicial officer. *McNabb v. U. S.,* 318 U.S. 332 (1943); *Mallory v. U. S.,* 354 U.S. 449 (1957). Although these decisions were grounded upon the Court's supervisory power over the federal courts, most commentators viewed them as attempts by the Court to avoid the tremendous problems inherent in the due process voluntariness test, and thus there was some expectation that the *McNabb-Mallory* rule (finally abolished by Title II of the Omnibus Crime Control and Safe Streets Act of 1968) would ultimately be rested upon a constitutional foundation and applied to the states.

This did not come to pass, perhaps because subsequent decisions holding that there was a constitutional right to counsel at certain pretrial "critical stages" provided a better stepping stone. The anticipated move away from sole reliance upon the voluntariness test occurred in *Escobedo v. Ill.,* supra, suppressing the defendant's confession because it was obtained in violation of his right to counsel at the time of interrogation. *Escobedo* was a cautious step, for the holding was carefully limited to the unique facts of the case (see § 26), but it was generally assumed that this newly established right to counsel in the police station would thereafter be expanded on a case-by-case basis. Instead, the Court

just two years later decided *Miranda v. Ariz.,* 384
U.S. 436 (1966), which was grounded upon the Fifth
Amendment privilege against self-incrimination and
prescribed a specific set of warnings as prerequisites
to all future custodial interrogations (see § 27).

It is *Miranda* which is of major current significance, and thus the emphasis in this chapter is upon
the basis and meaning of that decision. But the
voluntariness approach also deserves further attention, as does the right to counsel approach, which the
Court has more recently utilized in certain cases not
amenable to easy resolution under *Miranda,* e. g.,
Brewer v. Williams, 430 U.S. 387 (1977).

25. THE "VOLUNTARINESS"— "TOTALITY OF CIRCUM- STANCES" TEST

Objectives of the test. Although the Supreme
Court earlier had occasion to review the admissibility
of confessions in the federal courts, first under the
common law rule of evidence barring confessions
obtained by threats or promises, *Hopt v. Utah,* 110
U.S. 574 (1884), and later—at least in one case—
under a voluntariness test apparently derived from
the Fifth Amendment privilege against self-incrimination, *Bram v. U. S.,* 168 U.S. 532 (1897), it was not
until *Brown v. Miss.,* 297 U.S. 278 (1936), that the
Court barred the use of a confession in the state
courts. It could not, of course, dispose of the state
confession on the same grounds as were resorted to in

the earlier cases; under our federal system, the Supreme Court could not proscribe mere rules of evidence for the states, and the Fifth Amendment privilege was then not applicable to the states, *Twining v. N. J.,* 211 U.S. 78 (1908), overruled by *Malloy v. Hogan,* 378 U.S. 1 (1964). Thus the confessions in *Brown,* obtained by brutally beating the suspects, were struck down on the notion that interrogation is part of the process by which a state procures a conviction and thus subject to the requirements of the Fourteenth Amendment due process clause.

The interests to be protected under the due process test, and thus the true dimensions of that constitutional protection, remained somewhat obscure in the earlier cases. In *Brown,* the confessions clearly were of doubtful reliability, and thus that case might be read as announcing a due process test for excluding confessions obtained under circumstances presenting a fair risk that the statements are false. Concern with this risk was emphasized in subsequent cases, such as *Chambers v. Fla.,* 309 U.S. 227 (1940); *Ward v. Texas,* 316 U.S. 547 (1942); and *Lyons v. Okla.,* 332 U.S. 596 (1944), and this led many state courts to the conclusion that "unfairness in violation of due process exists when a confession is obtained by means of pressure exerted upon the accused under such circumstances that it affects the testimonial trustworthiness of the confession." *S. v. Schabert,* 15 N.W.2d 585 (Minn.1944).

While it is fair to say that ensuring the reliability of confessions is a goal under the due process voluntariness standard, it is incorrect to define the standard in terms of that one objective. In *Rogers v. Richmond,* 365 U.S. 534 (1961), defendant's confession was obtained after the police pretended to order his ailing wife arrested for questioning, and the state court had ruled that the statement need not be excluded "if the artifice or deception was not calculated to procure an untrue statement." The Supreme Court disagreed, emphasizing that convictions based upon coerced confessions must be overturned "not because such confessions are unlikely to be true but because the methods used to extract them offend an underlying principle in the enforcement of our criminal law: that ours is an accusatorial and not an inquisitorial system." *Rogers* thus made certain what was strongly intimated in several earlier cases, e. g., *Ashcraft v. Tenn.,* 322 U.S. 143 (1944); *Haley v. Ohio,* 332 U.S. 596 (1948), namely, that the exclusionary rule for confessions (in much the same way as the Fourth Amendment exclusionary rule, see p. 23) is also intended to deter improper police conduct.

In *Townsend v. Sain,* 372 U.S. 293 (1963), the ailing defendant had been given a drug with the properties of a truth serum, after which he gave a confession in response to questioning by police who were unaware of the drug's effect. Although the confession was not obtained by conscious police wrongdoing and apparently was reliable, the Court nonetheless held its use impermissible: "Any questioning by police officers which *in fact* produces a confession which is not the product of free intellect renders that confession inadmissible." *Townsend* thus highlights another theme which runs through many of the earlier cases, e. g., *Lisenba v. Cal.,* 314 U.S. 219 (1941); *Watts v. Ind.,* 338 U.S. 49 (1949): the confession must be a product of the defendant's "free and rational choice." This phrase, however, was not used in an absolute sense, but rather in conjunction with a recognized need to exert some pressure to obtain confessions. As the Court seems to have acknowledged in *Miranda,* the question of whether a confession was "voluntary" had theretofore been determined by a lesser standard than, say, the question of whether a testator's will was his voluntary act.

Viewing the voluntariness test in terms of its objectives, then, it could be said that the test was designed to bar admission of those confessions which: (a) were of doubtful reliability because of the practices used to obtain them; (b) were obtained by offensive police practices even if reliability was not in question (e. g., where there is strong corroborating evidence); or (c) were obtained under circumstances in which the defendant's free choice was significantly impaired, even if the police did not resort to offensive practices.

The relevant circumstances. Under the voluntariness test, the Supreme Court undertook a continuing re-evaluation on the facts of each case of how much pressure on the suspect was permissible. The rule required examination of the "totality of circumstances" surrounding each confession. *Haynes v. Wash.,* 373 U.S. 503 (1963). The factors deemed most important were: (1) physical abuse, *Lee v. Miss.,* 332 U.S. 742 (1948); (2) threats, *Payne v. Ark.,* 356 U.S. 560 (1958); (3) extensive questioning, *Turner v. Pa.,* 338 U.S. 62 (1949); (4) incommunicado detention, *Davis v. N. C.,* 384 U.S. 737 (1966); (5) denial of the right to consult with counsel, *Fay v. Noia,* 372 U.S. 391 (1963); and (6) the characteristics and status of the suspect, such as his lack of education, *Culombe v. Conn.,* 367 U.S. 568 (1961), emotional instability, *Spano v. N. Y.,* 360 U.S. 315 (1959), youth, *Gallegos v. Colo.,* 370 U.S. 49 (1962), or sickness, *Jackson v. Denno,* 378 U.S. 368 (1964). However, the voluntariness test is by its nature imprecise, and thus it could rarely be said that the presence of any one of these factors or any fixed combination of them clearly required exclusion of a confession.

Administration of the test. Although the *Miranda* dissenters saw the voluntariness test as "a workable and effective means of dealing with confessions in a judicial manner," many critics of the totality-of-circumstances approach had long been of the contrary view. The amorphous character of the test, together with the seeming reluctance of some courts to overturn the conviction of an apparently guilty defendant, led to divergent results in the lower courts. Not infrequently, confessions were upheld although they quite clearly appeared to have been obtained under circumstances previously condemned by the Supreme Court. For example, in *Davis v. N. C.,* supra, it was uncontested that no one other than the police had spoken to the defendant during the 16 days of detention and interrogation which preceded his confessions. The Court reversed, noting it had "never sustained the use of a confession obtained after such a lengthy period of detention and interrogation," but two state courts and two federal courts had previously upheld the confession notwithstanding these objective facts.

Davis was unique in that the relevant circumstances were revealed by police records; usually, an attempt at the trial level to ascertain the "totality of circumstances" has resulted in what has been commonly referred to as a "swearing contest" between the defendant and the police. The ultimate determination of whether the confession should be excluded, therefore, typically had to be made upon the basis of several hotly disputed questions of fact.

26.   THE RIGHT TO COUNSEL

Pre-Escobedo developments. Several developments in the late 1950's and early 1960's enhanced the prospect that the Supreme Court might ultimately resolve the confession issue in terms of the right to counsel. In *Crooker v. Cal.,* 357 U.S. 433 (1958), where defendant's confession was obtained following denial of his request to call an attorney, the Court held the confession voluntary and also rejected defendant's separate contention that he had a right to counsel at the police station. Recognition of such a right, asserted the majority, would preclude both fair and unfair questioning, a result not required under the "less rigid" due process concept. *Betts v. Brady* (p. 341), holding that due process did not impose a flat requirement of appointed counsel in all serious state trials, was cited in support. The four dissenters in *Crooker* asserted that under due process "the accused who wants a counsel should have one at any time after the moment of arrest." *Crooker* was followed in *Cicenia v. Lagay*, 357 U.S. 504 (1958), where defendant's requests to see his attorney were refused and his counsel turned away at the station, but again there was a strong dissent. The confession in *Spano v. N. Y.*, 360 U.S. 315 (1959), was found involuntary on traditional grounds, but four concurring justices accepted defendant's contention that his absolute right to counsel in a capital case attached at the time he was indicted (which was prior to his confession).

In *White v. Md.*, 373 U.S. 59 (1963), the absolute right to counsel in a capital case was held applicable to a pretrial "critical stage," a preliminary arraignment at which a guilty plea later introduced into evidence was obtained. Some commentators suggested that if, as in *White*, an uncounseled guilty plea

[221]

could not be admitted as evidence of guilt at trial, then it followed that the same should be true of an uncounseled confession. *White* took on greater significance when the *Betts* rule (relied upon in *Crooker*) was overruled in *Gideon v. Wainwright,* (p. 342), holding that the absolute right to counsel for indigent state defendants existed as to all serious cases and not merely capital cases.

The argument that the right to counsel attaches when the defendant is indicted and his status thereby changes from "suspect" to "accused," not reached by the majority in *Spano,* was accepted in a somewhat different context in *Massiah v. U. S.,* 377 U.S. 201 (1964). After defendant's indictment, he was engaged in an incriminating conversation by a bugged codefendant-turned-informer, about which the over-hearing agent testified at trial. Perhaps to avoid a difficult eavesdropping issue (see § 21), the Court held, 6–3, that the Sixth Amendment prohibits extraction of incriminating statements from an indicted person without presence of counsel. The majority indicated this would be equally true had the incriminating statements been obtained by police interrogation. Any thoughts that *Massiah* was limited to federal prosecutions or to cases in which the defendant had already retained counsel were dispelled by the per curiam decision in *McLeod v. Ohio,* 381 U.S. 356 (1965), but most lower courts refused to extend *Massiah* back to the point of earlier tentative charges. *U. S. ex rel. Forella v. Follette,* 405 F.2d 680 (2d Cir. 1969).

The Escobedo case. The confession in *Escobedo
v. Ill.,* 378 U.S. 478 (1964), was obtained after
defendant's repeated requests to consult with retained counsel were refused and after his attorney
had actually been turned away at the station. The
Court, 5–4, concluded that this pre-indictment
interrogation was just as much a "critical stage" as
the preliminary hearing in *White,* in that what
happened then could "affect the whole trial," and
that *Massiah* was apposite because "no meaningful
distinction can be drawn between interrogation of an
accused before and after formal indictment." Yet
the Court did not announce a broad right-to-
counsel-at-the-station rule, but instead cautiously
limited the holding to the facts of the case:

"We hold * * * that where, as here, [1] the
investigation is no longer a general inquiry into an
unsolved crime but has begun to focus on a particular
suspect, [2] the suspect has been taken into police
custody, [3] the police carry out a process of
interrogations that lends itself to eliciting incriminating statements, [4] the suspect has requested and
been denied an opportunity to consult with his
lawyer, and [5] the police have not effectively
warned him of his absolute constitutional right to
remain silent, the accused has been denied 'the
Assistance of Counsel' in violation of the Sixth
Amendment to the Constitution as 'made obligatory
upon the States by the Fourteenth Amendment,'
* * * and that no statement elicited by the police

during the interrogation may be used against him at a criminal trial."

The meaning of Escobedo. Because the much broader *Miranda* decision is not retroactive (see § 8), the precise meaning of *Escobedo* is still a matter of significance as to confessions admitted at trials occurring between the two decisions. This matter of interpretation has largely fallen upon the lower courts; they have reached diverse results, but (as in the representative cases cited below) have usually attributed significance to each of the five "elements" in the *Escobedo* holding enumerated above.

Thus: (1) While the Court said in *Miranda* that the focus requirement of *Escobedo* was really intended to mean deprivation of freedom in a significant way, this requirement has been utilized to find *Escobedo* inapplicable where the suspect was in custody on another charge and the interrogation was undertaken while the case was in the investigatory rather than accusatory stage, *P. v. Morse,* 452 P.2d 607 (Cal.1969). (2) *Escobedo* does not apply when the suspect is not in police custody, *S. v. Kelter,* 426 P.2d 500 (Wash.1967), although custody may be present without a formal arrest, *C. v. Brown,* 247 A.2d 802 (Pa.Super.1968). (3) *Escobedo* does not govern volunteered statements, *P. v. Taylor,* 55 Cal.Rptr. 521 (App.1966), or even interrogation undertaken primarily for another purpose, such as to locate a kidnap victim, *P. v. Modesto,* 398 P.2d 753 (Cal.1965). (4) *Escobedo* does not require a warning of the right to counsel, *S. v. Outten,* 206 So.2d 392 (Fla.1968), but applies only if the suspect makes a clear and unambiguous request for counsel. *Frazier v. Cupp,* 394 U.S. 731 (1969). (5) *Escobedo* is inapplicable if the police have warned the suspect of his right to remain silent, *Ward v. C.,* 138 S.E.2d 293 (Va.1964).

Consider also *Kirby v. Ill.,* discussed at p. 273, where the Court concluded that the Sixth Amendment right to counsel attaches "only at or after the time that adversary judicial proceedings have been initiated." Because *Escobedo* was the "only seeming deviation" from a long line of cases accepting this starting point, the Court "in retrospect concluded that the "'prime purpose' of *Escobedo* was not to vindicate the constitutional right to counsel as such, but, like *Miranda* to guarantee full effectuation of the privilege against self-incrimination." Moreover, *Kirby* noted, *Escobedo* is now limited in its "holding * * * to its own facts."

The Williams case. More then ten years following the *Miranda* decision, the Court "resurrected" the *Massiah* rule in *Brewer v. Williams,* 430 U.S. 387 (1977). Williams was arraigned in Davenport, Iowa, on an outstanding arrest warrant prior to his transportation to Des Moines on a murder charge. Though the police had assured Williams' lawyer that he would not be interrogated during the trip, a detective made a "Christian burial speech," to the effect that because of the worsening weather it would be necessary to find the body now to ensure the victim a Christian burial, after which Williams directed the police to the body. The Supreme Court, noting (i) that the right to counsel attaches when "judicial proceedings have been initiated" against the defendant, clearly the case here in light of the warrant issuance, arraignment on the warrant, and commitment to jail by the court, and (ii) that the detective "set out to elicit information from Williams" by a means "tantamount to interrogation," concluded the case fell within "the clear rule of *Massiah* * * * that once adversary proceedings have commenced against an individual, he has a right to legal representation when the government interrogates him." Though declining to hold that the right to counsel could be waived only upon notice to counsel, the Court rejected the state court's conclusion that waiver had occurred here merely because during the trip Williams did not assert that right or a desire not to talk in the absence of counsel.

The primary importance of *Williams* and the other right-to-counsel cases lie in their possible use to exclude incriminating statements not necessarily excludable under *Miranda*. This is because the definitions of "interrogation" under *Miranda* and of the conduct prohibited by the *Massiah-Williams* line of cases "are not necessarily interchangeable, since the policies underlying the two constitutional protections are quite distinct." *R. I. v. Innis,* —— U.S. —— (1980). The cases will be further considered in that respect later (see § 28F).

27. THE PRIVILEGE AGAINST
SELF–INCRIMINATION

The privilege in the police station. The Fifth Amendment provides that no person "shall be compelled in any criminal case to be a witness against himself." Although a literal reading of this language suggests that the privilege against self-incrimination has no application to unsworn statements obtained by station-house interrogation, in *Bram v. U. S.,* 168 U.S. 532 (1897), the Court asserted that "in criminal trials, in the courts of the United States, wherever a question arises whether a confession is incompetent because not voluntary, the issue is controlled by that portion of the Fifth Amendment." The Court's conclusion that there was a historical connection between the privilege and the confession doctrine appears incorrect, and was subsequently challenged by many commentators. The privilege was not expressly relied upon in later cases concerning the admissibility of confessions in federal courts, while the Court dealt with confessions used in state courts solely in terms of the due process voluntariness test (see § 25). But in *Malloy v. Hogan,* 378 U.S. 1 (1964), which did not involve a confession, the Court held the privilege applicable to the states, and in support of this result noted that the admissibility of a confession in a state trial had long been tested by the same standard as applied to federal prosecutions by *Bram.* Promptly thereafter, the Court decided the *Escobedo* case (see § 26), which, while grounded upon the Sixth Amendment right to counsel, spoke of "the right of the accused to be advised by his lawyer of his privilege against self-incrimination."

Any remaining doubts were dispelled by *Miranda v. Ariz.*, 384 U.S. 436 (1966), holding that the privilege against self-incrimination "is fully applicable during a period of custodial interrogation." Although the apparent assumption of the *Miranda* majority that this proposition was "settled" in the precedents is subject to question, this of course does not compel the conclusion that the *Miranda* holding was in error. Even the dissenters in *Miranda* conceded that the Fifth Amendment privilege "embodies basic principles always capable of expansion," although they forcefully argued that those principles would not be served by extending the privilege to the police station.

The Miranda rules. Apart from this reliance upon the Fifth Amendment rather than the Sixth, *Miranda* is striking in its contrast to *Escobedo*. The latter holding was carefully limited to the facts of the case before the Court while *Miranda* sets forth what the dissenters called a "constitutional code of rules for confessions":

(1) These rules are required to safeguard the privilege against self-incrimination, and thus must be followed in the absence of "other procedures which are at least as effective in apprising accused persons

of their right of silence and in assuring a continuous opportunity to exercise it."

(2) These rules apply "when the individual is first subjected to police interrogation while in custody at the station or otherwise deprived of his freedom of action in any significant way," and not to "general on-the-scene questioning as to facts surrounding a crime or other general questioning of citizens in the fact-finding process" or to "volunteered statements of any kind."

(3) Without regard to his prior awareness of his rights, if a person in custody is to be subjected to questioning, "he must first be informed in clear and unequivocal terms that he has the right to remain silent," so that the ignorant may learn of this right and so that the pressures of the interrogation atmosphere will be overcome for those previously aware of the right.

(4) The above warning "must be accompanied by the explanation that anything said can and will be used against the individual in court," so as to ensure that the suspect fully understands the consequences of foregoing the privilege.

(5) Because this is indispensible to protection of the privilege, the individual also "must be clearly informed that he has the right to consult with a lawyer and to have the lawyer with him during interrogation," without regard to whether it appears that he is already aware of this right.

(6) The individual must also be warned "that if he is indigent a lawyer will be appointed to represent him," for otherwise the above warning would be understood as meaning only that an individual may consult a lawyer if he has the funds to obtain one.

(7) The individual is always free to exercise the privilege, and thus if he "indicates in any manner, at any time prior to or during questioning, that he wishes to remain silent, the interrogation must cease"; and likewise, if he "states that he wants an attorney, the interrogation must cease until an attorney is present."

(8) If a statement is obtained without the presence of an attorney, "a heavy burden rests on the Government to demonstrate that the defendant knowingly and intelligently waived his privilege against self-incrimination and his right to retained or appointed counsel," and such waiver may not be presumed from the individual's silence after the warnings or from the fact that a confession was eventually obtained.

(9) Any statement obtained in violation of these rules may not be admitted into evidence, without regard to whether it is a confession or only an admission of part of an offense or whether it is inculpatory or allegedly exculpatory.

(10) Likewise, exercise of the privilege may not be penalized, and thus the prosecution may not "use at trial the fact that [the defendant] stood mute or claimed his privilege in the face of accusation."

[230]

The Supreme Court has more recently asserted that *Miranda* "recognized that these procedural safeguards were not themselves rights protected by the Constitution but were instead measures to insure that the right against compulsory self-incrimination was protected. * * * The suggested safeguards were not intended to 'create a constitutional straightjacket,' but rather to provide practical reinforcement for the right against compulsory self-incrimination." *Mich. v. Tucker*, 417 U.S. 433, 444 (1974). This approach is reflected generally in the cases interpreting *Miranda* (see § 28).

Criticism of Miranda. Not unexpectedly, the *Miranda* decision was greeted with criticism from many quarters. It was contended that police abuse was not so widespread as to call for such a far-reaching decision, and that confessions were essential to law enforcement but would be unobtainable under the new rules (see § 24). Recent empirical studies, however, have concluded that the impact of *Miranda* has been quite different than predicted by the Court's critics. In most instances the *Miranda* warnings have not appreciably reduced the amount of talking by a suspect, and the police are now obtaining about as many confessions as before *Miranda*.

These conclusions lend some support to the views of another group of critics, those who find a fundamental inconsistency in the majority's reasoning. They claim that the heavy emphasis on the inability of an uncounseled defendant to decide whether to incriminate himself when subject to the inherent pressures of custody is inconsistent with the conclusion that the decision whether to dispense with counsel can be voluntary in the same circumstances. As stated in one of the *Miranda* dissents: "But if the defendant may not answer without a warning a question such as 'Where were you last night?' without having his answer be a compelled one, how can the court ever accept his negative answer to the question of whether he wants to consult his retained counsel or counsel whom the court will appoint?"

The Crime Control Act. Title II of the Omnibus Crime Control and Safe Streets Act of 1968 amends existing legislation by adding 18 U.S.C.A. § 3501, which purports to "repeal" *Miranda* in federal prosecutions. The Act states that a confession is admissible in the federal courts if voluntarily given, and that whether the defendant was advised of his right to remain silent or his right to counsel and whether he was without counsel when he confessed are merely to be taken into consideration as circumstances bearing on the issue of voluntariness.

If viewed as a total "repeal" of *Miranda*, this statute is quite clearly unconstitutional, for rights derived from the Constitution cannot be repealed by legislation. However, in support of this legislation it has been noted that the *Miranda* Court indicated Congress might devise equally effective safeguards for protecting the privilege, and the argument is made that Title II does this by a less rigid formula than *Miranda*, permitting a confession to be used where a less than perfect warning was given or a less than conclusive waiver was obtained. In response, the contention can be made that compliance with Title II would result in courts returning to the old practice of considering all of the circumstances of the individual case, a procedure which the *Miranda* Court concluded had proven ineffective in protecting a suspect's constitutional rights.

28. THE MEANING OF MIRANDA

A. WHAT OFFENSES ARE COVERED?

Traffic and other minor offenses. A number of courts have held *Miranda* inapplicable to traffic and other minor crimes. Their underlying reasoning has been obscure; there have merely been general references to the volume of these lesser offenses, *S. v. Bliss*, 238 A.2d 848 (Del.1968), or to the "practical" and "historical" differences between them and serious crimes, *S. v. Zucconi*, 226 A.2d 16 (N.J.Super.1967). In *Campbell v. Superior Ct.*, 479 P.2d 685 (Ariz.1971), on the other hand, *Miranda* was applied to a defendant arrested for driving under the influence. In support of *Campbell*, it may be noted that the privilege against self-incrimination *at trial* (unlike the right to counsel or to jury trial) has never been limited to serious crimes.

Tax investigations. In *Mathis v. U. S.*, 391 U.S. 1 (1968), which concerned statements obtained by an internal revenue agent from a defendant incarcerated in jail on another matter, the government contended that the *Miranda* warnings were not required because the questions were asked as "part of a routine tax investigation where no criminal proceedings might even be brought." The Court acknowledged that such an investigation might be initiated for the purpose of a civil action, but ruled that the warnings are required because there is always the possibility that criminal prosecution will result.

B.   WHEN IS INTERROGATION "CUSTODIAL"?

"Custody" vs. "focus."   In the course of defining that interrogation which is "custodial," the *Miranda* Court dropped a footnote stating that was "what we meant in *Escobedo* when we spoke of an investigation which had focused on an accused." Some have thus suggested that custody and focus are alternative grounds for requiring the warnings. A more likely explanation for this footnote, which probably does not really state what was intended by the focus element when *Escobedo* was written (see § 26), is that the Court was attempting to maintain some continuity between that case and the new approach of *Miranda*, while in fact making a fresh start in describing the point at which the constitutional protections begin. The Court has since rejected the claim that "focus" involves psychological restraints equivalent of custody, necessitating the *Miranda* warnings. *Beckwith v. U. S.*, 425 U.S. 341 (1976).

Purpose of the custody. *Mathis v. U. S.*, supra, posed the question whether *Miranda* applies when the purpose of the custody is unrelated to the purpose of the interrogation, as there the defendant was in jail serving a state sentence when questioned by a revenue agent about his tax returns. The Court, 5–3, answered in the affirmative, asserting that a contrary result would go "against the whole purpose of the *Miranda* decision." The dissenters were unwilling to accept this conclusion, for they read *Miranda* as resting "not on the mere fact of physical restriction but on a conclusion that coercion— pressure to answer questions—usually flows from a certain type of custody, police station interrogation of someone charged with or suspected of a crime."

On-the-scene questioning. The *Miranda* Court stated that interrogation is custodial if it occurs while the individual is "in custody at the station or otherwise deprived of his freedom of action in any significant way." One reason for the latter part of this disjunctive definition is obvious: if *Miranda* governed only station-house interrogations, the police could easily circumvent the warning requirements by conducting interrogations in such places as hotel rooms or squad cars. But what of questions asked when the custody is arguably less coercive, such as just after arrest or during the brief on-the-street detention for investigation apparently permitted by the *Terry* case (see § 15)?

In *Orozco v. Texas,* 394 U.S. 324 (1969), where four policemen entered defendant's bedroom at 4 a.m. and questioned him without the *Miranda* warnings, the Court held that *Miranda* applied, not on the ground that these unique facts established a "potentiality for compulsion" equivalent to station-house interrogation, but rather because the officers had testified that defendant was "under arrest and not free to leave" when he was questioned. The dissenters thought this intention-of-the-officer test inappropriate, in that "it is difficult to imagine the police duplicating in a person's home or on the street those conditions and practices which the Court found prevalent in the station house and which were thought so threatening to the right to silence."

Some courts and commentators have questioned the intent-of-the-officer approach, preferring a test based upon whether the police had sufficient grounds to arrest or hold the suspect, whether the suspect subjectively thought he was not free to leave, or whether a reasonable person would believe his freedom was significantly impaired. It has been reasoned that the latter, objective test is consistent with *Miranda* and also most workable in that it avoids reliance upon self-serving statements of the police and the suspect, avoids the need to determine the officer's state of mind, and relieves the officer from the necessity of speculating as to the thoughts of the suspect. *U. S. v. Hall*, 421 F.2d 540 (2d Cir. 1969).

As *Orozco* shows, a person can be in "custody" for *Miranda* purposes even when outside the police station. But most lower courts are of the view that absent special circumstances (e. g., arresting a suspect at gun point or forcibly subduing him) police questioning outside the station is not "custodial." *U. S. v. Gallagher*, 430 F.2d 1222 (7th Cir. 1970). Cf. *Schneckloth v. Bustamonte* (§ 18) (no Fourth Amendment warnings needed for normal consent search on the street "under informal and unstructured conditions * * * immeasurably far removed from 'custodial interrogation' ").

Voluntary appearance. If the defendant's appearance at the stationhouse for questioning is truly voluntary, then there is no custody and *Miranda* does not apply. *Ore. v. Mathiason*, 429 U.S. 492 (1977). Where a burglary suspect came to the station in response to a telephoned request by an officer that he do so, was told upon his appearance there that he was not under arrest, and was allowed to go his way shortly thereafter, this was a noncustodial situation which was not converted into a custodial one by the coercive environment. *Ore. v. Mathiason*, supra. The result would not be the same if the defendant were picked up by the police and brought to the station, even if he was not told he was under arrest and was not booked. Cf. *Dunaway v. N. Y.*, 442 U.S. 200 (1979).

C. WHAT CONSTITUTES "INTERROGATION"?

"Volunteered" statements. The *Miranda* Court emphasized that "there is no requirement that police stop a person who enters a police station and states that he wishes to confess to a crime, or a person who calls the police to offer a confession or any other statement he desires to make. Volunteered statements of any kind are not barred by the Fifth Amendment and their admissibility is not affected by our holding today." Thus, it is clear that a statement not preceded by the *Miranda* warnings will be admissible when, for example, the defendant walks into a station and confesses, *Lung v. S.,* 420 P.2d 158 (Okla.Crim.1966), or he blurts out an admission when approached by an officer near a crime scene, *C. v. Boyd,* 239 A.2d 853 (Pa. Super.1968). Also, because the *Miranda* Court found custody-plus-interrogation coercive, rather than mere custody, it likewise seems clear that a statement may qualify as "volunteered" even though made by one in custody, *P. v. Mercer,* 64 Cal.Rptr. 861 (App.1967); *In re Orr,* 231 N.E.2d 424 (Ill.1967).

Follow-up questioning. Assuming a truly volunteered statement, may the police follow up that statement with some questions? *Miranda* is not entirely clear on this issue; at one point custodial interrogation is defined as "questioning initiated by law enforcement officers," suggesting that police questioning designed to clarify or amplify a volunteered statement is permissible, but elsewhere it is said that the suspect must be warned "prior to any questioning." So far, courts have been quite willing to admit the answers to follow-up questions on the ground that these answers are a continuation of the volunteered statement, *S. v. Intogna*, 419 P.2d 59 (Ariz.1966); *C. v. Eperjesi*, 224 A.2d 216 (Pa.1966). It may well be, however, that a distinction should be drawn between questions designed to clarify an ambiguous statement (e. g., "did what"? in response to "I did it"), and those which seek to enhance the defendant's guilt or raise the offense to a higher degree (e. g., "why did you do it?").

The "functional equivalent" of questioning. What if the police have done something (other than questioning the suspect) which appears to have prompted his statement, such as showing him incriminating physical evidence or confronting him with a confessing accomplice or the accusing victim? Though the cases had not been in agreement, compare *Combs v. Wingo,* 465 F.2d 96 (6th Cir. 1972), with *U. S. v. Pheaster,* 544 F.2d 353 (9th Cir. 1976), such actions will usually fall within the Court's recent holding in *R. I. v. Innis,* —— U.S. —— (1980):

"We conclude that the *Miranda* safeguards come into play whenever a person in custody is subjected to either express questioning or its functional equivalent. That is to say, the term 'interrogation' under *Miranda* refers not only to express questioning, but also to any words or actions on the part of the police (other than those normally attendant to arrest and custody) that the police should know are reasonably likely to elicit an incriminating response from the suspect. The latter portion of this definition focuses primarily upon the perceptions of the suspect, rather than the intent of the police. This focus reflects the fact that the *Miranda* safeguards were designed to vest a suspect in custody with an added measure of protection against coercive police practices, without regard to objective proof of the underlying intent of the police. A practice that the police should know is reasonably likely to evoke an incriminating response from a suspect thus amounts to interrogation. But, since the police surely cannot be held accountable for the unforeseeable results of their words or actions, the definition of interrogation can extend only to words or actions on the part of police officers that they *should have known* were reasonably likely to elicit an incriminating response."

In *Innis,* the defendant, who had already asserted his *Miranda* rights, made incriminating statements after one officer said to another, as they took defendant to the station after his arrest, that the missing shotgun might fall into the hands of students at a nearby school for handicapped children. The majority concluded this was a dialog between the police rather than questioning, and that it was not the "functional equivalent" of questioning because there was nothing in the record to suggest the officers should have known the brief conversation would prompt defendant to make an incriminating response.

It must be remembered that conduct which does not constitute "interrogation" under *Innis* may still amount to the eliciting of an incriminating statement in violation of defendant's right to counsel; see § 28F.

Purpose of the questioning. The Supreme Court has held that the privilege against self-incrimination offers no protection against requiring a suspect to appear in a lineup, to give a handwriting sample, or to speak for identification the words uttered by the offender at the scene of the crime (see § 30). Thus, *Miranda*-type warnings are not a prerequisite to these procedures. Some commentators have suggested that questions asked for purposes of identification (e. g., "what is your name?", "where do you live?") are likewise outside the privilege, and that therefore they may be put to a suspect in custody without first giving him the *Miranda* warnings. Cf. *Cal. v. Byers*, 402 U.S. 424 (1971), holding that a statute requiring a driver of a car involved in an accident to stop and give the driver of the other car his name and address does not violate the privilege. This conclusion is consistent with the *Innis* definition of "interrogation," supra.

What if the police engage in routine questioning, perhaps as a part of the booking process, which is not related to the investigation of the case nor designed, expected or likely to elicit information relevant to guilt, but the defendant responds with a remark which turns out to be incriminating? One view is that the intent with which the question is asked is not relevant, in that even an innocent question asked of one in custody may create the impression that he must answer, so that the response is not voluntary in the sense required by *Miranda*. *Proctor v. U. S.*, 404 F.2d 819 (D.C.Cir. 1968). But, it may be argued that such innocent inquiries do not add to the pressures generated by police custody and that therefore the reply, especially if unresponsive, should be viewed as equivalent to a volunteered statement. Cf. *Parsons v. U. S.*, 387 F.2d 944 (10th Cir. 1968). This latter view is consistent with the *Innis* definition of "interrogation," supra.

What if the purpose of the police was self-protection? In *S. v. Lane*, 467 P.2d 304 (Wash.1970), where, immediately after the arrest of an armed robber in his apartment, he was asked if he had a gun and replied in the negative, noting he would not be dumb enough to have the gun there, the statement was held admissible on the ground that the question was asked to protect the immediate physical safety of the officers and could not have been delayed until after the warnings were given. On the other hand, it might be contended that, unlike a routine question about employment or residence, such an inquiry does add to the pressures generated by police custody, and that considering the limitations on search incident to arrest imposed by *Chimel* (pp. 145–146) the need for such an inquiry is not great.

What if the purpose of the questioning was to rescue the victim? In *P. v. Dean,* 114 Cal.Rptr. 555 (App.1974), the court held admissible incriminating responses by a kidnapping suspect to questions about the victim's whereabouts, reasoning that the officer's interest in saving the victim's life justified not giving the *Miranda* warnings and thereby impeding the rescue efforts.

Questioning by non-police. In *Miranda,* the Court defined interrogation as "questioning initiated by law enforcement officers." This language has been relied upon by courts in holding *Miranda* inapplicable to questioning by a private investigator, *S. v. Hess,* 449 P.2d 46 (Ariz.App.1969), a high school principal, *P. v. Shipp,* 239 N.E.2d 296 (Ill.App.1968), and the victim, *S. v. Little,* 439 P.2d 387 (Kan.1969). It has also been held that *Miranda* is not applicable to interrogation by the defendant's parole or probation officer, *S. v. Johnson,* 202 N.W.2d 132 (S.D. 1972), although more persuasive is the contrary holding, based upon the fact that a probationer or parolee "is under heavy pressure to cooperate" with such a person, *S. v. Gallagher,* 313 N.E.2d 396 (Ohio 1974).

D. WHAT WARNINGS ARE REQUIRED?

Adequacy of the warnings. Although it is undoubtedly true that *Miranda* does not require slavish adherence to the precise words used therein for the necessary warnings, certainly the warnings given should be found inadequate if they fail to convey the substance of the *Miranda* requirements. Thus, it is not sufficient that the police told the defendant that "he didn't have to make any statement" (instead of that he had a right to remain silent), or that "he could consult an attorney prior to questioning" (instead of that he also had a right to have the attorney present during questioning), *U. S. v. Fox,* 403 F.2d 97 (2d Cir. 1968). Failure to advise the defendant of his right to have counsel appointed is also fatally defective, *Groshart v. U. S.,* 392 F.2d 172 (9th Cir. 1968), as is a warning that counsel will be furnished only at some future time, *U. S. ex rel. Williams v. Twomey,* 467 F.2d 1248 (7th Cir. 1972). A contrary result has been reached where the defendant later had retained counsel at trial and on appeal, *U. S. v. Messina,* 388 F.2d 393 (2d Cir. 1968), which seems inconsistent with footnote 43 in *Miranda*: "While a warning that the indigent may have counsel appointed need not be given to the person who is known to have an attorney or is known to have ample funds to secure one, the expedient of giving a warning is too simple and the rights involved too important to engage in *ex post* *facto* inquiries into financial ability when there is any doubt at all on that score." Warnings that anything the suspect says "might," "may," "can," or "could" be used against him have been sustained, *Davis v. U. S.,* 425 F.2d 673 (9th Cir. 1970), but a warning that the statement may be used "for or against" the suspect contains an improper inducement to speak, *C. v. Singleton,* 266 A.2d 753 (Pa.1970).

"Cutting off" the warnings. What if the warning officer never completes his task because the suspect cuts him off with the assertion that the warnings are unnecessary because he is fully aware of all of his rights? The prevailing view is that this is no excuse for not completing the warnings, *S. v. Ross,* 157 N.W.2d 860 (Nev.1968); *Brown v. Heyd,* 277 F.Supp. 899 (E.D.La.1967), and this is consistent with the language in *Miranda* which emphasizes that the expedient of giving adequate warnings is so simple that "we will not pause to inquire in individual cases whether the defendant was aware of his rights without a warning being given."

Multiple interrogation sessions. Once the warnings have been completely given and the defendant has given an effective waiver, must the warnings be repeated again at the outset of a subsequent interview? The courts have quite consistently answered in the negative, both when the later interview follows promptly after the first, *P. v. Hill,* 233 N.E.2d 367 (Ill.1968), and when several days have intervened, *Maguire v. U. S.,* 396 F.2d 327 (9th Cir. 1968). It might be argued, however, that the *Miranda* concern with the suspect's continuing right to invoke the privilege means that a substantial interval calls for repetition of the warnings, particularly so that the "warning will show the individual that his interrogators are prepared to recognize his privilege should he choose to exercise it."

Additional admonitions. Is the suspect entitled to notice from the police of the charge against him or, at least, of the nature and seriousness of the crime they are investigating? No, say most of the courts which have confronted this issue. *S. v. Lucero,* 445 P.2d 731 (Mont.1968); *S. v. McKnight,* 243 A.2d 240 (N.J.1968). This result is often justified by distinguishing confessions from guilty pleas. A plea of guilty, which involves a waiver of the privilege against self-incrimination as well as other rights, is constitutionally defective if the defendant is unaware of the precise nature of the charge. *Boykin v. Ala.,* 395 U.S. 238 (1969). But this, it is argued, is because a plea of guilty involves a legal conclusion (e. g., "I admit guilt as to the crime of battery"), while a confession or admission only involves an acknowledgment that certain possibly incriminating facts occurred (e. g., "I am the one who struck the victim"). And thus, while a plea to battery could not be converted into a homicide plea by the subsequent death of the victim, an acknowledgment of certain acts would be admissible whether the crime turns out to be battery or homicide, for (as the *McKnight* court put it) the privilege is not violated merely because the defendant "misconceived the inculpatory thrust of the facts he admitted."

However, it is said in *Miranda* that "any evidence that the accused was threatened, tricked, or cajoled into a waiver will, of course, show that the defendant did not voluntarily waive his privilege." Deliberate acts by the police to mislead the suspect as to the seriousness of the situation might be subject to attack on this basis. Thus, in *Schenk v. Ellsworth,* 293 F.Supp. 26 (D.Mont.1968), where defendant was suspected of murdering his wife but was only told the questioning would be "in connection with the shooting incident of his wife," the court noted he was "very likely misled" by his interrogator and thus had not intelligently waived counsel.

E. WHAT CONSTITUTES WAIVER?

Express or implied. In *No. Car. v. Butler,* 441 U.S. 369 (1979), it was held: "An express written or oral statement of waiver [of *Miranda* rights] is usually strong proof of the validity of that waiver, but is not inevitably either necessary or sufficient to establish waiver. The question is not one of form, but rather whether the defendant in fact knowingly and voluntarily waived [the *Miranda* rights]. The courts must presume that a defendant did not waive his rights; the prosecution's burden is great; but in at least some cases waiver can be clearly inferred from the actions and words of the person interrogated." But this does not mean waiver is established merely by the fact that the defendant thereafter answered questions, *Tague v. La.,* —— U.S. —— (1980), as *Miranda* cautions that "a valid waiver will not be presumed simply from the silence of the accused after warnings are given or simply from the fact that a confession was in fact eventually obtained."

If the defendant requests an attorney, this is per se an invocation of his Fifth Amendment rights, requiring that all interrogation cease. This is because of the "pivotal role" of counsel in the criminal process, and thus a comparable per se approach is not applicable to a request for a probation officer, clergyman, or close friend. *Fare v. Michael C.,* 442 U.S. 707 (1979).

Refusal to execute written waiver or confession. On the question of whether an effective waiver can be established in the face of defendant's refusal to sign a waiver-of-rights form, or to have his confession reduced to writing, the prevailing view is yes. *U. S. v. Frazier,* 476 F.2d 891 (D.C.Cir. 1973); *Hodge v. U. S.,* 392 F.2d 552 (5th Cir. 1968). That position is supported by the Supreme Court's approach in *No. Car. v. Butler,* discussed above. However, it does seem that under such circumstances no waiver should be found if other indications of the suspect's intentions to waive are at all ambiguous.

Thus, in *U. S. v. Nielsen,* 392 F.2d 849 (7th Cir. 1968), where the defendant said he would not sign the waiver or anything else until he consulted an attorney, who he preferred to call later, the court ruled the government had not met its "heavy burden" to establish waiver; the defendant's willingness to talk and unwillingness to sign anything were contradictory, suggesting that he did not fully appreciate that his oral statements could be just as damaging as a signed confession.

Multiple interrogation sessions. A suspect who has once refused to waive his *Miranda* rights may in some circumstances execute an effective waiver at a subsequent interrogation session.   In *Michigan v. Mosley,* 423 U.S. 96 (1975), the Court rejected the claim that assertion of *Miranda* rights creates "a per se proscription of indefinite duration upon any further questioning by any police officer on any subject," and concluded that instead the test is whether the defendant's right to cut off questioning was "scrupulously honored."   In *Mosley,* the defendant, after receiving the *Miranda* warnings, declined to discuss the robberies for which he was arrested, but two hours later waived his *Miranda* rights to a different officer with respect to an unrelated homicide.   In holding his incriminating statements admissible, the Court stressed that this was not a case "where the police failed to honor a decision of a person in custody to cut off questioning, either by refusing to discontinue the interrogation upon request or by persisting in repeated efforts to wear down his resistance and make him change his mind." Rather, "the police here [i] immediately ceased the interrogation, [ii] resumed questioning only after the passage of a significant period of time and the provision of a fresh set of warnings, and [iii] restricted the second interrogation to a crime that had not been a subject of the earlier interrogation." White, J., concurring, suggested that absent a request for counsel by the defendant (signalling that he is unwilling to make the decision on his own), a defendant's invocation of the right to remain silent could be followed rather promptly with an effective waiver of that right, at least where the police had in the interim supplied additional information relevant to the decision.

F. DOES THE RIGHT TO COUNSEL OR THE APPOINTMENT OR RETENTION OF COUNSEL HAVE ADDED SIGNIFICANCE?

Counsel's request to see client. What if defendant is arrested and taken to the station, where he receives the *Miranda* warnings and waives his rights, after which his attorney appears at or telephones the station with a request that he be allowed to see his client? The *Miranda* Court appears to have assumed that the request must be granted, for a footnote (n. 35) to a discussion of *Escobedo* reads: "The police also prevented the attorney from consulting with his client. Independent of any other constitutional proscription, this action constitutes a violation of the Sixth Amendment right to the assistance of counsel and excludes any statement obtained in its wake." But it is unclear why this should be so if the defendant has waived his Sixth Amendment rights, for the implication that the lawyer has a separate constitutional right to see his client is certainly questionable. (Cf. *P. v. Zuniga*, 202 N.E.2d 31 (Ill.1964), holding a lawyer cannot challenge the constitutionality of a statute limiting compensation for representation of indigents, as the Sixth Amendment right to effective representation is not his.)

More understandable is the position taken in *C. v. McKenna*, 244 N.E.2d 560 (Mass.1969), that the attorney's request must be communicated to the client so that he may reconsider his waiver of counsel in the light of this new fact. As the court noted, the defendant "might have chosen to go on with the interrogation," but nonetheless "he was entitled to know of his counsel's availability and, with that knowledge, to make the choice with intelligence and understanding." This position is particularly persuasive if, as held in some of the cases discussed earlier, a defendant who has not waived his rights may be confronted with new facts upon which he might change his mind in favor of waiver.

Questioning without retained or appointed counsel's presence or approval. If counsel has made no such request, but the right to counsel has attached under the *Massiah-Williams* rule (see § 26) or the police know that counsel has been retained or appointed, may they obtain an effective waiver from the defendant in custody without also contacting the lawyer and asking whether he wishes his client to be interrogated or whether he wishes to be present for the interrogation? Applying the above analysis here, it could be said that the Sixth Amendment is a right of the client and not the lawyer, and that (assuming the police did not withhold from the defendant the fact counsel had been appointed or retained for him) no new facts have been withheld from the defendant, so that his waiver will suffice. Such was the holding in *Coughlan v. U. S.,* 391 F.2d 371 (9th Cir. 1968).

Given the reluctance of most courts to extend the *Escobedo* rule beyond the facts of that case (see § 26), the *Coughlan* result is not surprising. *Massiah* has been deemed inapplicable to this situation because limited to cases where there were "circumstances preventing an effective exercise or waiver of rights to counsel," *U. S. v. Durham,* 475 F.2d 208 (7th Cir. 1973), as where the defendant was "coerced" or "tricked" into confessing, *S. v. Chabonian,* 185 N.W.2d 289 (Wis.1971). As for *Williams,* the Court in that case emphasized it was *not* holding waiver of Sixth Amendment rights was impossible "without notice to counsel."

Use of tactics other than "interrogation." Certain police tactics not amounting to questioning or its functional equivalent have been held not to fall within the protections of *Miranda* even when they have prompted an incriminating response from the suspect (see § 28C). But if these tactics were employed after "judicial proceedings had been initiated against" him, when his constitutional right to counsel had attached under *Massiah* and *Williams* (see § 26), their use may violate the Sixth Amendment. In *Massiah,* where incriminating statements were obtained by use of a police agent and eavesdropping equipment, it was enough that those statements were "deliberately elicited" by the police. And in *Williams* it sufficed that the "Christian burial speech" was made by a detective who "deliberately and designedly set out to elicit information from Williams just as surely as—and perhaps more effectively than—if he had formally interrogated him."

What, for example, if the police place an undercover agent into defendant's cell, where he succeeds in eliciting incriminating information from the defendant? The use of secret agents in other contexts has been upheld (see § 21), and it would be difficult to attack this tactic on *Miranda* grounds, for it seems unlikely that a violation of the privilege is involved. As the Court held in *Hoffa v. U. S.,* 385 U.S. 293 (1966), statements elicited by an undercover agent are not "the product of any sort of coercion, legal or factual," so that no right protected by the Fifth Amendment is violated. It might be argued, of course, that *Hoffa* is distinguishable in that the conversations there were "wholly voluntary" because of Hoffa's freedom to decide whether to speak *and* with whom to speak, while the jailed suspect cannot choose his cellmate and is induced to speak by the very presence of the cellmate. See the dissent by four Justices to the dismissal of the writ of certiorari in *Miller v. Cal.,* 392 U.S. 616 (1968).

But in *U. S. v. Henry,* —— U.S. —— (1980), where this tactic was used on an indicted defendant, the Court held it violated the Sixth Amendment. The scope of the *Henry* holding is unclear. For one thing, the majority repeatedly stressed that the confrontation was "after indictment," relied exclusively upon *Massiah* and other cases viewing the post-indictment stage as "critical" for right to counsel purposes, and never acknowledged the extension of Sixth Amendment protection to various preindictment situations. Secondly, it is uncertain exactly what kind of involvement by the government in obtaining an incriminating statement is forbidden. At one point the question is said to be whether "a government agent 'deliberately elicited' incriminating statements * * * within the meaning of *Massiah*." But the majority then concluded that though the government agent had told the cellmate-informer not to initiate conversations with Henry regarding the bank robbery but only to "pay attention to the information furnished by Henry," the *Massiah* test was met because the informant in

[254]

fact "was not a passive listener," he was on a contingent fee and would be "paid only if he produced useful information," the agent was aware the informer "had access to Henry and would be able to engage him in conversations without arousing Henry's suspicion," and even if the informant complied with the agent's instructions he "remained free to discharge his task of eliciting the statements in myriad less direct ways." Much to the consternation of the three *Henry* dissenters, the majority declared the Sixth Amendment was violated "even if the agent's statement is accepted that he did not intend that [the informer] would take affirmative steps to secure incriminating information," as "by intentionally creating a situation likely to induce Henry to make incriminating statements without the assistance of counsel, the government violated Henry's Sixth Amendment right to counsel." The Court in *Henry* added it was not "called upon to pass on the situation where an informant is placed in close proximity but makes no effort to stimulate conversation about the crime charged."

29. SELF–INCRIMINATION AND THE GRAND JURY WITNESS

Application of the privilege. Although this chapter is concerned primarily with police interrogation, it should be noted that prosecutors have even broader authority in interrogating witnesses before the grand jury. Acting as the legal advisor to the grand jury, the prosecutor may obtain a subpoena requiring that a person appear before the grand jury and testify under oath. While the police are subject to Fourth Amendment requirements in detaining a person for questioning (see § 15), those requirements do not apply to the decision to issue a grand jury subpoena (see § 16). Similarly, while the police have no authority to require a person to respond to interrogation, even apart from his self-incrimination privilege, the witness before the grand jury is required to respond to each question. Failure to do so may subject him to contempt, and if he lies under oath, he may be prosecuted for perjury. However, the witness may not be compelled to incriminate himself, and he may respond by claiming the privilege where it applies. *Counselman v. Hitchcock,* 142 U.S. 547 (1892). The privilege is available not only where the witness' answer would acknowledge an element of a crime, but wherever it would furnish "a link in the chain of evidence" that might be used to institute a prosecution. *Hoffman v. U. S.,* 341 U.S. 479 (1951). This standard applies to any potential state or federal prosecution, and thus the privilege may be claimed even though the potential incrimination applies to a jurisdiction other than that which compels the testimony. *Murphy v. Waterfront Comm.,* 378 U.S. 52 (1964).

Need for self-incrimination warnings. A subpoenaed grand jury witness may be an innocent third party or a potential defendant who is a "target" of the grand jury's investigation. *U. S. v. Winter,* 348 F.2d 204 (2d Cir. 1965). A few courts have suggested that the "target witness" is in a position comparable to the arrestee subject to custodial interrogation and therefore must be given *Miranda* warnings. However, most of the courts that have confronted that issue have held otherwise. *C. v. Columbia Inv. Corp.,* 325 A.2d 289 (Pa.1974). In *U. S. v. Mandujano,* 425 U.S. 564 (1976), the full Court found it unnecessary to reach this issue. Although the witness there had not been given full *Miranda* warnings, he was being prosecuted for having given false testimony before the grand jury; even if the lack of full *Miranda* warnings had resulted in a denial of his Fifth Amendment privilege, it would provide "no protection for the commission of perjury." See also *U. S. v. Wong,* 431 U.S. 174 (1977) (grand jury witness who misunderstood self-incrimination warnings cannot suppress her false testimony in subsequent perjury prosecution).

While the full Court did not reach the issue, a four-justice plurality opinion in *Mandujano* did consider and reject the need for full *Miranda* warnings. It stressed that: (1) grand jury questioning "takes place in a setting wholly different from custodial police interrogation"; (2) a grand jury witness has no absolute right to remain silent comparable to that of the person being interrogated by the police, but rather has an "absolute duty to answer all questions, subject only to a valid Fifth Amendment claim"; and (3) there was no Sixth Amendment basis for providing the witness with appointed counsel since "no criminal proceedings had [yet] been instituted" and the "Sixth Amendment right to counsel [therefore] had not come into play." Because the witness in *Mandujano* was told that he had a right not to answer incriminatory questions, the plurality noted it therefore was "unnecessary to consider whether any warning is required." Consistent with federal practice, the witness in *Mandujano* also had been told that he could consult with retained counsel (which he did not have) outside of the grand jury room. Two concurring justices argued that a witness could not be assumed to have knowingly waived his self-incrimination privilege without more complete warnings, including a notification that he was the target of the investigation. However, in a later case, *U. S. v. Washington,* 431 U.S. 181 (1977), the Court specifically rejected the need for a target notification, noting that a witness' target status "neither enlarges nor diminishes the constitutional protection against compelled self-incrimination."

Subpoenas for documents. We have considered so far the application of the privilege to the person subpoenaed to testify before the grand jury. The privilege also may apply to a subpoena duces tecum requiring the production of incriminating documents before the grand jury. Here, however, several limitations on the scope of the privilege sharply restrict its application. First, the privilege does not apply to the required production of records of corporations or similar collective entities (e. g., a labor union, or an ongoing business enterprise organized as a partnership). *Bellis v. U. S.,* 417 U.S. 85 (1974); *U. S. v. White,* 322 U.S. 694 (1944). As the Court noted in *Bellis* and *White,* the Fifth Amendment "respects a private inner sanctum of individual feeling and thought" which is not possessed by a corporation or other entity that "has a character so impersonal in the scope of its membership and activities that it cannot be said to embody or represent the purely private or personal interests of its constituents." Since the individual officer of the entity who presents the records is acting in a custodial, representative capacity, he also cannot claim the privilege even though the records are highly incriminating to him personally.

Second, the privilege can only be raised by the person actually being compelled to produce the records. Thus, a taxpayer could not claim the privilege where his accountant was required to produce the taxpayer's records that were in the accountant's possession. *Couch v. U. S.,* 409 U.S. 322 (1973). The accountant in that situation also could not claim the privilege since it is available only where the person compelled to produce the records will himself be incriminated, not where the only incrimination is to others. *Fisher v. U. S.,* 425 U.S. 391 (1976). See also *Roger v. U. S.,* 340 U.S. 367 (1951) (where a witness testifying before a grand jury had waived the privilege by acknowledging her own possession of records, she could not claim the privilege as to questions that might prove incriminating to others). However, in the case of an attorney possessing the records of a client, the attorney-client privilege will bar production if the self-incrimination privilege would have barred production from the client if he had possessed the records. *Fisher v. U. S.,* supra.

Finally, even where the subpoenaed records are not those of a collective entity and are incriminating to the person subpoenaed, the privilege does not apply unless the records are the "private papers" of the subpoenaed person. *Fisher v. U. S.,* supra, suggests that incriminatory records will constitute private papers for this purpose only if the testimonial aspects of their production are themselves incriminatory. Those testimonial aspects consist of (1) the implicit acknowledgment through production that the records exist and are in the possession of the subpoenaed person, and (2) the implicit authentication that the records produced are those described in the subpoena. *Fisher* noted that these testimonial aspects of production would not be incriminatory (and therefore the privilege would not apply) where a taxpayer was required to produce workpapers prepared by his accountant. The taxpayer's production of the workpapers would not authenticate their content since the taxpayer "did not prepare the papers and could not vouch for their accuracy," and the existence and location of the workpapers had been independently established without regard to the taxpayer's act. A commonly accepted illustration of a situation where production clearly would be incriminatory under *Fisher* is that of a subpoena directing a target witness to produce a personal diary that discusses the matter under investigation.

Immunity. The state may preclude a witness' reliance on the privilege against self-incrimination, with respect to either testimony or the production of documents, by an appropriate grant of immunity. The object of the privilege is to protect the witness against criminal prosecution, not to protect him against being compelled to give information that might tend to "disgrace him or bring him into disrepute." *Brown v. Walker,* 161 U.S. 591 (1896). Accordingly, if the state guarantees to the witness protection against prosecution equal to that which would exist if he claimed the privilege, it has effectively replaced the privilege and can compel him to testify. At one time, it was thought that equivalent protection required a grant of "transactional immunity"—i. e. immunity from prosecution for any offenses based on the transaction as to which the witness is compelled to testify. *Brown v. Walker,* supra. Under this type of immunity, which is still utilized in many states, a witness compelled to furnish information relating to a particular offense may not be prosecuted for that offense even if the state has obtained sufficient evidence to establish his guilt through sources other than his compelled testimony. In *Kastigar v. U. S.,* 406 U.S. 441 (1972), the Court held that it was sufficient to grant a less extensive immunity known as "use and derivative use" immunity. Such immunity, the Court noted, was coextensive with the privilege because it barred prosecution use of the witness' compelled statement and any information derived from that statement. Cf. § 34 (discussing the "fruit of the poison tree" doctrine). However, since the privilege extends to possible incrimination under both federal or state law, the protection against use and derivative use must extend to both jurisdictions. *Murphy v. Waterfront Comm.*, supra. Although the states lack the power to preclude federal prosecutions, the Supreme Court has lent the necessary scope to state immunity grants by holding that state immunized testimony and its fruits cannot be used in federal prosecutions. Congress has provided that federal witness immunity bars use and derivative use in both federal and state prosecutions. 18 U.S.C.A. § 6002.

For a grant of immunity to provide protection "coextensive" with the Fifth Amendment, it need not treat the witness as if he had remained silent. Thus, if the witness granted immunity gives false testimony, he may be prosecuted for that criminal conduct, and at his criminal trial the allegedly false testimony and also other testimony relevant to prove that the false statements charged were knowingly made are admissible in evidence. *U. S. v. Apfelbaum,* —— U. S. —— (1980).

CHAPTER 5

LINEUPS AND OTHER PRETRIAL IDENTIFICATION PROCEDURES

30. THE PRIVILEGE AGAINST SELF–INCRIMINATION

The Schmerber case. In *Schmerber v. Cal.*, 384 U.S. 757 (1966), the Court upheld the taking of a blood sample by a physician at police direction from a defendant over his objection after his arrest for drunken driving. Among the grounds upon which the defendant challenged the admission of this sample in evidence against him was that it violated his Fifth Amendment privilege not to "be compelled in any criminal case to be a witness against himself." The Court, in a 5–4 decision, rejected this contention and held that "the privilege protects an accused only from being compelled to testify against himself, or otherwise provide the State with evidence of a testimonial or communicative nature."

In defining the scope of the privilege, the majority noted that many identification procedures were not protected by the Fifth Amendment. *Holt v. U. S.*, 218 U.S. 245 (1910), holding that a defendant could be compelled to model a blouse, was cited as the "leading case," and it was observed that "both federal and state courts have usually held that it offers no protection against compulsion to submit to fingerprinting, photographing or measurements, to write or speak for identification, to appear in court, to stand, to assume a stance, to walk, or to make a particular gesture."

Application to pretrial identification. It is thus not surprising that the Court has subsequently relied upon *Schmerber* in holding that several identification practices do not conflict with the privilege: requiring the defendant to appear in a lineup and to speak for identification, *U. S. v. Wade*, 388 U.S. 218 (1967); or to provide handwriting exemplars, *Gilbert v. Cal.*, 388 U.S. 263 (1967). In both cases the Court split 5–4 on this issue. The majority relied upon the *Schmerber* distinction between an accused's "communications" in whatever form, vocal or physical, and "compulsion which makes a suspect or accused the source of 'real or physical evidence.'" The dissenters argued that *Schmerber* was wrongly decided, in that the privilege is designed to bar the government from forcing a person to supply proof of his own crime, and that even assuming the correctness of *Schmerber* the instant cases were distinguishable because each defendant was required "actively to cooperate—to accuse himself by a volitional act." Other courts have followed the majority view and have thus held the privilege inapplicable to such other identification procedures as fingerprinting, *Johnson v. C.*, 158 S.E.2d 725 (Va.1968), or examination by ultraviolet light, *U. S. v. Richardson*, 388 F.2d 842 (6th Cir. 1968).

Consequences of failure to cooperate. Although not protected by the Fifth Amendment, some identification procedures (such as speaking or writing for identification) require the active participation of the suspect. But, what if the suspect will not cooperate? One possibility, feared the dissenters in *Wade*, is that "an accused may be jailed—indefinitely—until he is willing to" cooperate. In *U. S. v. Hammond*, 419 F.2d 166 (4th Cir. 1969), a federal bank robbery defendant was held in criminal contempt for refusing to obey a court order requiring him to participate in lineups scheduled by the government. Cf. *U. S. v. Doe*, 405 F.2d 436 (2d Cir. 1968), where a federal grand jury witness was held in contempt and committed to custody until he provided handwriting samples. Another possibility is that the prosecution may be permitted to comment at trial on the lack of cooperation, as in *U. S. v. Parknes*, 424 F.2d 152 (9th Cir. 1970). Comment on the defendant's refusal to speak for identification was held improper in *P. v. Ellis*, 421 P.2d 393 (Cal.1966), but only because it was the direct result of a prior police warning of the right to remain silent and thus not an indication of guilt.

31. THE RIGHT TO COUNSEL AND CONFRONTATION

A. LINEUPS

Procedures required. At least after the accused has been indicted, ruled the Court in *U. S. v. Wade*, 388 U.S. 218 (1967), and *Gilbert v. Cal.*, 388 U.S. 263 (1967), he should not be exhibited to witnesses in a lineup conducted for identification purposes without notice to and in the absence of his counsel. Rather, both the accused and his counsel must be notified of the impending lineup, and the lineup must not be conducted until counsel is present (expressly left open was the possibility that the presence of substitute counsel might suffice where notification and presence of the suspect's own counsel would result in prejudicial delay). In the absence of "legislative or other regulations * * * which eliminate the risks of abuse and unintentional suggestion at lineup proceedings," the Court emphasized in *Wade*, the above procedures are required by virtue of the defendant's constitutional right to confrontation and his right to counsel at a critical stage of the proceedings. (Apparently no court has yet held any set of regulations to be adequate; see e. g., *P. v. Fowler*, 461 P.2d 643 [Cal.1969].)

As explained by the Court, the right to counsel in this context is supportive of another right—here, the right to confrontation—in much the same way that

[266]

the *Miranda* counsel requirement rests upon the privilege against self-incrimination. (But see *Kirby v. Ill.,* discussed at p. 273.) Under past lineup practices, the defense was often unable "meaningfully to attack the credibility of the witness' courtroom identification" because of several factors which militate against developing fully the circumstances of a prior lineup identification by that witness: (a) other participants in the lineup are often police officers, or, if not, their names are rarely recorded or divulged at trial; (b) neither witnesses nor lineup participants are apt to be alert for or schooled in the detection of prejudicial conditions; (c) the suspect (often staring into bright lights) may not be in a position to observe prejudicial conditions, and, in any event, might not detect them because of his emotional tension; (d) even if the suspect observes abuse, he may nonetheless be reluctant to take the stand and open up the admission of prior convictions; and (e) even if he takes the stand, his version of what transpired at the lineup is unlikely to be accepted if it conflicts with police testimony. Moreover, the Court pointed out, the need to learn what occurred at the lineup is great; the risk of improper suggestion is substantial, and once the witness has picked out the accused in a lineup, he is unlikely to go back on his word in court.

The three dissenters to this aspect of *Wade* and *Gilbert* saw no need for the imposition of such a "broad prophylactic rule" in the absence of evidence that improper police practices at lineups were wide-spread. They also expressed concern that the delays required to comply with the procedures prescribed by the majority would make prompt and certain identification impossible.

Although there are cases to the contrary, the better view is that *Wade* and *Gilbert* apply at the moment of actual identification and not merely the moment of viewing, as it is important for counsel to be able to reconstruct the former at trial. *P. v. Williams*, 478 P.2d 942 (Cal.1971). The contrary position is bolstered to some extent by the *Ash* decision (see § 31B). *Wade* and *Gilbert* apply to a one-on-one identification procedure as well, even if conducted in the course of a judicial proceeding. *Moore v. Ill.*, 434 U.S. 220 (1977).

Waiver of counsel. The Court in *Wade* indicated that there might be an "intelligent waiver" of counsel, in which case notice to and presence of an attorney would not be required. Although this may seem consistent with the waiver permitted in *Miranda* (see § 27), some have questioned whether the right to counsel at the lineup should be subject to waiver. The argument is that while waiver of counsel under *Miranda* serves the legitimate objective of permitting the suspect to bear witness to the truth, no comparable value is served by waiver under *Wade*.

The *Wade* opinion does not dwell upon the question of what is required to show an effective waiver, although it seems likely that the approach in *Miranda* is to be followed here. This means the defendant must be advised that he has a right to counsel for this particular purpose and that counsel will be provided for him if he is indigent, and "a heavy burden" rests upon the government to show an express waiver following the warnings. Moreover, waiver of counsel for another purpose will not suffice, and thus a waiver of counsel following the *Miranda* warnings does not carry over to the lineup.

Consequences of violation. If the required lineup procedures are not followed, then testimony as to the fact of identification at the lineup is inadmissible at trial. "Only a *per se* exclusionary rule as to such testimony can be an effective sanction to assure that law enforcement authorities will respect the accused's constitutional right to the presence of his counsel at the critical lineup." If such testimony is admitted, the defendant is entitled to a new trial unless it is determined that the error was harmless beyond a reasonable doubt (see § 38). *Gilbert v. Cal.*, supra.

But, what of subsequent in-court identification by a witness who earlier identified the defendant at an improperly conducted lineup? This presents a "fruit of the poisonous tree" problem, and consistent with the general approach to that kind of issue (see § 34), it must be determined "whether, granting establishment of the primary illegality, the evidence to which instant objection is made has been come at by

[269]

exploitation of that illegality or instead by means sufficiently distinguishable to be purged of the primary taint." Thus, the government will be afforded the opportunity to establish by clear and convincing evidence that the in-court identifications were based upon observations of the suspect other than the lineup identification. Relevant factors are "the prior opportunity to observe the alleged criminal act, the existence of any discrepancy between any pre-lineup description and the defendant's actual description, any identification prior to lineup of another person, the identification by picture of the defendant prior to the lineup, failure to identify the defendant on a prior occasion, and the lapse of time between the alleged act and the lineup identification," in addition to "those facts which, despite the absence of counsel, are disclosed concerning the conduct of the lineup." *U. S. v. Wade*, supra.

Justice Black, dissenting in part in *Wade*, argued that this "tainted fruit" determination is "practically impossible," in that the witness will be unable "to draw a sharp line between a courtroom identification due exclusively to an earlier lineup and a courtroom identification due to memory not based on the lineup." The majority rejected his contention that therefore all in-court identifications should be admissible, noting that if this were the case then the state could easily circumvent the lineup requirements by resting upon the witnesses' courtroom identification and thus leave the defendant in the same predicament as before. However, some have taken note of the difficulty in making the "tainted fruit" determination in questioning whether the Court went far enough; they fear that trial judges, inevitably left with considerable discretion in making this decision, will readily find an "independent source" for in-court identifications and in that way free the police from the necessity of complying with the *Wade-Gilbert* formula. Several commentators, upon review of lower court decisions, suggest that experience has shown this to be the case.

18 U.S.C.A. § 3502, a part of the Omnibus Crime Control and Safe Streets Act of 1968, provides that the "testimony of a witness that he saw the accused commit * * * the crime" is admissible in a federal court. Some have viewed this as a patently unconstitutional attempt to "repeal" *Wade*, but a Justice Department spokesman has argued that the statute merely makes the witness' statement that he is positive he saw the defendant commit the crime the "initially controlling factor" on the taint issue (instead of one of several, as in *Wade*), and thus is "an appropriate exercise of [Congress'] traditional rulemaking power."

Role of counsel. What, exactly, is the role of defense counsel at the lineup? *Wade* stresses the need to protect the defendant's "right meaningfully to cross-examine the witnesses against him and to have effective assistance of counsel at the trial itself," which most clearly suggests that counsel should function as an observer at the lineup. On the basis of his observations, he would then be in a position at trial to decide whether it is tactically wise to bring out the lineup identification in order to cast doubt upon an in-court identification. And, if he decides to do so, he will better know what questions to ask the witness about the circumstances of the lineup. The observer-counsel may also have to become a witness at the trial, for the Court in *Wade* emphasized that the suspect, other participants in the lineup, and the witnesses at the lineup are unlikely to observe or recognize prejudicial circumstances. Disciplinary Rule 5–102 of the ABA Code of Professional Responsibility, however, provides that if a lawyer learns he will be required to be a witness for his client, except as to merely formal or uncontested matters, he should withdraw from the case unless doing so "would work a substantial hardship on the client because of the distinctive value of the lawyer * * * as counsel in the particular case."

The majority in *Wade* implies that counsel might also take a more active role at the lineup; they say that "presence of counsel itself can often avert prejudice" and assist law enforcement "by preventing the infiltration of taint in the prosecution's identification evidence." The dissenters find in *Wade* "an implicit invitation to counsel to suggest rules for the lineup and to manage and produce it as best he can." Defense counsel obviously cannot compel the police to conduct the lineup in a certain way, although he might point out unfair features of the identification process and even suggest corrective measures. As a matter of tactics, however, counsel may prefer simply to allow the prejudicial practices so that he might bring them out in cross-examination, which raises the question of whether he should be permitted to stand silent and then challenge the police practices at trial. *U. S. v. Allen*, 408 F.2d 1287 (D.C.Cir. 1969), recommends that defense counsel be allowed to take an active role in setting up the lineup, in which case "it might well be that, absent plain error or circumstances unknown to counsel at the time of the lineup, no challenges to the physical staging of the lineup could successfully be raised beyond objections raised at the time of the lineup."

Pre-indictment identifications. Because both *Wade* and *Gilbert* involved lineups held after indictment and appointment of counsel, lower courts were in disagreement as to whether counsel was required at any pre-indictment identifications. In *Kirby v. Ill.*, 406 U.S. 682 (1972), the Court held that the *Wade-Gilbert* rule applies only to lineups occurring "at or after the initiation of adversary judicial criminal proceedings—whether by way of formal charge, preliminary hearing, indictment, information, or arraignment." The rationale was that the constitutional right to counsel has traditionally been so limited, and with good reason, in that only after such initiation is a defendant "faced with the prose-cutorial forces of organized society, and immersed in the intricacies of substantive and procedural criminal law." This conclusion, the three dissenters cogently pointed out, is based upon a misreading of *Wade* and *Gilbert* as purely right to counsel cases, rather than cases concerned with protecting the right to confrontation at trial, and ignores the fact that the practices condemned in those cases may just as easily occur during a pre-indictment lineup.

Except for the language quoted above, *Kirby* does not explore what it takes to "initiate" adversary judicial criminal proceedings, but that language was later relied upon in holding that a preliminary hearing suffices. *Moore v. Ill.*, supra. It is generally agreed that a warrantless arrest is not sufficient, *S. v. Anderson*, 505 P.2d 691 (Kan.1973), but the courts are not in agreement as to whether proceedings are initiated by issuance of an arrest warrant upon information and oath. Compare *U. S. v. Duvall*, 537 F.2d 15 (2d Cir. 1976), with *C. v. Richman*, 320 A.2d 351 (Pa.1974). Consider also *Brewer v. Williams* (p. 225) (concluding that adversary judicial proceedings clearly had been initiated where a warrant had been issued and defendant had been arraigned on the warrant and committed to jail).

B. OTHER IDENTIFICATION PROCEDURES

The use of pictures. Does it follow from *Wade* and *Gilbert* that an accused in custody has a right to have his counsel present while witnesses view still or motion pictures of him for purposes of identification? No, the Court concluded in *U. S. v. Ash*, 413 U.S. 300 (1973). Throughout the expansion of the constitutional right to counsel to certain pretrial proceedings, said the majority, "the function of the lawyer has remained essentially the same as his function at trial," namely, to give the accused "aid in coping with legal problems or assistance in meeting his adversary." This being so, there is no such right at photo-identification, as unlike a lineup, there is no "trial-like confrontation" involving the "presence of the accused." Moreover, even if a broader view were taken of the right to counsel, it need not extend "to a portion of the prosecutor's trial-preparation interviews with witnesses," given "the equal ability of defense counsel to seek and interview witnesses himself." Stewart, J., concurring, while objecting to the majority's distinction of *Wade* as a situation where the lawyer is giving advice or assistance to the defendant at the lineup, concluded that the lawyer's role "as an observer" need not be extended to photo identification, where "there are few possibilities for unfair suggestiveness."

The three dissenters in *Ash* objected that the risk of "impermissible suggestiveness" which led to *Wade* and *Gilbert* was equally present in the case of identification by pictures, and that because the defendant is not personally present for such identification there is less "likelihood that irregularities in the procedure will ever come to light" if counsel has not observed the identification. As for the majority's characterization of the right to counsel, the dissenters argued that historically the right to counsel attached at certain pretrial procedures not because of the assistance the attorney could immediately render at that time, but rather "to protect the fairness of the trial itself."

Scientific methods. In *Wade*, the government argued that a lineup is no different from other identification procedures, such as taking and analyzing "the accused's fingerprints, blood sample, clothing, hair, and the like," apparently in an attempt to bring the instant case within the ruling of *Schmerber v. Cal.*, 384 U.S. 757 (1966). The majority in *Schmerber* held that the taking of a blood sample was not covered by the Fifth Amendment, and thus found "no issue of counsel's ability to assist petitioner in respect of any rights he did possess." The Court in *Wade* distinguished the other procedures listed by the government on the ground that they do not present the risks attendant lineups: "Knowledge of the techniques of science and technology is sufficiently available, and the variables in techniques few enough, that the accused has the opportunity for a meaningful confrontation of the Government's case at trial through the ordinary processes of cross-examination of the Government's expert witnesses and the presentation of the evidence of his own experts." On this basis, the Court held in *Gilbert* that the taking of handwriting exemplars is not a critical stage entitling the suspect to the assistance of counsel. Thus, while the suspect might benefit from counsel's advice as to whether to give the exemplars or refuse and suffer the consequences (see p. 265), this does not involve a constitutional right to which the right to counsel might be linked.

32. DUE PROCESS: "THE TOTALITY OF THE CIRCUMSTANCES"

Generally. An identification made prior to the *Wade* and *Gilbert* decisions (which are not retroactive, see § 8), made thereafter but under circumstances in which counsel is not required, or perhaps even made in the presence of counsel, might be challenged on yet another ground. A "recognized ground of attack upon a conviction independent of any right to counsel claim" is that the defendant's identification was "so unnecessarily suggestive and conducive to irreparable mistaken identification that he was denied due process of law." *Stovall v. Denno*, 388 U.S. 293 (1967).

Unnecessary suggestiveness alone does not require the exclusion of evidence. The Court declined to hold otherwise as to an identification which predated the *Stovall* decision. *Neil v. Biggers*, 409 U.S. 188 (1972). If there has been suggestiveness, a subsequent in-court identification is inadmissible only if there is "a very substantial likelihood of irreparable misidentification," and "with the deletion of 'irreparable', [that test] * * * serves equally well as a standard for the admissibility of testimony concerning the out-of-court identification itself." *Neil v. Biggers*, supra. The Court later refused to apply a per se rule to post-*Stovall* identifications, and instead adhered to the "totality of the circumstances" test. *Manson v. Brathwaite*, 432 U.S. 98 (1977). Under this test, the factors to be considered in evaluating the likelihood of misidentification "include the opportunity of the witness to view the criminal at the time of the crime, the witness' degree of attention, the accuracy of his prior description of the criminal, the level of certainty demonstrated at the confrontation, and the time between the crime and the confrontation." *Manson v. Brathwaite*, supra.

In the *Wade-Gilbert* context, these same factors bear on the question of whether an in-court identification is a "fruit of the poisonous tree," as to which the government has the burden of proof (see § 31A). But in the context of the *Stovall* rule, these factors bear directly upon the question of whether there has been a violation of due process, which apparently means that the burden is on the defend-

ant. Cf. *P. v. Nelson*, 238 N.E.2d 378 (Ill.1968),
concerning proof of the suggestive nature of the
lineup.

Lineups. An apt illustration of a due process
violation in a lineup identification is provided by
Foster v. Cal., 394 U.S. 440 (1969). The Court
concluded it was "all but inevitable" that the victim
of a robbery would identify defendant "whether or
not he was in fact" the robber, as: (1) defendant
was placed in a lineup with two other men who were
half a foot shorter; (2) only he wore a jacket similar
to that worn by the robber; (3) when this did not
lead to positive identification, the police permitted a
one-to-one confrontation; and (4) because the witness' identification was still tentative, some days
later another lineup was arranged, but defendant was the only person in this lineup who had also
appeared in the first lineup.

The use of pictures. In *Simmons v. U. S.*, 390
U.S. 377 (1968), FBI agents identified a bank robbery suspect on the basis of his use of a car which
was similar to that used in the robbery. From a
relative of the suspect they obtained six snapshots,
mostly group pictures, in which the suspect appeared,
from which five bank employees separately identified the suspect the day after the robbery. Balancing the need against the risks, the Court concluded
that this procedure was not "unnecessarily suggestive." The use of the photos was justified, in that a
serious felony had occurred, the perpetrators were

still at large, inconclusive clues led to the suspect, and it was important for the FBI swiftly to determine whether they were on the right track so that they could properly deploy their forces. Also, there was little risk of misidentification, as the employees had all gotten a good look at the robber, they examined the pictures while their memories were still fresh, each witness examined the pictures separately, and the FBI agents disclosed nothing about the progress of the investigation or suggesting which persons in the pictures were under suspicion.

One-man showups. In contrast to a properly conducted lineup, the display of a single suspect to a witness carries with it a considerable risk of misidentification: the witness may well conclude that the individual displayed must be the offender, for otherwise he would not be in custody and singly displayed. In *Stovall v. Denno*, supra, the Court noted that "the practice of showing suspects singly to persons for the purpose of identification, and not as part of a lineup, has been widely condemned," but held that under the unique circumstances of the case the one-man showup was justified. The defendant was arrested because keys found at the scene of the murder were traced to him. The wife of the murder victim, who herself had been repeatedly stabbed while defending her husband, was hospitalized for major surgery to save her life. Two days after the crime, defendant was brought to her hospital room, where she identified him after he spoke a few words. Defendant was handcuffed to

one of the five police officers who were present
with two members of the prosecutor's staff, and he
was the only black in the room. The Court concluded that "an immediate hospital confrontation
was imperative," as no one knew how long the
witness might live, she could not visit the jail, and
she was the only person who could have exonerated
the defendant.

While *Stovall* thus rests upon a rather unique
showing of need for the one-man showup—the fact
that the sole eye witness was near death—there may
be other reasons why this less reliable procedure is
sometimes "imperative." For example, if *Stovall*
is considered with *Simmons*, where the recognized
need was for the police "swiftly to determine whether they were on the right track," it might be said
that an on-the-scene one-man showup of a suspect
who has just been arrested or detained for investigation does not violate due process. This is the conclusion which has been reached by the lower courts,
who have also stressed the increased reliability of
identifications made promptly after the event. *Bates
v. U. S.*, 405 F.2d 1104 (D.C.Cir. 1968); *P. v. Moore*,
244 N.E.2d 337 (Ill.App.1968). Similarly, some courts
have upheld a one-man showup where it was the
suspect who was seriously injured. *Johnson v. P.*,
470 P.2d 37 (Colo.1970). But failure to use a lineup
is not excused merely because it would be inconven-
ient or difficult to assemble a group of persons physi-
cally comparable to the suspect. *Neil v. Biggers*,
supra.

CHAPTER 6

APPLICATION OF THE EX-CLUSIONARY RULE

33. INTRODUCTION

The exclusion of unconstitutionally obtained evidence constitutes the primary method of implementing the constitutional rights discussed in Chapters 2–5. While other remedies also are available (e. g., tort actions, criminal prosecutions and injunctions), the Court has viewed the exclusionary rule as the key means of deterring unconstitutional police practices. The application of the exclusionary rule may vary according to the nature of the right violated (and, in that respect, we might more appropriately refer to exclusionary "rules"), but the basic issues relating to the scope of the exclusionary remedy are largely the same whether a physical search, electronic eavesdropping, interrogation, or special identification procedure is involved. Those issues include: (1) whether the remedy extends to all derivative evidence; (2) whether it bars use of evidence for purposes other than direct proof of guilt; (3) whether it can be utilized by defendants who were not the immediate victims of the violation; (4) whether the burden of proof in establishing the admissibility (or inadmissibility) of the evidence should fall upon prosecutor (or defendant) and the extent of that burden; and (5) whether the erroneous admission of excludable evidence may constitute a harmless error. The resolution of these issues has rested largely upon constitutional rulings. Though a few jurisdictions have adopted a more expansive version of the exclusionary rule than is constitutionally required, the vast majority have not extended the rule beyond what they consider the constitutional minimum.

In determining the constitutionally required scope of the exclusionary rule, courts have looked to various factors in different settings, but a recurring theme has been the impact of the particular ruling upon the two functions of the exclusionary rule that were stressed in *Mapp v. Ohio* (p. 23)—the deterrence of constitutional violations by eliminating the prosecutorial benefits of such violations, and the "imperative of judicial integrity" that demands that the courts not be made "party to lawless invasions of constitutional rights of citizens by permitting unhindered governmental use of the fruits of such invasions." *Terry v. Ohio*, 392 U.S. 1 (1968). Moreover, as between the two, far greater emphasis has been placed upon the impact of the ruling upon the deterrence function. See e. g. the discussion in §§ 34–36. But note *Harrison v. U. S.*, 392 U.S. 219, n. 10 (1968).

34. DERIVATIVE EVIDENCE

Fruits of the poisonous tree. In *Silverthorne Lumber Co. v. U. S.*, 251 U.S. 385 (1920), the Court held invalid a subpoena that had been issued on the basis of information acquired through an illegal search. "The essence of a provision forbidding the acquisition of evidence in a certain way," the Court noted, "is not that merely evidence so acquired shall not be used before the court but that it shall not be used at all." Just as the prosecution could not use in court evidence obtained directly from the unconstitutional search, neither could it use evidence obtained indirectly via a subpoena based upon that search. The exclusionary rule extended to all evidence "tainted" by the unconstitutional search, which included evidence subsequently obtained through use of the information acquired during that search.

The *Silverthorne* requirement of exclusion of "secondary" or "derivative" evidence is commonly described as the rule against admission of the "fruits of the poisonous tree." Though the rule was formulated in applying the exclusionary rule to unconstitutional searches, it generally is viewed as equally applicable to evidence derived from other constitutional violations. The Supreme Court has held the "poisonous tree" rule applicable to the evidentiary fruits of unconstitutional arrests, *Wong Sun v. U. S.*, 371 U.S. 471 (1963), unconstitutional lineup identification procedures, *U. S. v. Wade* (see p. 266), and violations of certain non-constitutional restrictions enforced by the exclusionary rule. See *Harrison v. U. S.,* 392 U.S. 219 (1968) (*McNabb-Mallory* violations); *Nardone v. U. S.,* 308 U.S. 338 (1939) (wiretaps violating § 605 of the Communications Act). In *Brewer v. Williams* (p. 225), the Court did not specifically rule on the issue, but it apparently assumed that the poisonous tree rule also applies to evidence derived from a statement obtained in violation of defendant's Sixth Amendment right to counsel. 430 U.S. 387, n. 12. Lower courts also have applied the rule to various other constitutional violations discussed in Chapters 2–5. See, e. g., *P. v. Ditson,* 369 P.2d 714 (Cal.1962) (involuntary confession); *S. v. Preston,* 411 A.2d 402 (Me.1980) (*Miranda* violation). Some lower courts have expressed doubt, however, as to whether the Supreme Court would require exclusion of all secondary evidence obtained through a violation of the "prophylactic *Miranda* rule." *C. v. Meehan,* 387 N.E.2d 527 (Mass.1979). In *Mich. v. Tucker,* 417 U.S. 433 (1974), the Court refused to exclude evidence derived from a *Miranda* violation that occurred before the *Miranda* case itself was decided, and reserved decision as to the application of the poisonous tree rule to post-*Miranda* case violations. See also *C. v. White,* 371 N.E.2d 777 (Mass.1977), aff'd by an equally divided court, 439 U.S. 280 (1978) ("evidence obtained in violation of *Miranda* may not be considered in determining whether there is probable cause to obtain a search warrant").

The "independent source" exception. In applying the poisonous tree rule, *Silverthorne* stressed that "facts" obtained through a constitutional violation were not necessarily "inaccessible" for court use. The facts could still be proved, the Court noted, "if knowledge of [the facts] is [also] gained from an independent source." Subsequent Supreme Court cases have cited the second decision in *Bynum v. U. S.*, 274 F.2d 767 (D.C.Cir. 1960), as a classic illustration of the proper application of *Silverthorne's* "independent source exception." The first *Bynum* decision, 262 F.2d 465 (D.C.Cir. 1958), excluded fingerprints obtained from the defendant after he had been illegally arrested. Cf. *Davis v. Miss.* (p. 163). At the time of that arrest, the police had reason to suspect the defendant had been involved in the robbery under investigation, although they lacked probable cause. When Bynum was subsequently reprosecuted, the government sought to use an older set of prints obtained from F.B.I. files, which also matched prints found at the scene of the crime. Since the police had reason to check for Bynum's prints without regard to the illegal arrest, and the older set of prints had been taken in connection with an unrelated matter, those prints were admitted as independently acquired evidence, "in no way connected with the unlawful arrest." *Bynum v. U. S.*, supra.

The "inevitable discovery" exception. Many courts hold that the independent source exception is not limited to evidence that was in fact obtained from an independent source. The same underlying justification, they contend, also supports admission of evidence derived solely from a constitutional violation if such evidence would "inevitably" have been discovered from lawful investigatory activities without regard to the violation. These courts argue that such an "inevitable discovery" exception does not permit the government to gain any special benefits from a constitutional violation and therefore is consistent with the deterrent function of the exclusionary rule. *P. v. Fitzpatrick*, 300 N.E.2d 139 (N.Y.1973). The exception generally is held to be applicable if the government can show, by a preponderance of the evidence, that the disputed evidence would have been found (usually through routine investigatory procedures) without the constitutional violation. *S. v. Williams*, 285 N.W.2d 248 (Iowa, 1979). In light of this evidentiary standard, some courts have preferred to describe the exception as "the hypothetical independent source rule." Id.

The inevitable discovery exception has been criticized on several grounds. Some critics contend that it too often is loosely applied so as to encompass any evidence that "could" rather than "would" have been otherwise discovered. *P. v. Fitzpatrick*, supra, at 146 (dis.). Other critics argue that the exception undercuts the exclusionary rule by providing an incentive for unconstitutional action. "Such a rule,"

the critics argue, "relax[es] the protection of [consti-
tutional] * * * rights in the very case in which,
by the government's own admission, there is no
reason for [unlawful action]." In their view, the rule
thereby encourages the government to take unconstitutional short cuts to acquire evidence that could
otherwise be obtained through longer, lawful chan-
nels. *U. S. v. Paroutian*, 299 F.2d 486 (2d Cir. 1962).

Such criticism has led several courts to reject any
form of inevitable discovery exception. *S. v. Williams*, supra (collecting cases). Other courts have
responded to the criticism by limiting application of
the exception. In *Williams*, for example, the Court
imposed two conditions for the application of the
exception: (1) that the state establish that "the
police have not acted in bad faith to accelerate the
discovery of the evidence in question"; and (2) that
the state prove "that the evidence would have been
found without the unlawful activity and how that
discovery would have occurred." These requirements, it was argued, would preclude police use of
"end runs and shortcuts" and would prevent application of the exception "on the basis of hunch or
speculation."

While the Supreme Court has not directly considered the validity of the inevitable discovery exception, a key opinion in *U. S. v. Crews*, —— U.S. ——
(1980), suggests acceptance of at least a very limited
form of inevitable discovery. In *Crews*, the defendant sought to quash his in-court identification as the

[288]

fruit of an illegal arrest. A series of earlier cases, including *Frisbie v. Collins* (p. 100), had held that an illegal arrest does not bar the subsequent prosecution of the arrestee. As the Court noted in *Crews,* the defendant "is not himself a suppressible 'fruit' and the illegality of his detention cannot deprive the Government of the opportunity to prove his guilt through the introduction of evidence wholly untainted by police conduct." Five justices concluded that the *Frisbie* ruling applied to all aspects of the defendants' presence in the courtroom, including the showing of his face. Three justices, in an opinion by Justice Brennan, argued that there was no need to decide that issue because, even if the showing of defendant's face could be an inadmissible fruit of an illegal arrest, there was an independent basis for the identification in the present case. Justice Brennan stressed that, prior to defendant's arrest, the police had received a description of the robber from the victim and had independently suspected that defendant was involved. Thus, the illegal arrest "yielded nothing of evidentiary value that the police did not already have in their grasp." It merely had served "to link together two extant ingredients in the identification." Although Justice Brennan's opinion is not entirely clear on this point, it appears to have relied on the assumption that the police inevitably would have obtained the identification even if defendant had not been arrested and brought into court. (Interestingly, the government in *Crews* had relinquished this type of argument as to the defendant's earlier photographic and lineup identifications, which they conceded to be a fruit of the illegal arrest).

The "purged taint" exception. Even where the secondary evidence would not have been discovered except for the constitutional violation (i. e., there was no independent source or inevitability of discovery), that evidence need not necessarily be classified as the fruit of the poisonous tree. The Court's decisions clearly indicate that the poisonous tree doctrine does not extend as far as a "but for" causation test might take it. If the means of acquiring evidence are substantially removed and distinguishable from the initial illegality, neither the "deterrence" rationale nor the "judicial integrity" rationale requires application of the exclusionary rule. *Harrison v. U. S.*, supra. Accordingly, as the Court noted in *Wong Sun v. U. S.*, 371 U.S. 471 (1963) the controlling question is: "[W]hether, granting establishment of the primary illegality, the evidence to which instant objection is made has been come at by exploitation of that illegality or instead by means sufficiently distinguishable to be purged of the primary taint." *Wong Sun v. U. S.*, 371 U.S. 471 (1963).

The application of this "purged taint" limitation is illustrated by the Court's rulings in *Wong Sun*. Narcotics agents there entered a dwelling without probable cause and chased down and arrested A,

[290]

who almost immediately thereafter made a statement accusing B of having sold narcotics. Narcotics
were subsequently seized from B, who in turn,
implicated C, who was also arrested illegally. Several days later, after having been arraigned and
released on his own recognizance, C voluntarily
made an oral confession to a narcotics agent during
interrogation. A argued that his statement and the
narcotics later seized from B were fruits of the
illegal entry into his dwelling and his illegal arrest.
The Court agreed and both items were excluded. It
rejected, however, C's claim that his statement was
the fruit of his illegal arrest. Even though C might
never have confessed if he had never been arrested,
his voluntary action after having been released and
warned of his rights had made the "connection
between the arrest and the statement * * * so
attenuated as to [have] dissipate[d] the taint."

As *Wong Sun* indicates, the taint of initial illegality may be purged by an "intervening independent
act by the defendant or third party which breaks
the causal chain linking the illegality and the evidence in such a way that the evidence is not in fact
obtained by 'exploitation of that illegality'". *P. v.
Sesslin*, 439 P.2d 321 (Cal.1968). Application of this
"intervening independent act" concept has caused
difficulty in several factual settings. Two that have
attracted particular attention are the situations in
which an illegality leads to discovery of a prosecution witness or to obtaining an incriminatory statement from the defendant himself.

The tainted witness. Prior to *U. S. v. Ceccolini*, 435 U.S. 268 (1978), lower courts had taken a variety of positions in cases in which a constitutional violation had led to the discovery of a prosecution witness. Some argued that the witness' testimony was never an inadmissible fruit since the witness' decision to testify was always an intervening act that purged the taint. Others argued that the witness' decision should largely be ignored and the testimony treated no differently than physical evidence. *Ceccolini* rejected both of these positions. The potentially tainted witness in *Ceccolini* was a clerk in a flower shop. While visiting the shop, a patrolman conducted an illegal search by opening an envelope lying on the cash register. The officer found that the envelope contained policy slips, but he did not tell the clerk of his discovery. He simply asked her about the ownership of the envelope and she responded that it belonged to her employer. Several months later, an F.B.I. agent, informed of the patrolman's discovery, questioned the clerk about her employer's activities. She expressed a willingness to help and related the incident involving the patrolman and the envelope. When the witness later testified against her employer at trial, the defense argued that her testimony should be excluded as the direct product of the officer's search. The Supreme Court rejected this contention.

The *Ceccolini* opinion initially rejected the contention that the case before it should be treated no differently than one in which police discovered physical evidence. The function of the exclusionary rule, the Court noted, requires that special consideration be given to the element of "free will" that might be involved in the witness' decision to testify. The "greater the willingness of the witness to freely testify, the greater the likelihood that he or she will be discovered by legal means and, concomitantly, the smaller the incentive to conduct an illegal search to discover the witness." The exclusion of a tainted witness also involves different considerations because it can "perpetually disable a witness from testifying about relevant and material facts, regardless of how unrelated such testimony might be to the purpose of the originally illegal search."

While *Ceccolini* stressed that the exclusionary rule should be invoked "with much greater reluctance" as applied to "live testimony" than to an "inanimate object," it refused to accept the government's position that the testimony of a witness should always be admissible "no matter how close and proximate the connection between it and a violation of the Fourth Amendment." In determining whether the taint was purged, consideration must be given to the "time, place, and manner," of the initial questioning of the witness and its relationship to the illegality that led to the questions. In this case, several factors led to the conclusion that the taint of the illegal search had been dissipated: (1) "the testimony given by the witness was an act of her own free

will in no way coerced or even induced by official
authority"; (2) the illegally discovered slips were not
used by either officer in questioning the witness; (3)
substantial time passed between the search and the
F.B.I. officer's contact with the witness and between that contact and her eventual testimony; (4)
though the subject of that testimony could be traced
to the discovery of the slips, the flower shop
had previously been under F.B.I. surveillance; and
(5) there was "not the slightest evidence" that the
patrolman made the search "with the intent of
finding a willing and knowledgable witness to testify
against [the defendant]."

Confessions as the fruit of the poisonous tree.
Wong Sun (p. 290) excluded from evidence the
incriminating statement of one defendant (A) on the
ground that it was the fruit of that defendant's
illegal arrest. At the same time, the Court also
admitted the incriminating statement of another
defendant (C) as the product of an "independent act
of free will" that purged the taint of his unconstitutional arrest. The two statements considered in
Wong Sun have been viewed as involving "opposite
ends of the pole." However, *Brown v. Ill.,* 422 U.S.
590 (1975), offered some guidance to the lower
courts in dealing with the wide range of fact situations that fall between those extremes. As in *Ceccolini*, the Court in *Brown* emphasized the need to
weigh several factors in light of the deterrent function of the exclusionary rule.

[294]

In *Brown* police officers arrested defendant without probable cause in order to interrogate him in connection with a murder investigation. Following the arrest, defendant was taken to the police station, warned of his *Miranda* rights, and questioned. Defendant made an initial incriminating statement within two hours after his arrest. He was interrogated again several hours later (after the *Miranda* warnings were repeated) and made a second incriminating statement. The state supreme court upheld the admission of both statements on the ground that the *Miranda* warnings automatically purged the taint of defendant's illegal arrest. The Supreme Court unanimously rejected the state court's view of the impact of the *Miranda* warnings. A majority also found that, on the facts of the case, both statements were the fruit of the illegal arrest.

With respect to the *Miranda* warnings, the *Brown* opinion noted: "[T]he *Miranda* warnings, *alone* and *per se*, cannot always make the act [of confessing] sufficiently a product of free will to break, for Fourth Amendment purposes, the causal connection between the illegality and the confession. * * * The *Miranda* warnings are an important factor, to be sure, in determining whether the confession is obtained by exploitation of an illegal arrest. But they are not the only factor to be considered. The temporal proximity of the arrest and the confession, the presence of intervening circumstances, and, particularly, the purpose and flagrancy of the official misconduct are all relevant."

After examining the *Brown* fact situation in light of the factors noted above, the majority concluded that the prosecution had failed to meet its burden of establishing the dissipation of the initial taint. Defendant's first statement was made within two hours of his arrest and the later, second statement was the fruit of the first. No intervening acts of significance (such as presentment before a magistrate, consultation with counsel, or release from custody) had occurred between the arrest and the first statement. Moreover, the majority emphasized, the illegality had "a quality of purposefulness." The "impropriety of the arrest was obvious"; it had been undertaken as an "expedition for evidence" and had been executed in a manner which "gave the appearance of having been calculated to cause surprise, fright, and confession." See also *Dunaway v. N. Y.,* 442 U.S. 200 (1979) (reaffirming *Brown* and stressing that the crucial test is not whether the statement is voluntary for Fifth Amendment purposes, but whether "intervening events broke the connection between petitioner's illegal detention and his confession); *Rawlings v. Ky.,* —— U.S. —— (1980) (where defendant was illegally detained for a short period in the "congenial atmosphere" of a friend's house, *Miranda* warnings were given shortly before he made an incriminating statement, the statement appeared to be a spontaneous reaction to a search of another person, and the police conduct did not rise to the level of "conscious or flagrant misconduct" involved in *Brown,* the state had carried its burden of showing that the statement was not the fruit of the illegal detention).

The relationship between an illegal search and a confession often is much closer than that between an illegal arrest and a confession. For example, when a suspect is confronted with illegally seized evidence, the resulting confession is likely to be placed in the same category as the contemporaneous confession in *Wong Sun* (i. e., the confession of A), and the fine-tuned assessment that the Supreme Court mandated in *Brown* will not be necessary. See *P. v. Robbins,* 369 N.E.2d 577 (Ill.1977); *P. v. Hines,* 575 P.2d 414 (Colo.1978). A similar situation is presented when an unconstitutionally obtained confession is followed by a subsequent confession given at a second interrogation session. In such cases, the second confession usually is presumed to be the fruit of the first unless significant factors clearly show "a break in the causative chain." *P. v. Spencer,* 424 P.2d 715 (Cal.1967); *Harrison v. U. S.,* 392 U.S. 219 (1968). The Supreme Court has recognized that, "after an accused has once let the cat out of the bag by confessing, no matter what the inducement, he is never thereafter free of the psychological and practical disadvantages of having confessed." *U. S. v. Bayer,* 331 U.S. 532 (1947). At the same time, however, it also has noted that there is no per se rule that "perpetually disables the confessor from making a usable [confession] after those conditions [which produced the first inadmissible confession] have been removed." Id.

When will the "coercive influence" of the first confession be offset by other factors? In *U. S. v. Bayer,* supra, the first confession, obtained in violation of *McNabb-Mallory,* had been given 6 months earlier and the defendant, a soldier, had subsequently been released from the major restrictions of his prior confinement. Where, on the other hand, the confessions are separated only by several hours, the second confession is very likely to be found the fruit of the first, at least when factors such as consultation with counsel, arraignment before a magistrate, and release from custody are not present. *C. v. Meehan,* 387 N.E.2d 527 (Mass.1979). Even when those factors are present, their significance has varied with the particular circumstances of the case (e. g., the scope of the magistrate's statement as to defendant's rights) and the attitude of the court. Compare *Killough v. U. S.,* 315 F.2d 241 (D.C.Cir. 1962) with *Lyons v. Okla.,* 322 U.S. 596 (1944). Various decisions suggest that the second confession is more likely to be rendered admissible by intervening events where the initial confession was not involuntary, but was simply inadmissible because of a *Miranda* violation. See *S. v. Miranda,* 450 P.2d 364 (Ariz.1969); *U. S. v. Trabucco,* 424 F.2d 1311 (5th Cir. 1970). Of course, even though several factors might otherwise suggest that the second confession constituted an "act of free will" purging the taint, they may be offset by extensive reliance upon the earlier confession in the production of the second. *Gilpin v. U. S.,* 415 F.2d 638 (5th Cir. 1969).

Thus, in an analogous situation, *Harrison v. U. S.,*
supra, the defendant's testimony at his initial trial,
offered to explain a confession that had been admitted erroneously in violation of *McNabb-Mallory,* was
viewed as the fruit of that confession even though
defendant was represented by counsel at the trial
and was aware that he was not legally required to
testify.

Guilty pleas as the fruit of the poisonous tree.
In *Pa. ex rel. Herman v. Claudy,* 350 U.S. 116
(1956), the Court noted that a plea of guilty entered
by an uncounseled defendant was "involuntary" (and
therefore invalid, see p. 43) if the plea was "based
on a confession extorted [from defendant] by violence or mental coercion." This aspect of the law
governing guilty pleas is viewed as a special application of the poisonous tree rule since the characterization of the plea as involuntary rests largely on the
finding that it is the fruit of the coerced confession.
Dorsciak v. Gladden, 425 P.2d 177 (Ore.1967). Consistent with this analysis, the fact that the plea
might not have been entered "but for" the earlier
constitutional violation does not necessarily render it
invalid; the taint of the initial violation may have
been "purged" by intervening events. Thus, in
McMann v. Richardson, 397 U.S. 759 (1970), a
divided Court held that "a defendant [represented
by counsel at the time of the plea] who alleges that
he pleaded guilty because of a prior coerced confession" does not thereby establish the invalidity of the

plea. Though defendant pleaded guilty on counsel's mistaken belief that the confession would probably be admissible and produce a conviction, that factor alone does not render the plea involuntary. Assuming that counsel's advice was competent, the consultation with counsel and the subsequent determination to plead are viewed as independent intervening acts that "purged" the taint. As the Court later noted, in the absence of special circumstances, a "guilty plea represents a break in the chain of events which has preceded it in the criminal process." *Tollet v. Henderson,* 411 U.S. 258 (1973).

The *McMann* analysis does recognize certain exceptional circumstances which permit a successful challenge to a guilty plea based upon a prior constitutional error. Thus, the *McMann* Court noted that a plea would be open to challenge where the defendant acted without counsel and entered the plea based upon evidence obtained unconstitutionally. See *Pa. ex rel. Herman v. Claudy,* supra. Similarly, a plea may be challenged where the oppressive circumstances that produced a constitutional violation (e. g., a coerced confession) had an "abiding impact and also taint[ed] the plea." Cf. *Chambers v. Fla.,* 309 U.S. 227 (1940). A challenge will also be sustained where counsel's advice was outside the range of normal competence (see § 43). Finally, as discussed at p. 409, there are certain constitutional violations that may be raised through a collateral attack notwithstanding a voluntary guilty plea.

[300]

35. THE COLLATERAL USE EXCEPTIONS

Grand jury proceedings. In *U. S. v. Calandra,*
414 U.S. 338 (1974), a divided Court held that a
grand jury witness could not refuse to answer questions on the ground that the questions were based on
evidence obtained from an unlawful search. The
majority concluded that the "speculative and undoubtedly minimal advance in the deterrence of police
misconduct" that might result from allowing such an
objection was outweighed by the likely deleterious
impact upon the effective and expeditious discharge
of the grand jury's duties. "Permitting witnesses to
invoke the exclusionary rule before the grand jury,"
the majority noted, "would halt the orderly progress
of an investigation and might necessitate extended
litigation of issues only tangentially related to the
grand jury's primary objective." On the other
side, application of the exclusionary rule in grand
jury proceedings could only strengthen the rule's
deterrent impact in the rather unique situation
where an investigation was "consciously directed"
toward obtaining a grand jury indictment notwithstanding "the inadmissibility of the illegally seized
evidence in a subsequent criminal prosecution of the
search victim."

Impeachment at trial. In *Walder v. U. S.,* 347
U.S. 62 (1954), the defendant, charged with purchas-
ing and possessing heroin, asserted on direct examination that he had never purchased, sold or handled

narcotics at any time "in [his] life." On cross-examination, the government questioned defendant about a heroin capsule that had been seized in his presence approximately two years earlier, and when defendant denied the prior possession, introduced police testimony concerning the seizure. Defense objected on the ground that the capsule had been illegally seized and the defendant had secured its suppression in a earlier prosecution. The trial court, however, admitted the evidence, and "carefully charged the jury" that it was to be considered "solely for the purpose of impeaching the defendant's credibility." A divided Supreme Court affirmed on the basis of that limitation. The Court noted that "it is one thing to say that the Government cannot make any affirmative use of evidence unlawfully obtained, [but] * * * quite another to say that the defendant can turn the illegal method by which evidence in the Government's possession was obtained to his own advantage, and provide him with a shield against contradiction of his untruths." The majority reasoned that the defendant "must be free to deny all the elements of the case against him without thereby giving lease to the Government to introduce by way of rebuttal evidence illegally secured to it * * *. Beyond that, however, there is hardly justification for letting the defendant affirmatively resort to perjurious testimony in reliance on the Government's disability to challenge his credibility." Such an "extension of the [exclusionary] rule," it concluded, "would be a perversion of the Fourth Amendment."

In *Harris v. N. Y.*, 401 U.S. 222 (1971), a divided Court relied upon *Walder* to uphold the use of defendant's prior statement, obtained in violation of *Miranda*, to impeach his trial testimony. Unlike *Walder*, the illegally obtained evidence in *Harris* had been acquired in the investigation of the offenses currently charged against defendant. Also, defendant was impeached "as to testimony bearing more directly on the crimes charged" than the "collateral" matter included in Walder's testimony. The majority concluded, however, that neither distinction suggested any "difference in principle that warrants a result different from * * * *Walder*." The majority also rejected the contention that *Walder* should not apply to *Miranda* violations because of *Miranda's* Fifth Amendment foundation. Viewing *Miranda* as serving a deterrent function similar to *Mapp*, it concluded that that function was adequately served by excluding evidence from the prosecution's case in chief and did not require providing "a license to use perjury." See also *Ore. v. Hass*, 420 U.S. 714 (1975) (impeachment use permitted where officer obtained statement, in violation of *Miranda*, by continuing interrogation after defendant asked for a lawyer; "speculative possibility" that this interrogation technique would be employed purposely to gain impeachment evidence was not sufficient to change the "balance * * * struck in *Harris*").

The *Harris* opinion suggested that the ruling there might not apply to involuntary confessions. The Court mentioned that the case did not involve a "coerced confession," and it also noted that, "of course," the "trustworthiness" of any statement used for impeachment must satisfy "legal standards." In *Mincey v. Ariz.,* 437 U.S. 385 (1978), the *Harris* suggestion was converted into a direct ruling that involuntary statements could not be used for impeachment purposes. This ruling was later explained as resting on more than the potential untrustworthiness of involuntary confessions. A coerced confession, it was noted, involves the application of the privilege "in its most pristine form," while *Miranda* violations involve a rule designed "to deter unlawful police conduct." Because of *Miranda's* prophylactic function, some balancing was permissible in *Harris,* but not in *Mincey.* See *N. J. v. Portash,* 440 U.S. 450 (1979) (holding that grand jury testimony given pursuant to a grant of immunity was coerced testimony, similar to an involuntary confession, and therefore could not be used for impeachment even though it was at least as reliable as the statements used for that purpose in *Harris*).

In *U. S. v. Havens,* —— U.S. —— (1980), the Supreme Court partially accepted and partially rejected another possible limitation upon the *Harris* ruling. The defendant in *Havens,* on direct examination, denied that he had been "engage[d]" in the smuggling activities of his traveling companion. On cross-examination, defendant was asked whether he had anything to do with his companion's makeshift underwear pockets in which the smuggled cocaine was carried. When defendant gave a negative response, the prosecutor sought to impeach that denial by reference to an illegal search of defendant's suitcase in which the material for the pockets had been found. Defendant argued that the illegally seized material should not be available for impeachment because that evidence did not "squarely contradict" his direct testimony, as opposed to his cross-examination testimony. A divided Supreme Court rejected that argument. It refused to adopt a "flat rule" that would restrict *Harris* to the impeachment of direct testimony, but it also noted that the extension of *Harris* to impeachment of cross-examination testimony was not without limits. In particular, in distinguishing a pre-*Walder* ruling, *Agnello v. U. S.,* 269 U.S. 20 (1925), the Court suggested a limit based upon the relationship of the prosecutor's cross-examination to the defendant's direct testimony. The *Havens* majority noted that *Agnello* had been a case in which "the government had 'smuggled in' the impeaching opportunity in the course of cross-examination." While defendant's direct testimony in *Agnello* presumably had not been inconsistent with his prior possession of narcotics, the prosecutor there had asked about prior possession on cross-examination, and after eliciting the expected denial, sought to produce narcotics previously seized illegally from defendant's apartment. In that situation, impeachment by reference to the illegally seized evidence had been inappropriate since the defendant "had done nothing to justify cross-examination in respect of the [illegally seized] evidence." In *Havens,* on the other hand, the questions asked on cross-examination "would have been suggested to a reasonably competent cross-examiner by Havens' direct examination." Under that circumstance, prohibiting impeachment by reference to reliable but illegally obtained evidence would be contrary to the emphasis in *Harris* and *Walder* on the "defendant's obligation to speak the truth in response to proper questions."

In *Doyle v. Ohio,* 426 U.S. 610 (1976) and *Jenkins v. Anderson,* —— U.S. —— (1980), the Court moved from impeachment by reference to illegally seized evidence to impeachment by reference to defendant's prior silence. In *Doyle,* the Court rejected the contention that *Harris* should be extended to allow general impeachment by reference to the fact that defendant, in contrast to his exculpatory testimony at trial, had refused to give any statement to the police after receiving his *Miranda* warnings. The Court stressed that "silence in the wake of warnings may be nothing more than the arrestee's exercise of *Miranda* rights." Moreover, it noted, the implicit message of the warnings is that the defendant's exercise of his right of silence will "carry no penalty"; it therefore would be "fundamentally unfair," after giving the warnings, to then use the silence to "impeach an explanation subsequently offered at trial."

Distinguishing *Doyle, Jenkins v. Anderson* held that the constitution did not bar impeachment by reference to the defendant's prearrest silence. When the defendant in *Jenkins* testified at trial that he had killed in self-defense, the prosecutor forced him to acknowledge on cross-examination that he had not reported the killing to the police until two weeks later. Here, unlike *Doyle,* the defendant's silence had not been "induced by governmental action" since "the failure to speak occurred before he had been taken into custody and given *Miranda* warnings." Two concurring justices argued that the defendant's prearrest silence should not even be viewed as the exercise of a Fifth Amendment right as the defendant had been under "no official compulsion whatever, either to speak or remain silent." The majority concluded, however, that it was unnecessary to reach that issue. Past precedent, most noteably *Raffel v. U. S.,* 271 U.S. 494 (1926), established that, where there would be no fundamental unfairness as in *Doyle,* the possibility of an impeachment reference to prior silence would not impose an "impermissible burden" upon a person's right to remain silent, even where (as in *Raffel*) the silence reflected a clear exercise of his Fifth Amendment privilege in a previous judicial proceeding.

Sentencing. The Supreme Court has not yet ruled upon the application of the exclusionary rule to the sentencing process. But cf. *Gilbert v. Cal.,* 388 U.S. 263, 272 (1967) (unconstitutional lineup identification testimony excluded from penalty hearing before jury). Lower courts generally hold that illegally seized evidence is admissible, but recognize certain exceptions to that rule. Thus, *U. S. v. Schipani,* 315 F.Supp. 253 (S.D.N.Y.1970), upholding a sentencing court's consideration of information derived from illegal wiretaps, stressed that "no appreciable increment in deterrence would result from applying a second exclusion at sentencing after the rule has been applied at the trial itself." The Court noted, however, that it was not considering a situation in which the illegal search "was undertaken not to obtain evidence to support an indictment and conviction, but to * * * enhance the possibility of a heavier sentence after the basic investigation has been completed." See *Verdugo v. U. S.,* 402 F.2d 599 (4th Cir. 1968). The court also distinguished cases prohibiting consideration of involuntary confessions in sentencing [e. g., *U. S. ex rel. Brown v. Rundle,* 417 F.2d 282 (3d Cir. 1969)]. The "genesis" of the involuntary confession prohibition was as a means of excluding unreliable evidence (see § 25). Also, the involuntary confession related to a direct violation of the self-incrimination prohibition rather than a failure to comply with prophylactic rules designed to implement that prohibition.

A general extension of the exclusionary rule to sentencing has also been questioned on the basis of "practical considerations." *U. S. v. Schipani,* supra. Serious enforcement of the rule would be difficult under current sentencing practices, which do not require that the judge state his reasons for imposing a particular sentence and often deny defendant a right to examine the presentence report. Moreover, it is argued, even if these practices were changed, it would be "almost impossible for a district judge, who had screened proffered evidence on the motion to suppress, to banish it entirely from his mind at sentencing." Id. Proponents of applying the exclusionary rule argue that these objections are not insurmountable and similar problems of enforcement have not prevented the courts from establishing other limitations upon factors that can be considered in sentencing. See *U. S. v. Weston,* 448 F.2d 626 (9th Cir. 1972) (where trial judge relied upon "evidence obtained in violation of constitutional rights [including illegally seized evidence], * * * the case will be remanded for resentencing without considering the evidence so obtained").

Related civil or quasi-criminal proceedings. In *One 1958 Plymouth Sedan v. Pa.,* 380 U.S. 693 (1965), the exclusionary rule was held applicable to a proceeding for the forfeiture of an automobile on the ground that it had been used in the illegal transportation of alcohol. The Court emphasized that the proceeding was "quasi-criminal in character" because its object was to "penalize for the commission of an offense against the law." In *U. S. v. Janis,* 428

U.S. 433 (1976), the Court refused to extend *Plymouth Sedan* to a civil tax proceeding. In that case, local police seized wagering records and cash in an unconstitutional search, and then notified federal authorities, who imposed an assessment against *Janis* for wagering excise taxes and levied upon the seized cash. The Court refused to quash the assessment simply because it was based upon illegally seized evidence. The majority opinion suggested that it would take strong evidence of a substantial additional deterrent effect before it would consider extending the exclusionary rule to what was simply a civil suit for liability that existed without regard to the criminality of defendant's wagering activities. Here, such evidence was lacking: "Working, as we must, with the absence of convincing empirical data, common sense dictates that the deterrent effect of the exclusion of relevant evidence is highly attenuated when the 'punishment' imposed upon the offending criminal enforcement officer is the removal of that evidence from a civil suit by or against a different sovereign."

36. STANDING

A. THE PERSONAL INTEREST REQUIREMENT

Source of the limitation. In order to employ the exclusionary rule, a defendant must have "standing" to challenge the constitutional violation which serves as the basis for the rule's application. This requirement of an appropriate interest or "standing" to invoke a constitutional remedy is not unique to the exclusionary rule, but is applicable generally to all constitutional challenges. As a constitutional minimum, standing requires that the party seeking relief have an adversary interest in the "outcome of the controversy." *Flast v. Cohen,* 392 U.S. 83 (1968). That standard presumably is met in the criminal case by the very position of the defendant as the person against whom the challenged evidence will be used. But in most areas of constitutional law, the Court has also required that the adverse interest be based upon a violation of the rights of the individual raising the claim rather than the violation of the rights of a third party which indirectly affects the claimant. *Tileston v. Ullman,* 318 U.S. 44 (1943). As applied to the exclusionary remedy, this principle limits standing to the defendant who is also the victim of the constitutional violation that necessitates the exclusion of evidence. Thus, in *Wong Sun* (p. 290), where the illegal arrest of A led to the seizure of narcotics in the home of B and the subsequent arrest of C at another location, the narcotics could not be introduced in evidence against A, but could be introduced against C. A had standing because the seizure of the narcotics was the fruit of his illegal arrest, but C lacked standing because neither the arrest of A nor the subsequent seizure of narcotics violated his constitutional rights.

[311]

Application in state and federal courts. The prohibition against permitting a litigant to assert the rights of third parties "has not been imposed uniformly as a firm constitutional mandate," *Flast v. Cohen,* supra, and several authorities have argued that an exception should be made in the application of the exclusionary rule in order to preserve the deterrent function of that rule. This view was accepted in *P. v. Martin,* 290 P.2d 855 (Cal.1955), holding that a defendant could require exclusion of evidence obtained through an illegal search that violated the constitutional rights of a third party. The court reasoned that the traditional bar against "third-party" or "vicarious" standing "virtually invites law enforcement officers to violate the rights of third parties and to trade the escape of a criminal whose rights are violated for the conviction of others by the use of the evidence illegally obtained against them." It therefore concluded that the defendant's right "to object to the use of evidence must rest, not on a violation of his own constitutional rights, but on the ground that the government must not be allowed to profit by its own wrong and thus encouraged in the lawless enforcement of the law." [The California court subsequently refused, however, to extend the *Martin* analysis to permit a defendant to exclude evidence derived from statements of third parties that were obtained in violation of *Miranda. P. v. Varnum,* 427 P.2d 772 (Cal.1967)].

In *Alderman v. U. S.,* 394 U.S. 165 (1969), the Supreme Court rejected the *Martin* analysis in the context of a claim for "third-party" standing to challenge unconstitutional electronic surveillance. The majority there denied the alternative contentions that (1) all defendants should derive standing to challenge evidence obtained from the violation of the constitutional rights of others; (2) at least co-defendants and co-conspirators should have such standing to suppress evidence obtained in violation of the rights of other co-defendants or co-conspirators, or (3) a special standing rule should be recognized to permit a defendant to exclude evidence obtained unlawfully from another through a search "directed at" the prosecution of the defendant. Two dissenters supported the latter position, but the majority concluded that there was "no necessity" to depart from "the general rule that Fourth Amendment rights are personal rights which   *   *   *   may not be vicariously asserted." It did not follow from the adoption of the exclusionary rule "that anything which deters illegal searches [must] thereby [be] commanded by the Fourth Amendment." The majority was "not convinced that the additional benefits of extending the exclusionary rule to other defendants [i. e., non-victims] would justify further encroachment upon the public interest in prosecuting those accused of crime and having them acquitted or convicted on the basis of all the evidence which exposes the truth." In reaching this conclusion, the *Alderman* majority relied in part on the protection against illegal electronic eavesdropping provided in Title III (see § 20). However, in *Rakas v. Ill.,* 439

U.S. 128 (1978), the Court made it clear that the *Alderman* analysis rejected third party standing as a constitutional requirement for all Fourth Amendment cases.

In rejecting third party standing, *Alderman* and *Rakas* did not foreclose its adoption by state courts under state law. The Court emphasized that third party standing was neither required not prohibited by the constitution. On the other hand, the standing of a victim of a constitutional violation is constitutionally mandated. A state may not use a narrow definition of standing to deny the benefits of the exclusionary rule to a defendant who is constitutionally entitled to that remedy by virtue of a violation of his personal rights. With respect to many constitutional rights, the nature of the constitutional right clearly identifies the person who may be the victim of an alleged violation. In the case of an allegedly coerced confession, for example, the potential victim is the defendant from whom the confession was obtained and there is no question as to his standing to raise that objection. In the search and seizure area, on the other hand, the issue is more complex. There are several factors that must be considered in determining whether a defendant was the "victim" of an unconstitutional search.

B.   SEARCH AND SEIZURE OBJECTIONS

Identifying the issue. The Supreme Court usually has described the issue as to whether defendant was the "victim" of an unconstitutional search as an issue of "standing." However, in *Rakas,* supra, the Court suggested that it served no "useful analytical purpose" to consider the issue as a matter "apart from the merits of the defendant's Fourth Amendment claim." The appropriate question, the Court noted, is whether the "disputed search infringed an interest of the defendant which the Fourth Amendment was designed to protect." This was more direct, it reasoned, than asking whether the defendant's alleged standing is based on his own rights or those of a third party. The Court noted, however, that looking directly at the merits would not alter the results in past cases or make the issue any easier to resolve, and many cases continue to discuss the issue as one of standing. See *Ark. v. Sanders* (p. 155) at n. 8.

Whether the issue is described as one of standing or defining the scope of Fourth Amendment rights, particular attention must be given to the precise police conduct being called into question. It must be recalled that the poisoned fruit doctrine can readily give the defendant the right to challenge evidence obtained during a search at the premises of another, even though the defendant has no expectation of privacy in those premises and clearly is not a victim of that search. In *Wong Sun* (p. 290), for example, defendant A was allowed to object to the prosecution's use of narcotics found in B's house because the search of B's house was the fruit of the illegal entry into A's home and A's illegal arrest. In the cases

discussed below, the challenges generally were
directed at the searches that directly produced the
seized evidence, and the basic issue presented was
whether, under the standards discussed in § 11, the
defendant had a protected expectation of privacy in
the premises searched.

Legitimate presence at the site of the search. In
Jones v. U. S., 362 U.S. 257 (1960), an occasional
occupant of an apartment was held to have standing
to object to a search of that apartment conducted
while he was present. *Jones* rejected the view that a
party whose privacy was interrupted by an unlawful
search only had standing if he had some special
property right in the premises. The Court noted that
property distinctions such as those between "lessee,
licensee, invitee, and guest, often only of gossamer
strength, ought not to be determinative in fashioning
procedures ultimately referable to constitutional
safeguards." It concluded that "anyone legitimately
on the premises where a search occurs may challenge
its legality * * * when its fruits are proposed to
be used against him."

In *Rakas* (p. 313), the majority reexamined and,
perhaps, recast the *Jones* ruling. The Court reaffirmed that the "arcane distinctions" of property
law were not controlling. It did not follow, however,
that any person legitimately on the premises necessarily had an expectation of privacy in the searched
portion of the premises. Jones, the Court noted,
occasionally stayed at the apartment searched in that

case and had been given a key to the apartment by
the owner. At the time of the search, he was the
only occupant of the apartment. Under these
circumstances, he had a legitimate expectation of
privacy in the apartment, but this did not mean that
all persons legitimately on the premises would have
such an expectation. The Court offered two
illustrations of cases in which legitimate presence
would not be sufficient. A "casual visitor who had
never seen, or been permitted to visit the basement
of another's house" could not object to a search of the
basement simply because he happened to be in the
kitchen of the house at the time of the search.
Likewise, "a casual visitor who walks into a house
one minute before the search commences and leaves
one minute after the search ends" would not have a
reasonable expectation of privacy in the search of the
house. (It should be noted, however, that the Court
left open the possibility that the casual visitors might
have standing to contest the seizure of evidence as
the fruit of any violation of their own rights that
occurred during the course of the search. Cf. *Wong
Sun,* supra).

Once the *Rakas* majority had rejected legitimate
presence as an "automatic measure" of standing, it
had little difficulty with the case before it. The
defendants in *Rakas* were two passengers in a car
that had been stopped in connection with the
investigation of a robbery. After they were ordered
out of the car, the police searched the car and found a

sawed-off rifle under the front passenger seat and a
box of rifle shells in the glove compartment. The
Court found that the defendants had no protected
Fourth Amendment interests in the areas searched.
The glove compartment and the area under the seat,
"like the trunk of the automobile, are areas in which a
passenger qua passenger simply would not have a
legitimate expectation of privacy." The *Rakas*
majority stressed, however, that it was dealing with
defendants whose only claim of privacy rested on
their status as passengers in the automobile. It noted
that the petitioners "asserted neither a property nor
a possessory interest in the automobile, nor an
interest in the property seized." (See p. 321). A
concurring opinion further noted that neither had the
defendants challenged the "constitutionality of the
police action in stopping the automobile" or in
ordering the defendants out of the automobile. Cf.
Wong Sun, supra.

Presence as a trespasser. The *Jones* ruling was
specifically limited to persons "legitimately" on the
premises. The Court noted that its rejection of
property distinctions "would of course not avail
those who, by virtue of their wrongful presence,
cannot invoke the privacy of the premises search."
Thus, standing clearly would be denied "a trespasser or a burglar who entered another's home
and is there when the home is searched." *Cotton v.
U. S.,* 371 F.2d 385 (9th Cir. 1967). The lower
courts are divided, however, over the standing of a

driver to challenge the search of a stolen vehicle. Most courts have ruled that the driver may challenge the search where it was the fruit of his unlawful arrest, but, if the arrest was lawful, he lacks standing to challenge the search on other grounds (e. g., the lack of a warrant). *Harper v. S.,* 440 P.2d 893 (Nev.1968); *Palmer v. S.,* 286 A.2d 572 (Md. App.1972). Other courts have argued that the driver should not be placed in the same category as the temporary trespasser or burglar. They note that "even a trespasser, if he has also taken actual possession of the premises, acquires possessory rights against all the world except the true owner," and contend that such limited interest should be sufficient to establish standing. *Cotton v. U. S.,* supra. The *Rakas* majority indicated that it was not favorably impressed by this argument. The majority opinion noted that, notwithstanding *Jones'* "clear statement" on "wrongful presence," some lower courts "inexplicably have held that a person present in a stolen automobile at the time of the search may object to the lawfulness of the search of the automobile [citing *Cotton,* supra]."

Possessory interest in the premises. A defendant with a present possessory interest in the premises searched, such as the owner or lessee of a house, is generally recognized as automatically having a legitimate expectation of privacy in those premises. That interest gives him standing to challenge the search even though he was not present when the search was made. *Chapman v. U. S.*, 365 U.S. 610 (1965). The "possessory" interest which provides standing under this analysis ordinarily encompasses any interest which grants the defendant a general right to occupy the premises. That right need not be exclusive. Occupants of hotel rooms have been held to have a sufficient interest, *Stoner v. Cal.*, 376 U.S. 483 (1964), and a few decisions suggest that a business associate or friend who has a key to the suite of another and regularly uses that suite may also have a sufficient "possessory" interest to establish standing. *Baker v. U. S.*, 401 F.2d 958 (D.C.Cir. 1968). Cf. *Mancusi v. DeForte*, infra. The defendant's interest must relate, however, to current use. Thus, a tenant who has abandoned the premises may not challenge a subsequent search. *Parman v. U. S.*, 399 F.2d 559 (D.C.Cir. 1968).

Mancusi v. DeForte, 392 U.S. 364 (1968), although involving a defendant who also was present at the time of the search, reflects the Court's general approach in determining whether an interest in the premises searched is a sufficient basis in itself to justify standing. The Court there held that an employee had standing to object to a search of an office which he shared with several other people. The Court reasoned that defendant clearly would have had standing if the office had been his alone, and the joint use of the office had not so diminished his expectation of privacy as to eliminate standing. Defendant's "capacity to claim the protection of the

[Fourth] Amendment," it noted, "depends not upon a property right in the invaded place but upon whether the area was one in which there was a reasonable expectation of freedom from government intrusion."

Prior to *Rakas,* a non-owner driver of an automobile generally was viewed as having a protected expectation of privacy in the automobile, provided he had permission to use the car. *S. v. Boster,* 539 P.2d 294 (Kan.1975). While the *Rakas* dissent questioned whether the majority's position there might not also extend to a driver, the majority did note that the defendants-passengers there had not claimed a "possessory interest" in the car. Having been given possession of the car, including the keys, the driver certainly would appear to have a greater expectation of privacy than a passenger, particularly as to such areas as the glove compartment or trunk.

Property interest in the item seized. Various lower court opinions and a few Supreme Court opinions have suggested that, even though a defendant lacks a possessory interest in the premises searched, he still may challenge a search if he has a property interest in the item seized. In support of this conclusion, the courts usually have referred to the language of the Fourth Amendment, noting that it protects an individual's "effects" as well as his home against unreasonable searches and seizures. However, most personal effects, not being containers, are simply seized without themselves being

[321]

searched, and the seizure is usually lawful standing
by itself. Consider, for example, a case in which the
counterfeit plates of A are located in the house of B.
As the owner of the plates, A might be able to
challenge their seizure without probable cause, but
probable cause to seize the plates will exist as soon as
the officer sees them. The constitutional violation
usually exists in the search of the house of B without
probable cause or a warrant. The question largely
left unanswered by the courts is why the presence of
A's personal effects in B's house gives A standing to
challenge the search of B's house. The answer
offered by some commentators is that A, in receiving
permission to store his effects in B's home, has a
legitimate expectation of privacy in their undisturbed
presence on that property. Recent Supreme Court
decisions appear to support this explanation, although
it has not been fully explored.

Prior to the recent decisions, the leading Supreme
Court case on standing obtained through a property
interest in the item seized was *U. S. v. Jeffers,* 342
U.S. 48 (1951). *Jeffers* permitted the defendant to
challenge the search of his aunts' hotel room, where
police found 19 bottles of cocaine that he had stored
in a closet. The Court emphasized that the search
and seizure were directed at obtaining defendant's
"property." The *Jeffers* opinion also noted, however, that the "[aunts] had given [defendant] a key to
their room, that he had their permission to use the
room as well, and that he often entered the room for

[322]

various purposes." This aspect of *Jeffers* suggested that the defendant's access to his aunts' room may have been as important as his ownership of the seized item in establishing standing. Lower courts, however, tended to focus primarily upon Jeffers' interest in the item seized. (This focus may be explained in part by a portion of the *Jeffers* opinion that concentrated upon Jeffers' "ownership" interest in the course of rejecting the government's contention that he could not object to the seizure since Congress had abolished all property rights in contraband drugs). Subsequently, in *Rakas v. Ill.,* supra the Court noted that *Jeffers* was a case in which defendant's standing was "based on Jeffers' possessory interest in both the premises searched and the property seized."

The *Rakas* description of *Jeffers* was reiterated and given special emphasis in *U. S. v. Salvucci,* —— U.S. —— (1980). *Salvucci* overturned the previously accepted doctrine of "automatic standing" for cases involving possessory offenses (see p. 327). In reaching that result, the Court rejected the contention that the prosecution was engaged in self-contradiction when it alleged, on the one hand, that the defendant violated a statute prohibiting possession of contraband and, on the other, that he lacked standing to challenge the search of the home of another in which the contraband was seized. The Court noted that the challenge before it was not to the legality of the seizure in itself, but to the legality of the preceding search of the premises. It could not be assumed that "a person in legal possession of the goods seized during an illegal search has * * * necessarily been subject to a Fourth Amendment deprivation" since such possession "does not invariably represent the protected Fourth Amendment interest" violated by the illegal search. While possession is a factor to be considered, the Court noted, it could not be made into a "substitute" or "proxy" for a factual finding that the defendant had a "legitimate expectation of privacy in the area searched."

Rawlings v. Ky., —— U.S. —— (1980), furnishes an illustration of this point made in *Salvucci* that possession of the seized goods and an expectation of privacy in the area searched do not invariably coincide. Defendant in *Rawlings* was charged with possession of drugs that he had placed in the purse of an acquaintance [Cox]. Assuming that the search of Cox's purpose was illegal, the Court held that the defendant could not challenge the legality of that search. The record below amply supported the lower court's conclusion that Rawlings "had no legitimate expectation of privacy in Cox's purse at the time of the search." When Rawlings "dumped thousands of dollars worth of illegal drugs into Cox's purse," shortly before the police arrived on the scene, he had "known her only a few days" and "had never received access to her purse prior to that sudden bailment." He had no right to exclude others from her purse, and a longtime companion had, in fact, had free access to the purse. While there was some question as to whether Cox had consented to the "bailment," even if she had, "the precipitous nature of the transaction hardly support[ed] a reasonable inference that petitioner took normal precautions to maintain his privacy." Finally, the Court noted, petitioner had "frank[ly] admitt[ed] * * * that he had no subjective expectation that Cox's purse would remain free from government intrusion." Cf. *U. S. v. Lisk,* 552 F.2d 228 (7th Cir. 1975) (opinion by Stevens, J.) (where defendant placed an explosive device in the trunk of a friend's car, telling the friend to hold the device until he asked for it, defendant had no Fourth Amendment interest in the trunk, and since the device was seized in plain view after the trunk was opened, he could not object to the seizure).

Establishing standing. In *Simmons v. U. S.,* 390 U.S. 377 (1968), the defendant, seeking to establish standing to challenge the search of a suitcase, testified that he was the owner of the suitcase. His motion to suppress was subsequently denied, and the government used his testimony at trial in establishing guilt. In finding the use of the testimony unconstitutional, the Supreme Court noted that, at least in marginal cases where the defendant is uncertain as to the probable outcome of his motion, the potential use of such testimony at trial obviously would have a deterrent impact upon the assertion of Fourth Amendment rights. Moreover, the placement of this condition upon the assertion of those rights raised self-incrimination difficulties since "the defendant who wishes to establish standing must do so at the risk that the words which he utters may later be used to incriminate him." The Court acknowledged that, as an "abstract matter," such incrimination might be viewed as entirely "voluntary"—compulsion existed only in the sense that the defendant would forgo a "benefit" if he refrained from testifying. However, where that lost "benefit" was a remedy afforded by another provision of the Bill of Rights, the defendant was, in effect, subjected to a "Hobson's choice". Accordingly, the Court held, "when a defendant testifies in support of a motion to suppress evidence on Fourth Amendment grounds, his testimony may not thereafter be admitted against him at trial on the issue of guilt unless he makes no objection."

Although the *Simmons* ruling concerned Fourth Amendment claims, a similar restriction has been applied to defendant's testimony on motions to suppress based upon other constitutional grounds. As many lower courts have noted, the dilemma that *Simmons* sought to avoid is equally present whether defendant is objecting on the basis of an illegal search, confession, or lineup identification. *P. v. Walker,* 132 N.W.2d 87 (Mich.1965). It is not clear, however, whether *Simmons,* in eliminating that dilemma, goes so far as to prohibit use of the defendant's suppression testimony for impeachment at trial. The *Simmons* opinion referred only to use of defendant's testimony "on the issue of guilt." Relying on that language and on *Harris* (p. 303) and *Walder* (p. 301), *P. v. Sturgis,* 317 N.E.2d 545 (Ill.1974), permitted impeachment use. However, since the *Simmons* decision viewed the suppression testimony as basically a "compelled" statement, the post-*Sturgis* rulings in *Mincey v. Ariz.* and *N. J. v. Portash* (p. 304) would appear to provide a basis for distinguishing *Harris* and *Walder.* On the other hand, in *U. S. v. Kahan,* 415 U.S. 239 (1974), the Court did comment that "the protective shield of *Simmons* is not to be converted into a license for false representation." *Kahan* did not involve suppression testimony, but rather a false statement made by defendant in seeking to obtain court appointed counsel. (Noting that the defendant was not in any way compelled to make the false statement, *Kahan* held defendant's falsehood could be used to establish his knowledge of the incriminating nature of the assets that he had failed to disclose.) The *Kahan* comment was subsequently repeated, however, in the discussion in *U. S. v. Salvucci* (p. 328), of the treatment of suppression testimony under *Simmons.*

Automatic standing. Prior to *Simmons,* in *Jones v. U. S.,* 362 U.S. 257 (1960), the Court held that a defendant charged with a crime requiring proof of his possession of seized property automatically had standing to challenge the search that led to the seizure of that property. In reaching this conclusion, the Court stressed two factors. First, without automatic standing, the defendant would be forced, in establishing standing, to "allege facts the proof of which would tend * * * to convict him", and lower courts had held that those allegations might then be used against him at trial. Second, automatic standing followed from the prosecution's allegation of possession since it would be a "contradictory position" to allege that defendant had possession yet lacked standing. In *U. S. v. Salvucci,* —— U.S. —— (1980), the Court discarded the *Jones* automatic standing rule in light of subsequent developments. *Simmons,* the Court noted, eliminated the defense dilemma that *Jones* had sought to avoid. Under *Simmons* the defendant's allegation of possession for the purpose of establishing standing could no longer be used against him in proving the offense charged. As to *Jones'* second point, in light of the *Rakas* analysis focusing upon the defendant's legitimate expectation of privacy, it could no longer be assumed that the government's position of alleging possession and challenging standing was necessarily contradictory (see p. 323).

37. BURDEN OF PROOF

Allocation of the burden. The Supreme Court has held that the prosecution must bear the burden of proving several elements that relate to the application of the exclusionary rule. *Miranda v. Ariz.* (p. 230) (waiver of privilege against self-incrimination and right to counsel); *Bumper v. N. C.* (p. 173) (consent to a search); *U. S. v. Wade* (p. 270) (in-court identification not based upon an unconstitutional lineup identification). With respect to the voluntariness of a confession, *Lego v. Twomey* (p. 331) strongly suggests that the burden here also falls on the prosecution. The Supreme Court opinions do not distinguish between the burdens of production and persuasion, and it generally is assumed that the rulings noted above place both burdens on the prosecution. We accordingly will refer to the burden of proof as encompassing both burdens unless a distinction is drawn in their allocation.

In those areas where the Court has not spoken, there tends to be some diversity in the allocation of the burden of proof. This is particularly true as to establishing the reasonableness of a search or seizure. Several jurisdictions always put the burden of proof on the prosecution. See Mo.Rev.Stat. § 542.296(b). They take the view that no sufficient basis exists for distinguishing search issues from other constitutional issues (e. g., voluntariness of a confession) on which the prosecution traditionally carries that burden. Several states also take the opposite position. See Mont.Code § 46–13–302. They argue that defendant, as the party seeking to suppress the evidence, should bear the burden of proving the illegality of a search. But cf. *P. v. Berrios,* 270 N.E.2d 709 (N.Y.1971) (ultimate burden of persuasion is on defendant, but prosecution must initially present evidence showing legality). States placing the burden on the defendant do recognize, as required by *Bumper,* supra, that the burden shifts to the prosecution when it relies on consent as the justification for the search. Some also shift the burden when the prosecution relies on information obtained from informers to establish probable cause.

Most jurisdictions follow the federal court pattern in allocating the burden of proof; the prosecution bears the burden where the search was made without a warrant, while the defendant bears the burden on searches made with a warrant. *C. v. Antobenedetto,* 315 N.E.2d 530 (Mass.1974). Tying allocation of the burden to the presence of a warrant is justified as a logical extension of Supreme Court rulings noting a Fourth Amendment presumption in favor of the use of warrants (see p. 140). *U. S. v. Pearson,* 448 F.2d 1207 (5th Cir. 1971). Also, the presence of the warrant, setting forth the government's basis for finding probable cause, arguably makes it easier for the defendant to prepare his attack on the probable cause determination than in the instance of a warrantless search. When the police have acted without a warrant "the evidence comprising probable cause is particularly within the knowlege and control of the arresting agencies." *C. v. Antobenedetto,* supra.

Quantum of proof. In a few areas, the Supreme Court has spoken on both the allocation of the burden of proof and the level of that burden. Thus, *Miranda v. Ariz.,* supra, noted that the prosecution bears a "heavy burden" in showing a valid waiver of the rights recognized in that decision. Similarly, *U. S. v. Wade,* supra, noted that the prosecution must show by "clear and convincing evidence" that an in-court identification is not the product of an unconstitutional lineup identification. Where the Court has not spoken, states usually use the preponderance of the evidence standard, since that is the standard commonly applied to factual issues relating to the admissibility of evidence. Thus, aside from the issue of consent (on which Supreme Court decisions suggest a higher standard, cf. *Miranda*), factual questions relating to the validity of a search commonly are resolved by application of the preponderance standard. *Zehrung v. S.,* 569 P.2d 189 (Alaska 1977).

In *Lego v. Twomey,* 404 U.S. 477 (1972), the Court found the preponderance standard constitutionally acceptable as applied to the prosecutor's burden of establishing the voluntariness of a confession. The majority rejected the contention, advanced in the dissent, that proof of admissibility beyond a reasonable doubt was needed "to give adequate protection to these values that the exclusionary rules are designed to serve." The majority found it "very doubtful that escalating the prosecution's burden of proof in Fourth and Fifth Amendment suppression hearings would be sufficiently productive [in implementing the deterrent impact of the exclusionary rule] to outweigh the public interest in placing probative

evidence before juries for the purpose of arriving at
truthful decisions about guilt or innocence." Moreover, the defendant had "offer[ed] nothing to suggest that admissibility rulings [based upon a preponderance of the evidence standard] have been unreliable or otherwise wanting in quality because not
based on some higher standard." *Lego*, of course,
left the states free to apply a higher standard of
proof if they so desired, and several have adopted a
reasonable doubt standard. *S. v. Collins*, 297 A.2d
620 (Me.1972).

38.   HARMLESS ERROR

Application to constitutional errors.   All jurisdictions have "harmless error" provisions that prohibit appellate reversals based upon errors which do
not "affect the substantial rights" of the defendant.   Fed.R.Crim.P. 52(b).   Prior to *Chapman v.
Cal.*, 386 U.S. 18 (1967), it frequently was assumed
that the harmless error principle did not apply to
review of constitutional errors because such errors
were "per se injurious to the defendant".   *Allen v.
S.*, 137 S.E.2d 711 (Ga.App.1964).   *Chapman*, however, rejected this position.   The Court there held
that at least some constitutional errors could constitute "harmless errors" and therefore not require an
appellate reversal.   The *Chapman* opinion acknowledged that "prior cases have indicated that there are
some constitutional rights so basic to a fair trial that
their infraction can never be treated as harmless

error", but noted that other precedent "beli[ed] any belief that all trial errors which violate the constitution automatically call for reversal". The opinion concluded "that there may be some constitutional errors which in the setting of a particular case are so unimportant and insignificant that they may, consistent with the Federal Constitution, be deemed harmless". The majority indicated that a violation of the *Griffin* ruling (prohibiting prosecutorial comment upon defendant's failure to take the stand, see p. 178) could fall within that category, but found that the particular *Griffin* violation in *Chapman* was not harmless and therefore required reversal.

The applicable federal standard. *Chapman* also held that the substantive standard for determining whether an error was harmless, as applied to constitutional errors, was a matter of federal rather than state law: "Whether a conviction for crime should stand when a state has failed to accord federal constitutionally guaranteed rights is every bit as much a matter of a federal question as what particular constitutional provisions themselves mean, what they guarantee and whether they had been denied." The state court in *Chapman* had applied a harmless error standard that placed primary emphasis upon the "presence of other substantive evidence that proof of guilt was overwhelming," but the Supreme Court stressed that the standard should emphasize the impact of the error upon the "substantial rights" of the defendants. Accordingly, the

Court ruled that a constitutional error could be viewed as harmless only if the "beneficiary" of the error (i. e., the prosecution) could "prove beyond a reasonable doubt that the error * * * did not contribute to the verdict obtained."

Harrington v. Cal., 395 U.S. 250 (1969), provided further amplification of the federal standard. The Court there held that the determination as to whether the unconstitutional admission of evidence constituted harmless error was to be based upon the "probable impact of the [evidence] in the minds of an average jury" in the context of the particular case. The majority noted that this evaluation was to be applied to the jury as a whole; a conviction need not be reversed simply because the reviewing court could "imagine a single juror whose mind might have been made up because of [the illegally admitted evidence]." Moreover, while the *Chapman* definition was designed to avoid giving "too much emphasis to overwhelming evidence of guilt," the nature of the other evidence in the case remained an important factor in evaluating the impact of the illegally admitted evidence. Thus, the majority stressed that the illegally admitted evidence in that case, confessions of co-defendants admitted in violation of the *Bruton* ruling (p. 37), only supplied evidence relating to a single element that was well established by other testimony, including defendant's own admission. The majority concluded: "The case against [the defendant] is so overwhelming that unless we say that no violation of *Bruton* can constitute harmless error, we must leave this state conviction undisturbed." A dissenting opinion contended that this conclusion departed from *Chapman* by shifting the relevant inquiry from the impact of the tainted evidence to the weight of the untainted evidence, but the majority responded that it was only reaffirming *Chapman*. The majority noted in this regard that it was "not suggesting that, if evidence bearing on all ingredients of the crime is tendered," the unconstitutional admission of "cumulative evidence" necessarily constitutes harmless error. Its decision was based only on the "evidence in this record."

The *Harrington* analysis was also applied in *Milton v. Wainwright*, 407 U.S. 371 (1972) and *Brown v. U. S.*, 411 U.S. 223 (1973). In *Milton*, the Court concluded that, assuming arguendo that admission of defendant's post-indictment confession violated his Sixth Amendment rights under *Massiah v. U. S.* (p. 222), that error nevertheless "was, beyond a reasonable doubt, harmless." The majority stressed that the jury had been presented with "overwhelming evidence, including no less than three full confessions that were made by petitioner prior to his indictment" and found not to violate constitutional standards. In *Brown*, the Court reached a similar conclusion as to a *Bruton* error, noting that "the testimony erroneously admitted was merely cumulative of other overwhelming and largely uncontroverted evidence properly before the jury."

Automatic reversals. As the *Chapman* opinion acknowledged, earlier cases, such as *Gideon v. Wainwright,* had "indicated that there are some constitutional rights so basic to a fair trial that their infraction can never be treated as harmless error." However, neither *Chapman* nor the earlier opinions suggested any clear line for distinguishing between those errors that require automatic reversal and those to which the *Chapman* harmless error standard is applied. Justice Harlan, dissenting in *Chapman,* suggested that two factors are relevant in making such a distinction—certain errors "have an effect which is so devastating or inherently unreliable" as to require automatic reversals while others involve those "types of official misbehavior [that] require [automatic] reversal because society cannot tolerate giving final effect to a judgment tainted with such intentional misconduct." *Chapman v. Cal.,* supra (dis.). As an illustration of the former category, Justice Harlan cited the admission of a coerced confession and the failure to appoint counsel at trial. As an illustration of the second type, he cited a prosecutor's use of improper assertions and insinuations calculated to mislead a jury, *Berger v. U. S.,* 295 U.S. 78 (1935), and the trial of a defendant before a judge with a direct pecuniary interest in the outcome of the case, *Tumey v. Ohio,* 273 U.S. 510 (1927). It is debatable, however, whether either *Chapman* or post-*Chapman* decisions are entirely consistent with the distinctions advanced by Justice Harlan.

Chapman and subsequent decisions have held the *Chapman* standard applicable on a case-by-case basis to violations of: (1) the self-incrimination prohibition against prosecutorial comment on the defendant's failure to testify (*Chapman*); (2) the confrontation clause limitations upon the use of a co-defendant's confession (*Harrington*); (3) the prohibition against admission of eye-witness identification derived from a lineup at which the right to counsel was denied (*Gilbert v. Cal.*, p. 269); (4) the denial of right to counsel at a preliminary examination (*Coleman v. Ala.*, p. 362); (5) the prohibition against the admission of evidence obtained by an unconstitutional search and seizure (*Chambers v. Maroney*, p. 152); and (6) the prohibition against admission of incriminating statements obtained in violation of defendant's right to counsel (*Milton*). On the other hand, in *Mincey v. Ariz.*, 437 U.S. 385 (1978), the Court reaffirmed its earlier ruling that any use of an involuntary confession at trial, even if only for impeachment, requires automatic reversal. Lower courts generally have treated statements obtained in violation of *Miranda* as subject to the harmless error rule, rather than to the automatic reversal requirement applied to involuntary statements. *Smith v. Estelle*, 527 F.2d 430 (5th Cir. 1976). This position is justified on the ground that a confession obtained in violation of *Miranda* "may not be nearly as untrustworthy * * *, or nearly as shocking to our notions of fundamental due process, as an involuntary confession." Id. Support for application of the

Chapman rule to *Miranda* violations also is found in the analogous treatment of statements obtained in violation of the Sixth Amendment in *Milton,* supra.

CHAPTER 7

RIGHT TO COUNSEL

Introduction. The Sixth Amendment provides that, "in all criminal prosecutions, the accused shall enjoy the right * * * to have the Assistance of Counsel for his defense." This right was held fully applicable to the states, via the Fourteenth Amendment, in *Gideon v. Wainwright* (p. 15). The right to be represented by counsel has been described as "the most pervasive" of all of the defendant's rights "for it affects his ability to assert any other rights he may have." Schaefer, *Federalism and State Procedure*, 70 Harv.L.Rev. 1, 8 (1957). It is for this reason, perhaps, that it has been a focal point of the criminal law "revolution" of the past two decades.

Most of the Supreme Court decisions dealing with the right to counsel have been concerned with the state's failure to appoint counsel, at its expense, to assist the indigent defendant, rather than the right of the more affluent defendant to utilize the assistance of privately retained counsel. The latter right is so clearly established by the Sixth Amendment's language and history that it rarely has been the subject of litigation, at least as applied to the formal stages of the criminal prosecution. The Supreme Court has characterized that right as "unqualified," and early established that it included, as a "necessary corollary," the right to a reasonable delay in the proceedings to permit the defendant to employ and consult with counsel. *Powell v. Ala.*, 287 U.S. 45 (1932); *Chandler v. Fretag*, 348 U.S. 3 (1954); *Reynolds v. Cochran*, 365 U.S. 525 (1961). The scope of the indigent's right to appointed counsel, on the other hand, has been far more controversial.

39. THE RIGHT TO APPOINTED COUNSEL

A Sixth Amendment requirement. The constitutional right of an indigent defendant to the assistance of court appointed counsel was first recognized by the Supreme Court in *Powell v. Ala.*, supra, but that decision was carefully limited to situations similar to that before the Court—a "capital case" in which the defendant was "incapable adequately of making his own defense because of ignorance, feeble mindedness, illiteracy or the like." The *Powell* Court concluded that, at least under those circumstances, the appointment of counsel to assist the indigent was a "logical corollary" of the right to a fair hearing. Despite its limited holding, the *Powell* opinion suggested the need for the appointment of counsel generally. The opinion stressed the inability of even the "intelligent and educated layman" to properly represent himself, and concluded that there was a need for "the guiding hand of counsel at every step of the proceedings." The Court noted, for example, that the defendant ordinarily would be incapable of determining the validity of an indictment, applying the rules of evidence, or preparing his defense. "Left without the aid of counsel he may be put on trial without a proper charge, and convicted upon incompetent evidence, or evidence irrelevant to the issue or otherwise inadmissible."

In *Johnson v. Zerbst*, 304 U.S. 458 (1938), the Court relied heavily upon *Powell's* statement as to the general need for counsel in holding that the Sixth Amendment required federal courts to appoint counsel in all felony cases. But in *Betts v. Brady*, 316 U.S. 455 (1942), the Court refused to apply the *Johnson* ruling to the states via the Fourteenth Amendment. The majority held that due process did not necessarily require appointment of counsel in all criminal cases, but only in those cases where the particular circumstances indicated that the absence of counsel would result in a trial lacking "fundamental fairness." The Court ruled that these circumstances were not present in the case before it since the trial rested upon the "simple issue" of evaluating conflicting testimony, and the defendant, a man of ordinary intelligence and some familiarity with the courts, had been able to present adequately his case. Over the next twenty years, the Court decided over thirty cases involving application of the *Betts* standard. In all except a few, it found that "special circumstances," such as the complexity of the legal issues presented, the youth or mental incapacity of the defendant, or the fact that the offense charged was punishable by death, required the appointment of counsel to ensure fundamental fairness.

Gideon v. Wainwright, 372 U.S. 335 (1963), overruled *Betts*. *Gideon* held that the Fourteenth Amendment fully incorporated the Sixth Amendment right and accordingly required the state to make appointed counsel available to indigent defendants in all felony cases. The opinion for the Court relied essentially upon *Johnson*'s application of the *Powell* rationale and argued that *Betts'* case-by-case approach had departed from the basic thrust of that rationale. It concluded that "in our adversary system of criminal justice, any person hauled into court, who is too poor to hire a lawyer cannot be assured a fair trial unless counsel is provided for him." The "obvious truth" of this conclusion, the Court noted, was evidenced by the fact that "lawyers to prosecute are everywhere deemed essential" and "there are few defendants charged with crime * * * who fail to hire the best lawyers they can get." A concurring opinion suggested that decisions applying *Betts* had so frequently found "special circumstances" requiring appointment of counsel that the *Betts* rule was no longer a reality, and retention of a rule emphasizing a case-by-case analysis would only lead astray the state courts "charged with the front line responsibility for the enforcement of constitutional rights."

An equal protection requirement. Both Supreme Court and lower court opinions have suggested that, aside from the Sixth Amendment requirements of *Gideon*, appointment of counsel to assist the indigent may be required by the equal protection clause of the Fourteenth Amendment and the equal protection concept incorporated within the Fifth Amendment due process clause. Primary support for this position is found in *Griffin v. Ill.*, 351 U.S. 12 (1956), and *Douglas v. Cal.*, 372 U.S. 353 (1963). *Griffin* did not deal directly with appointment of counsel, but was based on a principle that was later extended to include counsel in *Douglas*. *Griffin* held that where state law conditioned appellate review upon the availability of a stenographic transcript or report of the trial proceedings, the state must make such a transcript or report available without charge to indigent defendants so they would have equal access to appellate review. The plurality opinion stressed that, although the state was not required by due process to afford appellate review, once it did so, it could not condition such review "in a way that discriminates against some convicted defendants on account of their poverty." "There can be no equal justice," the opinion noted, "where the kind of trial a man gets depends on the amount of money he has." In *Douglas*, the Court relied upon the "*Griffin* principle" to hold invalid the California practice of refusing to appoint counsel on an appeal by an indigent when the appellate court, after reviewing the trial record, concluded that "no good whatever could be served" by appointment. The Court noted that the more affluent defendant was not required to run the "gauntlet of a preliminary showing of merit" to have his appeal presented by counsel. The indigent defendant, it concluded, was entitled to equal treatment, at least on a first appeal granted by the state as a matter of right. The state therefore was required to appoint counsel for all indigent defendants on first appeal, just as it was required by *Gideon* to provide counsel at the trial level.

Construed broadly, the *Griffin-Douglas* concept of equal protection could require the appointment of counsel to assist the indigent at every stage in the administration of criminal justice at which the more affluent defendant is allowed by state law to be represented by privately retained counsel. The question of appointment would rest on the need for providing equal treatment rather than the need for a lawyer's assistance to assure a fair hearing. Thus, even though due process did not require appointment of counsel at a parole proceeding or at a trial of a misdemeanor punishable only by a fine, equal protection would require appointment if the more affluent defendant had a right under state law to be represented by counsel at those proceedings. This view of *Griffin-Douglas* was suggested in several lower court opinions decided before *Ross v. Moffitt*, 417 U.S. 600 (1974). See, e. g., *Earnest v. Willingham*, 406 F.2d 681 (10th Cir. 1969). In *Ross*, however, the Supreme Court appears to have adopted a considerably narrower view of *Griffin-Douglas.*

Ross involved a state practice of appointing counsel to assist indigent appellants on their appeals to the state intermediate appellate court, but not on their applications for review by the State Supreme Court or their petitions for certiorari to the United States Supreme Court. A divided Court (6–3) held that the failure to appoint counsel at these later stages of the appellate process did not deprive the appellants of equal protection. The Court stressed that the indigent defendant did not need counsel to have "meaningful access" to the higher appellate courts. On application for review, the State Supreme Court would have before it a transcript, the lower court brief, and, in many cases, an opinion of the state intermediate court. These materials, supplemented by any personal statement of appellant, provided an "adequate basis" for the state court to determine whether to grant review—especially since the "critical issue" for that decision was not whether there had been "a correct adjudication of guilt in every individual case," but whether the appeal presented issues of general legal significance. The same factors, the Court noted, also applied to its own consideration of petitions for writ of certiorari.

The *Ross* majority acknowledged that a lawyer skilled in preparing petitions for review "would * * * prove helpful" to an appellant (a point emphasized by the dissenters). But, it noted, "the fact that a particular service might be of benefit to an indigent defendant does not mean that service is constitutionally required." Equal protection "does not require absolute equality or precisely equal advantages". "The duty of the state * * * is not to duplicate the legal arsenal that may be privately retained by a criminal defendant in a continuing effort to reverse his conviction, but only to assure the indigent defendant an adequate opportunity to present his claims fairly in the context of the State's appellate process."

Selection of appointed counsel. Numerous lower courts have held that the indigent defendant's right to appointed counsel does not include the right to select the counsel who will represent him. *Davis v. Stevens*, 326 F.Supp. 1182 (S.D.N.Y.1971). The state's obligation, it is noted, is simply to appoint competent counsel, not the counsel whom defendant would prefer. The trial court may often choose to appoint counsel requested by the defendant where that counsel is willing to accept the appointment, but it has no constitutional duty to do so. *Drumgo v. Superior Court*, 506 P.2d 1007 (Cal.1973). *Harris v. Superior Court*, 567 P.2d 750 (Cal.1978), did hold, however, that a trial court abused its discretion in failing to appoint requested counsel under the circumstances of that case. The court there noted that the requested lawyers had represented the defendants in a related prosecution, possessed a familiarity with the factual and legal background of the case that could be acquired by new counsel only through a substantial investment of time and effort, and were supported for appointment by the counsel actually appointed because of their greater familiarity with the case. The *Harris* court emphasized that its ruling was not based simply on the "subjective factor" that defendants had greater confidence in the requested lawyers.

Determining indigency. Supreme Court opinions have referred generally to the "indigent defendant" without offering any specific definition of "indigency." Although it has described indigent defendants as persons "lack[ing] funds to hire a lawyer," the Court has not indicated what sources of funds and what alternative expenditures are to be considered in determining whether a particular defendant falls in this category. Lower courts considering these issues generally have held that the separate financial resources of a spouse or relatives will not be considered in determining indigency. *P. v. Gustavson*, 269 N.E.2d 517 (Ill.App.1971). Lower courts also have ruled that a defendant should be classified as indigent if his resources are not sufficient to both retain counsel and post bond—i. e., that he cannot be made to choose between personal liberty and representation at trial. *P. v. Eggers*, 188 N.E.2d 30 (Ill.1963). In evaluating defendant's resources, reference is made only to defendant's current financial status, not to his future earning potential. *March v. Municipal Court*, 498 P.2d 437 (Cal.1972) (determination of non-indigency could not be based on premise that college student defendants were capable of finding part-time employment).

Recoupment programs. Many states have "recoupment programs" requiring indigent defendants to reimburse the state for the costs of their legal defense if the defendant subsequently becomes financially able to make reimbursement. The Supreme Court has upheld such programs in principle, but has insisted that they not discriminate arbitrarily against indigent defendants generally or particular groups of defendants. Thus, *Rinaldi v. Yeager*, 384 U.S. 305 (1966), invalidated a state law that required only those indigent defendants sentenced to prison to reimburse the state; the statute invidiously discriminated between those imprisoned defendants and other convicted defendants sentenced only to probation or the payment of a fine. *James v. Strange*, 407 U.S. 128 (1972), similarly held invalid a state recoupment statute because it failed to permit the indigent defendant to avail himself of the restrictions on wage garnishment and other protective exemptions afforded to other civil judgment debtors (including debtors under recoupment laws relating to other forms of public assistance). *Fuller v. Ore.*, 417 U.S. 40 (1974), on the other hand, upheld a recoupment program that applied only to convicted defendants. The Court noted initially that the distinction drawn between those defendants convicted and those acquitted "reflect[ed] no more than an effort to achieve elemental fairness and is a far cry from * * * invidious discrimination." It also rejected a contention that recoupment imposed an improper burden on the indigent's right to appointed counsel that would "chill" his exercise of that right. A defendant "who is just above the line separating the indigent from the nonindigent," the Court noted, is subjected to considerable financial hardship to retain a lawyer. The Constitution does not "require that those only slightly poorer must remain forever immune from any [similar] obligation to shoulder the expenses of their legal defense."

40. THE SCOPE OF THE RIGHT TO COUNSEL

A. INTRODUCTION

Perhaps the two most significant problems involving the right to counsel are the determination of (1) the level of the charge to which the right applies and (2) those stages in the prosecution to which the right applies. These determinations usually have been made in the context of an indigent's demand for appointed counsel, and the decisions generally have referred only to that element of the right to counsel. Depending upon outcome and analysis, such decisions may or may not be controlling as to the defendant's right to be represented by privately retained counsel. As noted at p. 339, the Court has given special recognition to that aspect of the Sixth

Amendment right. Moreover, it has suggested that the right to be heard by retained counsel has an independent due process foundation that extends beyond the criminal prosecution. *Powell v. Ala.,* supra at 69; *Manness v. Meyers,* 419 U.S. 449, 470 (1975) (Stewart, J., con.).

A decision finding a constitutional right to appointed counsel at a particular stage in the criminal process should *a fortiori* support the right of a defendant to be represented by a retained counsel at the same stage. On the other hand, decisions finding no right to appointed counsel ordinarily should not be read to suggest that the state could constitutionally exclude retained counsel from the same proceeding. Thus, while the Court has held that there is no constitutional right to the assistance of appointed counsel in the trial of a misdemeanor punished only by fine (see p. 351), it does not necessarily follow that there is no constitutional right to be assisted by retained counsel at the same trial. Cf. *Hendrix v. Seattle,* 456 P.2d 696, 703 (Wash.1969); *Ross v. Moffitt,* supra. In some instances, however, a finding that the special function of a particular proceeding eliminates the need for appointed counsel may at least raise the possibility that the state could exclude counsel altogether from that proceeding. *Gagnon v. Scarpelli,* discussed at p. 364, is illustrative. The Court there held that, in light of various factors, including the impact of counsel upon the "nature of the proceeding," due process did not require the appointment of counsel in all probation revocation proceedings. It added that, since the particular case did not present the issue, there was no need to decide whether a probationer has "a right to be represented * * * by retained counsel" in those revocation proceedings that would not require appointed counsel for the indigent. See also *Morrissey v. Brewer* (p. 82) (a pre-*Gagnon* ruling establishing the right to a parole revocation hearing, but leaving open the question "whether the parolee is entitled to the assistance of [either] retained counsel or * * * appointed counsel").

B. THE LEVEL OF THE CHARGE

Misdemeanors and sentences of imprisonment. Prior to *Argersinger v. Hamlin*, 407 U.S. 25 (1972), some doubt existed as to whether the constitutional right to appointed counsel applied to any misdemeanor prosecutions. *Gideon v. Wainwright* (p. 342) itself involved a felony case, and later opinions referred to *Gideon* only as establishing a right to counsel in "felony prosecutions." *Mempa v. Rhay*, 389 U.S. 128, 134 (1967). *Argersinger*, however, held *Gideon* applicable to all indigent misdemeanor defendants who are sentenced to a jail term. The Court rejected the state's contention that the Sixth Amendment right to counsel, like the Sixth Amendment right to a jury trial (see p. 54), should not apply to "petty offenses" even where a jail sentence was imposed. While there was "historical support" for the jury trial limitation, "nothing in the history of the right to counsel" suggested a "retraction of the right in petty offenses wherein the common law previously did require that counsel be provided." Moreover, there was no functional basis for drawing the line at petty offenses. The "problems associated with * * * petty offenses," the Court noted, "often require the presence of counsel to insure the accused a fair trial." It could not be said that the legal questions involved in a misdemeanor trial were likely to be less complex because the jail sentence did not exceed six months. Neither is there less need for advice of counsel prior to entering a plea of guilty to a petty offense. Indeed, petty misdemeanors may create a special need for counsel because their great volume "may create an obsession for speedy dispositions, regardless of the fairness of the result."

Since the defendant in *Argersinger* had been sentenced to jail, the Court found it unnecessary to rule on the defendant's right to appointed counsel where "a loss of liberty was not involved." The opinion laid the foundation, however, for distinguishing between cases involving sentences of imprisonment and those in which only fines are imposed. Quoting from *Baldwin v. N. Y.* (p. 54), the Court noted the special qualities of imprisonment, "for however short a time," including its possible "serious repercussions affecting [defendant's] career and reputation." In *Scott v. Ill.*, 440 U.S. 367 (1977), the Court adopted the dividing line of imprisonment, as suggested by *Argersinger*. Defendant there was convicted of shoplifting, an offense punishable by a maximum sentence of imprisonment for one year, but was sentenced to only a fine of $50.00. The Court held that he had not been entitled to appointed counsel since the Sixth Amendment "require[s] only that no indigent criminal defendant be sentenced to a term of imprisonment unless the State has afforded him the right to assistance of appointed counsel." "*Argersinger*," it noted, "has proved reasonably workable, whereas any extension would create confusion and impose unpredictible, but necessarily substantial costs to 50 quite diverse states." The Court later added that the imprisonment dividing line of *Scott-Argersinger* encompassed imprisonment subsequently imposed through a recidivist provision. See *Baldasar v. Ill.*, —— U.S. —— (1980) (where the state failed to provide counsel at defendant's original misdemeanor conviction, for which he received a non-imprisonment sentence, it could not later use that conviction under an enhanced penalty provision to obtain an additional prison term on a subsequent charge). Cf. *Burgett v. Tex.* (p. 363).

Scott was a 5–4 decision, and Justice Powell noted that he joined the opinion only to provide "clear guidance" to the lower courts. The preferred approach, he argued, was a more flexible due process analysis that looked to the nature of the particular case, without relying solely on the sentence imposed. In light of Justice Powell's concurrence, and the majority's failure to refer to *Mayer v. Chicago*, 404 U.S. 189 (1971), some commentators have assumed that there still may be some non-imprisonment misdemeanor cases where the special circumstances of the case—particularly the serious consequences of conviction itself and the complexity of the issues presented—create a right to appointed counsel. *Mayer* also involved a non-imprisonment misdemeanor conviction, but was concerned with equal protection and the right to an appellate transcript, rather than the right to counsel. The Court there extended the *Griffin-Douglas* analysis to require that an indigent defendant, fined $500.00 for disorderly conduct and interference with a police officer, be provided a free transcript needed to present an appeal. The *Mayer* opinion stressed, inter alia, the potential significance of conviction for "even petty offenses" of the "kind involved here." "A fine," it noted, "may bear as heavily upon an indigent accused as forced confinement," and "the collateral consequences may be even more severe, as when (as was apparently a possibility in this case) the impecunious medical student finds himself barred from the practice of medicine because of [the] conviction * * *." Of course, providing a transcript may be distinguished from providing a lawyer on the ground that the lack of the transcript would have effectively denied Mayer all access to the appellate process, while Scott had access and could represent himself at his bench trial. But cf. *Douglas v. Cal.* (p. 343).

C. THE STAGE OF THE PROCEEDING

The Sixth Amendment recognizes the right of an "accused" to the assistance of counsel in "all criminal prosecutions." The Court has held that this right "attaches only at or after the time that adversary judicial proceedings have been initiated." *Kirby v. Ill.* (p. 273). That point marks the "commencement of the 'criminal prosecutions' to which alone the explicit guarantees of the Sixth Amendment are applicable." Id. Once adversary judicial proceedings have been initiated, the indigent defendant's right to appointed counsel extends to every "critical stage" of the prosecution—i. e. every stage "where substantial rights of the accused may be affected," and the "guiding hand" of counsel is therefore necessary. *Mempa v. Rhay,* supra.

The Sixth Amendment is not the only potential source of a constitutional right to appointed counsel at a particular proceeding. *Douglas v. Cal.* (p. 343) required appointment of counsel at the appellate level on equal protection grounds. Other cases have noted that, even though a proceeding is not part of the "criminal prosecution," the right to appointed counsel may be necessary to protect the exercise of another constitutional right, *Miranda v. Ariz.* (p. 228), or to provide a fair hearing as required by due process, *Gagnon v. Scarpelli* (p. 364).

Police investigation. As noted in the discussion of *Kirby* at p. 274), some uncertainty exists as to exactly what constitutes the initiation of adversary judicial proceedings. Once such proceedings have been initiated (e. g., by the filing of a formal charge), police investigatory operations are subject to the Sixth Amendment right to appointed counsel if they constitute a critical stage in the criminal proceedings (e. g., lineup identification). See § 31A. However, many police investigatory operations, though involving the accused's personal participation, are not viewed as critical stages in the criminal prosecution. See § 31B.

Though a particular aspect of the investigatory process is not subject to the Sixth Amendment, it may be subject to other constitutional protections, and these protections, in turn, may require the appointment of counsel. *Miranda v. Ariz.* (p. 228) represents exactly such a development. The Court there held that custodial interrogation must be accompanied by an opportunity to consult with counsel in order to protect the suspect's self-incrimination rights. On the other hand, in *Kirby* (p. 273), the Court rejected the argument that counsel was needed at a pre-Sixth Amendment lineup to support the defendant's constitutional right to confront identification witness when they testified at trial.

[356]

Grand jury proceedings.   A person who is being considered for possible indictment by the grand jury has no constitutional right to present his case, either by himself or by counsel, before that body. Grand jury sessions are protected by secrecy restrictions, and the target of a grand jury investigation need not even be informed of the ongoing investigation. The grand jury is viewed as performing an essentially discretionary function, similar to that performed by the prosecutor (whose decision it screens), rather than an adjudicative function requiring representation of the prospective defendant.

As noted at p. 257, the Supreme Court found it unnecessary in *U. S. v. Mandujano* to determine whether an indigent "target witness" before the grand jury had a right to appointed counsel. However, a four-justice plurality opinion argued that the Sixth Amendment did not apply since grand jury witnesses testify prior to the institution of "criminal proceedings." The plurality opinion cited in support of this conclusion *Kirby* (p. 273) and *In re Groban*, 352 U.S. 330 (1957). In *Groban,* a witness was not allowed to have retained counsel present during his examination by a state fire marshall in a proceeding to determine the cause of a fire. In finding that this denial of counsel did not violate due process, the majority cited as an analogy the grand jury proceeding, noting that "a witness before a grand jury cannot insist, as a matter of constitutional right, on being represented by his counsel." The dissent argued that the fire marshall's investigation was not analogous, but agreed that a witness did not have a right to counsel before the grand jury. The dissent emphasized that the presence of the grand jurors, as representatives of the community, distinguished a grand jury examination from interrogation by the fire marshall. The dissent noted that "it would be very difficult for officers of the state [i. e., the prosecuting attorney] to seriously abuse or deceive a witness in the presence of the grand jury." Consider also p. 257, noting the grounds offered by the plurality in *Mandujano* in distinguishing *Miranda.*

As a matter of practice, jurisdictions commonly permit grand jury witnesses to interrupt their testimony for the purpose of consulting with retained counsel located in an adjoining room. A few courts have suggested that this may be a due process right, at least where the witness desires to consult relating to his exercise of a legal right (e. g., his privilege against self-incrimination). *P. v. Iannielo,* 235 N.E. 2d 439 (N.Y.1968). The *Mandujano* plurality found it unnecessary to consider this issue because the witness there had been informed that he could leave the grand jury room to consult with retained counsel (which he did not have). Several states have statutory provisions allowing retained counsel to accompany the witness before the grand jury, and a few afford appointed counsel to the indigent witness.

Initial appearance. One of the earliest formal steps in the criminal case is the defendant's initial appearance before the magistrate, which ordinarily follows defendant's arrest. At that point, the defendant is informed of the charges against him (as stated in the complaint) and his rights to the assistance of counsel, to remain silent, and to a preliminary examination (in felony cases). In addition, the magistrate usually will set bail.

With the initial appearance, adversary judicial proceedings have been initiated. See *Brewer v. Williams* (p. 274). Where the state requires the defendant to make an election at the initial appearance that may be prejudicial, *White v. Md.,* 373 U.S. 59 (1963), establishes that the initial appearance also constitutes a "critical stage," requiring appointment of counsel. In *White* the state followed a practice, utilized in several jurisdictions, of requesting a felony defendant to enter an initial, non-binding plea before the magistrate. The defendant there, without the assistance of counsel, entered a plea of guilty. Subsequently, at the formal arraignment before the trial judge, defendant was assisted by appointed counsel and entered a plea of not guilty. The initial plea of guilty was nevertheless introduced as evidence against him at trial. The Supreme Court reversed the conviction, holding that the use of the plea rendered defendant's appearance before the magistrate a critical stage where counsel should have been made available to assist the "accused to * * * plead intelligently."

The combination of *White* and *Coleman v. Ala.,* discussed below, provides grounds for arguing that the first appearance also is a "critical stage" even when defendant makes no significant election at that point. In holding that the preliminary examination was a "critical stage," *Coleman* noted the value of counsel in making effective arguments on bail. The setting of bail is also a major element in the first appearance. However, since *Coleman* pointed to several functions requiring counsel's assistance at the preliminary examination, the bail function alone may not be sufficient to require appointment of counsel at the first appearance. Cf. *Gerstein v. Pugh* (discussed at p. 133) (initial judicial determination of probable cause following warrantless arrest is not critical stage because of "its limited function and its nonadversary character").

Preliminary hearing. The preliminary hearing or "examination," also conducted by the magistrate, is usually held at least several days after the defendant's initial appearance. In most jurisdictions, the basic function of the preliminary hearing is to determine whether there is probable cause to "hold" the accused for possible prosecution. If the accused is "boundover" for prosecution, the magistrate also may reconsider the appropriate level of bail.

Coleman v. Ala., 399 U.S. 1 (1970), held that the preliminary hearing was a "critical stage" under the Sixth Amendment. While there was no opinion for the Court, a majority agreed that the failure to appoint counsel at a typical state preliminary hearing resulted in a constitutional violation, though not necessarily requiring reversal of a subsequent conviction. The majority stressed the practical importance of the preliminary hearing and noted various advantages that could result from assistance of counsel:

"First, the lawyer's skilled examination and cross-examination of witness may expose fatal weaknesses in the State's case that may lead the magistrate to refuse to bind the accused over. Second, in any event, the skilled interrogation * * * by an experienced lawyer can fashion a valuable impeachment tool for use in cross-examination of the State's witnesses at the trial, or preserve [favorable] testimony * * * of a witness who does not appear at trial. Third, trained counsel can more effectively discover the case the state has against his client and make possible [better] preparation * * * [for] trial. Fourth, counsel can also be influential at the preliminary hearing in making effective arguments for the accused on such matters as the necessity for an early psychiatric examination or bail."

Arraignment. The formal arraignment occurs after the information or indictment is issued, and involves a reading of the charges contained therein and the entry of a plea (guilty, not-guilty, or nolo contendere) in response to those charges. Although the defendant is entitled to consultation with counsel before entering a guilty plea, the denial of counsel has been viewed as harmless error where the defendant was later allowed to withdraw the guilty plea and the fact that he originally entered such a plea could not be used against him in evidence. *Vitoratos v. Maxwell,* 351 F.2d 217 (6th Cir. 1965); cf. *White v. Md.,* supra. Similarly, failure to appoint counsel at arraignment will not constitute grounds for reversal where the defendant entered a not-guilty plea, unless the jurisdiction is one that views entry of the plea as barring the defendant from subsequently raising objections (e. g., attacks on the indictment) or defenses (e. g., insanity). In that situation, *Hamilton v. Ala.,* 368 U.S. 52 (1961), holds that the failure to appoint counsel requires reversal of a subsequent conviction. In *Hamilton,* local law treated certain defenses, such as insanity, as "irretrievably lost" if not raised at arraignment. The Court rejected the contention that the critical nature of the proceeding should depend upon a showing of actual prejudice—i. e., a showing that defendant would have raised one of the "lost" defenses if he had been assisted by counsel. It concluded that the degree of prejudice "can never be known" because only counsel present at the time "could have enabled the accused to know all the defenses available to him and to plead intelligently." Compare *Coleman v. Ala.,* supra (denial of counsel at preliminary hearing could constitute harmless error where the advantages lost through the lack of counsel, see p. 361, had no bearing on the subsequent trial).

Trial. The earliest right to counsel cases dealt primarily with assistance of counsel at trial, and such assistance is clearly recognized as the "core" of the Sixth Amendment right. See *Powell v. Ala.,* (p. 340); *Gideon v. Wainwright* (p. 342). Denial of the right to counsel at trial requires the automatic reversal of defendant's conviction. Here again, prejudice is presumed. See *Gideon,* supra. See also *Loper v. Beto,* 405 U.S. 473 (1973) (where indigent defendant was denied his right to appointed counsel under *Gideon,* the resulting conviction was void and could not be used to impeach his credibility when he testified at a subsequent trial on a different charge); *Burgett v. Tex.,* 389 U.S. 109 (1967) (conviction void under *Gideon* could not be used as a prior conviction under recidivist statute). But cf. *Lewis v. U. S.,* 100 U.S. 915 (1980) (federal statute prohibiting possession of a firearm by convicted felon could be applied to defendant with an uncounseled felony conviction where the defendant had failed to obtain a qualifying pardon or special permission as provided by the federal statute; Congress could rationally conclude that any felony conviction, even an allegedly invalid one, is a sufficient basis on which to prohibit the possession of a firearm unless the convicted person first obtains an exemption). Consider also *Baldasar v. Ill.* (p. 353).

Sentencing, probation and parole. *Mempa v. Rhay,* 389 U.S. 128 (1968), confirmed the implications of prior decisions in holding that sentencing was a "critical stage" of a criminal prosecution requiring the assistance of appointed counsel: *Mempa* held, moreover, that sentencing remained a "critical stage" even though deferred to a probation revocation proceeding. In *Mempa,* the trial judge placed the defendant on probation without fixing the term of imprisonment that would be imposed if probation was later revoked. The Court concluded that the subsequent determination and imposition of a prison sentence at the probation revocation proceeding was as much a part of the "criminal prosecution" as sentencing imposed immediately after trial. The Court rejected the state's contention that counsel was not needed since the term of the prison sentence was set by state law. The trial judge was required to submit a recommendation to the parole board as to the portion of the sentence to be served, and counsel could assist the defendant in presenting his case on that matter. Also, certain legal rights (e. g., withdrawal of a guilty plea) could be lost if not raised at the time the prison sentence was imposed, and counsel also was needed to protect those rights. Cf. *Hamilton v. Ala.* (p. 347).

In *Gagnon v. Scarpelli,* 411 U.S. 778 (1973), the Court held that *Mempa* did not extend to a probation revocation proceeding that involved only a determination as to revocation, a prison sentence previously having been imposed and suspended in favor of probation. The probation revocation determination is not based on the commission of the original offense and accordingly is not part of the "criminal prosecution" governed by the Sixth Amendment. The Court noted, however, that the "loss of liberty entailed [in a probation revocation] is a serious deprivation requiring that [the probationer] be accorded due process." Under *Morrissey v. Brewer* (p. 82), the probationer has a due process right to a preliminary and a final revocation hearing that includes the right to present evidence, confront witnesses, etc. *Gagnon* concluded that due process also requires that the state provide appointed counsel where, under the facts of the particular case, counsel is needed to assure the "effectiveness of the [hearing] rights guaranteed by *Morrissey*."

The *Gagnon* Court considered, but refused to impose, a flat requirement of counsel in all cases. While such a requirement had the "appeal of simplicity, it would impose direct costs and serious collateral disadvantages" without regard to the need for counsel. In most cases, the Court noted, the probationer has been convicted of committing another crime or admits the probation violation. Mitigating circumstances, if advanced, often are "not susceptible of proof" or are "so simple as not to require either investigation or exposition by counsel." Moreover, the introduction of counsel would "alter significantly the nature of the [probation-revocation] proceeding." The state would, in turn, retain its own counsel, and the role of the hearing body would become "more akin to that of a judge at trial and less attuned to the rehabilitative needs of the individual probationer." The Court acknowledged that a case-by-case evaluation of the need for counsel departed from the approach taken in *Gideon* (p. 342) and *Argersinger* (p. 351), but that departure was justified by "critical" distinctions between the functions and nature of criminal trials and revocation hearings. Indeed, in light of those distinctions, the Court left open the issue as to whether the probationer must be afforded the right to have retained counsel in hearings where appointed counsel would not be required (see p. 350).

The *Gagnon* opinion refused to attempt to formulate "a precise and detailed set of guidelines" to be followed in individual cases. It did note that "presumptively" counsel should be provided where, after being informed of his right, the indigent probationer requests counsel on the basis of a "timely and colorable claim" that (1) he has not committed the alleged violation or (2) that there are "substantial reasons which justified or mitigated the violation and made revocation inappropriate, and that the reasons are complex or otherwise difficult to develop or present." The opinion further noted that, "especially in doubtful cases," consideration should be given as to "whether the probationer appears to be capable of speaking effectively for himself." Finally, where a request for counsel is refused, grounds for refusal must be succinctly stated in the record.

While *Gagnon* itself involved a probation revocation proceeding, the opinion made clear that the same standards also applied to parole revocation hearings under *Morrissey v. Brewer,* supra. See *Russell v. Douthitt,* 304 N.E.2d 793 (Ind.1973). As noted at p. 351, *Morrissey,* like *Gagnon,* leaves open the issue as to whether there is a constitutional right to be represented by retained counsel in those revocation proceedings that do not require appointed counsel for the indigent. See also *Wainwright v. Cottle,* 414 U.S. 895 (1973) (Douglas and Blackmun, JJ., dis. from denial of cert.) (urging the Court to decide whether, where a state grants a statutory right to be assisted by retained counsel at revocation hearings, equal protection requires appointed counsel for the indigent).

Appeals. As discussed at p. 343, *Douglas v. Cal.* requires appointment of counsel to assist the indigent defendant at the first level of appellate review granted as a matter of right. *Ross v. Moffitt* (p. 345) held, however, that appointed counsel need not also be provided to prepare an application for review at subsequent levels of the appellate process, where review is discretionary. *Ross* did not involve appointment of counsel where discretionary review is granted by a higher appellate court, but counsel regularly is provided at that point as a matter of local practice.

In finding no constitutional right to the assistance of appointed counsel, *Ross* considered the applicability of due process as well as equal protection. In that connection, the Court emphasized the different constitutional status of the trial and the appellate process. While a state could not dispense with the trial stage of criminal proceedings, it could refuse to provide "any appeal at all." *McKane v. Durston,* (p. 82). Similarly, while due process requires that the state provide an attorney to serve as a "shield to protect [defendant] against being 'haled into court' by the State and stripped of his presumption of innocence," it does not require, absent unconstitutional discrimination, that the state also provide an attorney to "serve as a sword to upset the prior determination of guilt."

Where *Douglas* requires appointment of counsel, it also bars the state from adopting a procedure that invites counsel to evade his obligation of advocacy on his client's behalf. Thus, *Anders v. Cal.,* 386 U.S. 738 (1967), found a denial of defendant's rights under *Douglas* when appointed counsel filed a statement simply noting that the appeal had no merit, and the appellate court, without further briefing, then examined the record and affirmed the judgment. The Court held that, while appointed counsel may request the right to withdraw when he finds a case to be "wholly frivolous," he cannot do so by simply stating his conclusion that the appeal lacks merit. His request must be accompanied by a brief discussing all points in the record "that might arguably support the appeal." The appellate court may then dismiss the appeal (or affirm the conviction) if it finds that none of the legal points are "arguable." Otherwise, the appellate court "must, prior to its decision, afford the indigent the assistance of counsel to argue the appeal."

Collateral proceedings. The Supreme Court has not ruled directly on whether an indigent prisoner has a constitutional right to appointed counsel in challenging his conviction through collateral proceedings (e. g., habeas corpus, see §§ 44, 45). Its opinions appear to rest on the premise, however, that a state need not provide the assistance of counsel, at least for the filing of the collateral challenge. *Johnson v. Avery,* 393 U.S. 483 (1969), held that a state regulation prohibiting prisoners from assisting each other in preparing federal habeas corpus petitions violated the prisoner's right of access to federal habeas corpus. The majority opinion noted that federal courts generally do not appoint lawyers to assist prisoners in preparing habeas petitions, but it did not rule on the constitutionality of that practice. Three justices specifically noted, however, that it was "neither practical nor necessary to require the help of lawyers" in the preparation of habeas corpus petitions. *Bounds v. Smith,* 430 U.S. 817 (1977), later extended *Johnson v. Avery* to hold that "the fundamental right of access to the courts requires prison authorities to assist inmates in the preparation and filing of meaningful legal papers by providing prisoners with adequate libraries or adequate legal assistance from persons trained in the law." The Court noted that adequate libraries "are one constitutionally acceptable method to assure meaningful access to the courts," though it commended the state programs that also provide "some degree of professional or quasi professional legal assistance." Cf. *Procunier v. Martinez*, 416 U.S. 396 (1974) (holding invalid a California regulation barring attorney use of law students to interview inmate clients).

Johnson and *Bounds* were concerned primarily with the assistance necessary to file petitions. If a court grants a hearing on a prisoner petition, is the prisoner then entitled to the appointment of counsel? The lower courts have divided on this issue. Several lower courts have argued that there is no constitutional right to appointed counsel at any stage of a collateral proceeding. *Honore v. Wash. S. Bd.*, 466 P.2d 485 (Wash.1970) (collecting cases). Support for this position is based on several arguments. First, collateral proceedings are deemed not to be part of the "criminal prosecution" encompassed by the Sixth Amendment. Those proceedings have traditionally been designated as civil, and, in any event, are not a part of the process of conviction. Equal protection is also rejected as a basis for appointing counsel, although the *Griffin-Douglas* (p. 343) analysis has been applied by the Supreme Court to require that the state furnish indigents other assistance (transcripts) in post-conviction proceedings, *Long v. Dist.*

Ct., 385 U.S. 192 (1966). Assistance of counsel, it is contended, is no more essential in collateral proceedings, than it is on the second level of appellate review, where equal protection claims also have been rejected. See *Ross v. Moffitt* (p. 345). But note *Bounds v. Smith,* supra (distinguishing applications for discretionary review, which are based on lower court rulings and briefs, from habeas corpus petitions, which often raise "heretofore unlitigated issues").

On the other side, several lower courts have argued that due process does require the appointment of counsel for those aspects of collateral proceedings in which a lawyer's assistance is necessary for a "fair and meaningful hearing." *Dillon v. U. S.,* 307 F.2d 445 (9th Cir. 1962). They have required appointment at either all evidentiary hearings, *P. v. Shipman,* 397 P.2d 993 (Cal.1965), or at least those hearings where the issues raised, "by their nature and character, indicate the necessity for professional legal assistance." *Honore v. Wash. S. Bd.,* supra. Most jurisdictions now appoint counsel, as a matter of local rule, when the prisoner's petition requires an extensive hearing.

41. WAIVER OF THE RIGHT TO COUNSEL

Introduction. The Supreme Court frequently has noted that the defendant may waive his constitutional right to assistance of counsel provided he does so "knowingly and intelligently." *Johnson v. Zerbst,* 304 U.S. 458 (1938). At the same time, it has emphasized that waiver will not be "lightly assumed." "Trial courts must indulge every reasonable presumption against waiver." Id. Thus, *Carnley v. Cochran,* 369 U.S. 506 (1962), holds that waiver will not be presumed from a "silent record"; the evidence must show that the defendant was informed specifically of his right to the assistance of appointed or retained counsel and that he clearly rejected such assistance. "No amount of circumstantial evidence that the person may have been aware of his right [and intended to silently relinquish it] will suffice" as a replacement for specific notice and rejection. *Miranda v. Ariz.* (p. 230).

Even though the formal prerequisites of *Carnley* are established, the rejection of counsel still may not have been made "knowingly and intelligently"—i. e., it may not have been the product of a reasoned and deliberate choice based upon adequate knowledge of what the assistance of counsel encompasses. In determining whether defendant's rejection reflects such a choice, courts rely upon an analysis of the particular facts of the case, including defendant's age, mental condition, and experience, the particular setting in which the offer of counsel was made, and the manner in which it was explained. Moreover, a valid waiver at one stage of the proceeding (e. g., preliminary examination) does not necessarily indicate an intent to waive at a later stage (e. g., trial), and the prosecution must show that the defendant was given the opportunity to exercise his right to counsel at each separate stage.

Waiver prior to the entry of a guilty plea. Very frequently the defendant at arraignment may seek to waive counsel and enter a plea of guilty. The constitutional limitation upon waiver in this circumstance is supplemented by the due process requirement that the guilty plea be voluntary. To insure that both requirements are met, the Court has insisted that the trial judge, in addition to specifically advising defendant of his right to counsel, also make a careful inquiry into the basis of defendant's waiver. In *Von Moltke v. Gillies,* 332 U.S. 708 (1948), four justices suggested that the trial court must seek to insure that waiver is made "with an apprehension of the nature of the charges, the statutory offenses included within them, the range of allowable punishments thereunder, possible defenses to the charges and circumstances in mitigation thereof, and all other facts essential to a broad understanding of the whole matter." Lower courts generally view this standard as a basic guideline, rather than a precise formula, and will not hold a waiver invalid, for example, merely because the trial court failed to inform the defendant of the specific potential maximum sentence. *Cox v. Burke,* 361 F.2d 183 (7th Cir. 1966). They do stress, however, that the defendant must be fully aware of the significance of his decision, including the general nature of the particular charge made against him. Id. *Molignaro v. Smith*, 408 F.2d 795 (5th Cir. 1969). See also the discussion at p. 44 on the acceptance of guilty pleas.

Waiver and the right to proceed pro se. In *Faretta v. Cal.*, 422 U.S. 806 (1975), a divided Court held that the Sixth Amendment guarantees to the defendant the right to proceed *pro se* (i. e., to represent himself without counsel). *Faretta* relied upon the "structure of the Sixth Amendment, as well as * * * the English and colonial jurisprudence from which the Amendment emerged." The Court noted that, while the Sixth Amendment does not specifically refer to the right of self-representation, that right is "necessarily implied" by the Amendment's provisions for the accused's presentation of his defense. The Sixth Amendment it noted, refers to rights of confrontation, compulsory process, and notice as rights of "the accused." Similarly, the counsel provision speaks only of the "assistance" of counsel, and suggests thereby that "counsel, like the other defense tools guaranteed * * * shall be an aid to a willing defendant—not an organ of the State interposed between an unwilling defendant and his right to defend himself personally."

Faretta also reasoned that forcing counsel upon an unwilling accused would be contrary to "the logic of the Amendment," as reflected by the consequences of legal representation. Thus, when a defendant chooses to be represented by counsel, "law and tradition may allocate to the counsel the power to make binding decisions of trial strategy in many areas." (See p. 377). But this "allocation can only be justified * * * by the defendant's consent, at the outset, to accept counsel as his representative." Without such acquiescence, the defense presented is not in any "real sense" the accused's defense and cannot be attributed to him.

Faretta recognized that a constitutional right to proceed *pro se* "seems to cut against the grain" of decisions, like *Gideon*, that are based on the premise that "the help of a lawyer is essential to assure a fair trial." It rejected, however, the dissent's contention that the state's interest in providing a fair trial permitted it to insist upon representation by counsel. An analysis of the historical roots of the Sixth Amendment suggested that the founders had placed on a higher level the right of "free choice." Moreover, where the defendant opposes representation by counsel, "the potential advantage of a lawyer * * * can be realized, if at all, only imperfectly. To force a lawyer on a defendant can only lead him to believe that the law contrives against him."

Faretta stressed that the defendant who proceeds *pro se* must act "knowingly and intelligently" in giving up those "traditional benefits associated with the right to counsel": "Although a defendant need not himself have the skill and experience of a lawyer

[375]

in order competently and intelligently to choose self-representation, he should be made aware of the dangers and disadvantages of self-representation, so that the record will establish that 'he knows what he is doing and his choice is made with eyes open.' *Adams v. U. S. ex rel. McCann*, 317 U.S. 269 (1942)." The Court also noted that the right to self-representation "is not a license to abuse the dignity of the courtroom." Under *Ill. v. Allen* (p. 71), the judge may terminate self-representation by a defendant "who deliberately engages in serious and obstructionist misconduct." Similarly, self-representation is "not a license" for failure to comply with "relevant rules of procedural and substantive law." Thus, "whatever else may or may not be open to him on appeal, a defendant who elects to represent himself cannot thereafter complain that the quality of his own defense amounted to a denial of 'effective assistance of counsel.'"

Client participation. While not commonly described as an aspect of defendant's Sixth Amendment right, courts frequently have noted that decisions to relinquish or exercise certain constitutional rights must reflect the "considered choice" of the defendant rather than his attorney. Decisions falling in this category include the decisions to plead guilty or not guilty, to have or not have a jury trial, to testify or not testify, and to appeal or not appeal. See *Winters v. Cook,* 489 F.2d 174 (5th Cir. 1973). Thus, where defense counsel agreed to a procedure that was tantamount to pleading guilty, his action could not be accepted as a waiver of the rights of his client who was not aware of the nature of the particular procedure. *Brookhart v. Janis,* 384 U.S. 1 (1966). As the Court noted, counsel could not "override his client's desire * * * to plead not guilty and enter in the name of his client another plea" which had the same effect as a guilty plea. Of course, counsel can seek to persuade his client to exercise or relinquish any of the rights in this category, but the final decision must be that of the client. As to many other rights, however, counsel may act on his own initiative without first gaining client approval. That authority is not viewed as inconsistent with defendant's right to proceed *pro se.* As the Court noted in *Faretta,* when a defendant accepts counsel, he also accepts the role of counsel as "manager" of the lawsuit, and "law and tradition may allocate to counsel [as manager] the power to make binding decisions of trial strategy in many areas."

What places a particular decision in the domain of counsel or client? The issue typically arises in the course of determining whether a particular decision made by counsel alone (i. e., without the client's agreement or disagreement) constituted a waiver of a constitutional right. The usual answer is that decisions of "trial strategy" may be made by counsel alone, while decisions to relinquish "inherently personal rights of fundamental importance" require the personal choice of the client. *Winters v. Cook,* supra; *Henry v. Miss.,* 379 U.S. 443 (1965). The trial strategy category clearly includes "on-the-spot-decisions" made at trial, even though they involve the relinquishment of significant constitutional rights (e. g., the decision not to object to evidence that could be excluded on constitutional grounds). *Wainwright v. Sykes* (p. 406); *Henry v. Miss.,* supra. However, it also includes other decisions (e. g., whether to object to discrimination in the grand jury selection) that are made substantially before trial and with ample opportunity for client consultation. *Tollett v. Henderson* (p. 300). See also *Estelle v. Williams* (p. 71) (decision not to object to being tried in prison garb); *U. S. ex rel. Agron v. Herold,* 426 F.2d 125 (2d Cir. 1970) (decision to relinquish a "pre-trial publicity claim"). Thus while courts frequently emphasize considerations relating to the timing of counsel's decisions, *Lanier v. S.,* 486 P.2d 981 (Alaska 1971), they also consider other factors, such as the nature of the right involved and "the practical necessities of the adversary system." *U. S. ex rel. Brown v. Warden,* 417 F.Supp. 970 (N.D.Ill. 1976).

Several courts have suggested that the number of decisions requiring defendant's personal participation must be limited, lest counsel, client, and court be so "burdened" by the requirement of consultation that it will be "virtually impossible to conduct a criminal trial." *Winters v. Cook,* supra. As stated in *Win-*

ters, apart from the "disruptive effect on counsel and the confusing impact on the defendant himself, it would be a futile command to require that a trial judge continually satisfy himself that defendant was fully informed as to, and in complete accord with, his attorney's every action or inaction that involved any possible constitutional right." Courts also have stressed that certain decisions involve primarily matters of strategy and tactics, on which counsel clearly has special competence. As to these, they argue, counsel's wisdom must prevail, "for if such decisions are to be made by the defendant, he is likely to do himself more harm than good." *Nelson v. Cal.,* 346 F.2d 73 (9th Cir. 1965) (involving an objection to illegally obtained evidence). On the other hand, other decisions are viewed as including considerations of a personal nature, rather than simply determining what constitutes the best route to an acquittal. Here the defendant's choice must prevail even if, "in the final analysis, [his choice] might be harmful to his case." *P. v. Robles,* 466 P.2d 710 (Cal.1970) (right to testify on his own behalf). See also *Townsend v. Superior Ct.,* 543 P.2d 619 (1975) (counsel may not waive right to a speedy trial over his client's objections, though he may waive statutory right to be tried in 60 days, which "cannot properly be termed 'fundamental' ").

42. EFFECTIVE ASSISTANCE
OF COUNSEL

The constitutional right to counsel is based on the premise that counsel will effectively assist the defendant. Accordingly, counsel's failure to render adequate assistance results in a denial of defendant's constitutional right and requires reversal of his conviction. The Supreme Court has examined the requirement of effective assistance on only a few occasions, and then not at considerable length. The lower courts, on the other hand, have dealt with it rather frequently, but they have varied considerably in both the standard adopted to judge counsel's performance and the application of that standard.

The applicable standard. In examining most types of ineffective assistance claims, lower courts traditionally asked whether counsel's inadequacy had turned a trial into a "farce or mockery" or otherwise deprived defendant of "fundamental fairness." See *Beasley v. U. S.,* 491 F.2d 687 (6th Cir. 1974) (collecting cases). Several courts still adhere to this standard, but others have rejected it as too "subjective" and too reflective of a due process analysis rather than the "more stringent requirements" of the Sixth Amendment. Id. These courts apply a standard of "reasonably effective assistance," measured against the customary performance of the lawyer "with ordinary training and skill in the criminal law." Id. The Supreme Court also has utilized such a standard in determining when counsel's misevaluation of a constitutional claim might provide a basis for challenging a subsequent guilty plea. See *McMann v. Richardson* (p. 49) and *Tollett v. Henderson* (p. 300) ("within the range of competence demanded of attorneys in criminal cases"). These Supreme Court decisions arguably cast doubt on the constitutionality of the "farce or mockery" test. See *Marzullo v. Md.,* 561 F.2d 540 (4th Cir. 1977), 435 U.S. 1011 (1978) (White, J., dis. from cert. denial).

Retained vs. appointed counsel. Prior to the Supreme Court's decision in *Cuyler v. Sullivan,* 100 U.S. 1708 (1980), many lower courts suggested that the standard for judging ineffective assistance claims varied with the status of counsel as privately retained or court appointed. *Fitzgerald v. Estelle,* 505 F.2d 1334 (5th Cir. 1974). Noting that the Fourteenth Amendment applies only to "state action," these courts argued that counsel's inadequacies did not reach the level of a constitutional violation until the state became responsible for those inadequacies. They saw that responsibility as arising automatically from the trial court's selection of appointed counsel, but not applying to privately retained counsel unless counsel's inadequacies were so obvious that they should have been apparent to the trial court. *Fitzgerald v. Estelle,* supra; *U. S. ex rel. Hart v. Davenport,* 478 F.2d 203 (3d Cir. 1973). Other courts rejected this view. They argued that the crucial

state involvement was the trial of the defendant
without competent counsel and that involvement did
not hinge on counsel's appointed or retained status.
In *Cuyler,* supra, the Supreme Court appeared to
endorse this position. The prosecution there argued
that a retained counsel's representation of codefendants with conflicting interests could not result in a
constitutional violation "because the conduct of
retained counsel does not involve state action."
Rejecting this contention, the Court noted: "A
proper respect for the Sixth Amendment disarms
[the prosecution's] contention that defendants who
retain their own counsel are entitled to less protection
than defendants for whom the State appoints counsel.
*   *   *   The vital guarantee of the Sixth
Amendment would stand for little if the often
uninformed decision to retain a particular lawyer
could reduce or forfeit the defendant's entitlement to
constitutional protection. Since the State's conduct
of a criminal trial itself implicates the State in the
defendant's conviction, we see no basis for drawing a
distinction between retained and appointed counsel
that would deny equal justice to defendants who must
choose their own lawyers."

Application of the standard. To a large extent,
application of the effective assistance standard—
whichever standard it may be—depends upon an
analysis of the particular facts of the individual case.
Aside from certain cases involving multiple representation (see p. 387), a defendant ordinarily must show

not only an inadequacy, but also a likelihood that counsel's inadequacy actually prejudiced the defendant (i. e., had a probable effect on the outcome of his case). *U. S. v. Decoster,* 598 F.2d 311 (D.C.Cir. 1979). But see id. (Bazelon, J., dis.) (violation of usual duty of competent counsel should shift to the government the burden of establishing a lack of prejudice). The inquiry into possible prejudice necessarily requires consideration of the total fact situation. Case-by-case analysis also follows from the general unwillingness of the courts to classify particular acts or omissions as per se instances of inadequacy. As noted in *U. S. v. Decoster,* supra, the very nature of counsel's function suggests "a non-categorical approach" to the determination of incompetence. Since the defense counsel is constantly applying "professional judgment to an infinite variety of decisions," a "determination whether any given action or omission * * * amounted to ineffective assistance cannot be divorced from consideration of the peculiar facts and circumstances that influenced counsel's judgment."

Trial errors. Perhaps the most common ground for challenging counsel's competency is the failure of counsel to take advantage of certain procedures at trial—e. g., counsel's failure to object to inadmissible evidence or to vigorously cross-examine witnesses. Courts often express concern that an overly critical, "perfectionist approach" in judging counsel's performance at trial will: (1) force the trial judge to intervene whenever possible error is being committed and thereby "open the door to a fundamental reordering of the adversary system," *U. S. v. Decoster,* supra; (2) make lawyers more reluctant to take criminal assignments; (3) place a premium on the lawyer who performs poorly; and (4) permit a lawyer with a desperate case to assure his client a new trial by deliberately committing error. Accordingly, the courts stress that an incompetency claim must be based on an "eggregious shortfall," not merely a modest error that simply shows that counsel is fallible. *U. S. v. Decoster,* supra; *C. v. Saferian,* 315 N.E.2d 878 (Mass.1974) (requiring "behavior of counsel falling measurably below that which might be expected from an ordinary fallible lawyer" and thereby depriving defendant of an "otherwise available substantial ground of defense").

Appellate courts also commonly question their ability to properly evaluate counsel's judgment, noting that what may look like errors in retrospective could well have reflected sound trial strategy at the time. Accordingly, they generally hold that "mistakes" in "judgment" or "strategy" do not reach the level of constitutional incompetency unless totally without justification. *Frand v. U. S.,* 301 F.2d 102 (10th Cir. 1962). Many courts also tend to assume that counsel's failure to utilize a particular defense right reflects a strategic decision rather than negligence. Others, however, are more critical in considering alleged tactical justifications, and will not assume a tactical decision was made where other action "would have better protected the defendant and was reasonably forseeable." *Beasley v. U. S.,* supra. The easiest cases are those in which counsel's own statements or action clearly indicate that alleged mistakes were the product of his ignorance of a legal rule "commonplace to any attorney engaged in criminal trials." In such cases, courts generally find a denial of effective assistance, even where a single mistake was made, provided it was substantial and related to a crucial issue in the case. *P. v. McDowell,* 447 P.2d 97 (Cal.1968).

Failure to investigate. The failure to conduct a full factual investigation is another common ground for attacking the effectiveness of counsel. Courts have recognized that competent counsel need not interview all available witnesses or track down all leads suggested by their client. *Jackson v. Cox,* 435 F.2d 1089 (4th Cir. 1970). The failure to investigate "must be appraised in light of the information known to the attorney." Consideration must be given to the information furnished by the client (in particular, the defendant's explanation of the factual circumstances), the nature of the prosecution's case, and the extent of the investigation actually undertaken. *U. S. v. Decoster,* supra. Cf. *Tollett v. Henderson,* 411 U.S. 258 (1973) (counsel was not incompetent when he advised defendant to plead guilty without considering a possible objection based upon discrimination in the selection of the grand jury; "often the interests of the accused are not advanced by challenges that would only delay the inevitable date of prosecution").

Late appointment. Competent assistance of counsel necessarily requires adequate time for preparation. *Coles v. Peyton,* 389 F.2d 224 (4th Cir. 1968). If counsel is appointed only shortly before trial, should that factor in itself establish ineffective assistance of counsel? In *Chambers v. Maroney,* 399 U.S. 42 (1970), the Court refused to adopt a "per se rule requiring reversal of every conviction following tardy appointment of counsel." Instead, it emphasized examination of the totality of the circumstances surrounding the tardy appointment. In *Chambers,* one legal aid attorney adequately represented defendant at his original trial, but the second legal aid attorney, who represented him on retrial, did not consult with defendant until a few minutes before the retrial. *Chambers* thus was not a typical late appointment case since the second attorney had the advantage of the case file from the previous trial and might have been working on the case before his last minute consultation. However, there had not been an evidentiary hearing as to how counsel actually prepared. The Supreme Court concluded that such a hearing was not necessary in light of the trial record. It stressed that the lower court, on close examination of the record, "found ample grounds for holding that the appearance of a different attorney at the second trial had not resulted in prejudice to petitioner."

The *Chambers* rejection of a per se rule does not bar a lower court from recognizing a prima facie presumption of ineffective assistance upon a showing of tardy appointment. Under this approach, followed by several courts, the burden is then shifted to the prosecution to show that the late appointment did not result in prejudice to the defendant. *Garland v. Cox,* 472 F.2d 875 (4th Cir. 1973).

Multiple representation and conflicts of interest. In contrast to the position taken in *Chambers,* the Court has adopted a per se rule for cases in which counsel's performance was influenced by his joint representation of codefendants with conflicting interests. If a convicted defendant can establish that his attorney's performance was affected by a conflict of interest between himself and his jointly represented codefendant, there is no need to show that counsel's performance was so deficient as to have had a probable impact upon the outcome of the case. As the Court noted in *Glasser v. U. S.,* 315 U.S. 60, 76 (1942), the defendant's right to the undivided loyalty of his attorney is "too fundamental and absolute to allow courts to indulge in nice calculations as to the amount of prejudice resulting from its denial." A showing that the attorney "actively represented conflicting interests" is sufficient in itself to require reversal of the conviction. *Cuyler v. Sullivan,* 100 U.S. 1708 (1980). Indeed, where the defendant called a potential conflict of interest to the trial judge's attention, the showing of an actual conflict may not be necessary; reversal will be required if the trial court simply failed to afford defendant an adequate opportunity to show that the potential conflict might "imperil his right to a fair trial." Id.

Cases involving conflict of interest claims have focused primarily on three issues: (1) what action must a trial court take when the defense calls a potential conflict to the court's attention; (2) when must a court initiate its own inquiry as to the existence of a conflict of interest; and (3) what showing is needed as to the existence of a conflict. *Holloway v. Ark.,* 435 U.S. 475 (1978), is the leading case on the first issue. In *Holloway,* a public defender appointed to represent three codefendants informed the trial court that, because of confidential information received from his clients, he faced a likely conflict of interest. Counsel noted, in particular, that as each defendant testified, he would not be able to effectively cross-examine that defendant on behalf of the others. The trial court pushed aside counsel's concern, suggesting that counsel simply should let each defendant testify as to "what he wants to." The Supreme Court held that, "in the face of the representations made by counsel," the trial court failed to safeguard the defendant's constitutional right to the assistance of counsel and thereby committed reversible error. Even if counsel had not provided the trial court with sufficient information to establish the need for separate representation, that court could not simply disregard counsel's repeated warnings as to a probable conflict. It at least had the obligation to make sufficient inquiry to ensure that the "risk [of conflict] was too remote to warrant separate counsel."

The *Holloway* opinion specifically left open the trial court's responsibility "where the trial counsel did nothing to advise the trial court as the actuality or possibility of a conflict." In the subsequent decision of *Cuyler v. Sullivan,* supra, the Court held that a considerably different standard applied to that situation. *Cuyler* initially rejected the contention that a trial court had a constitutional duty to make some inquiry as to a possible conflict in all cases of multiple representation. Ordinarily, the Court noted, the trial judge could rely upon the absence of any objection by counsel, since counsel has "an ethical obligation to avoid conflicting representations and to advise the court promptly when a conflict arises during the course of the trial." Thus, "absent special circumstances," where counsel has raised no objection, the trial court "may assume either that multiple representation entails no conflict or that the lawyer and his clients knowingly accept such a risk of conflict as may exist." The Court noted, however, that there may be cases where the trial court "reasonably should know" from the surrounding circumstances that a conflict probably exists and therefore should make an inquiry on its own initiative. Such circumstances were not present in *Cuyler,* where the defense attorneys' presentation was consistent on its face with the protection of the interests of all the codefendants they represented.

The *Cuyler* opinion also held that where the trial court had no duty to make an inquiry, a defendant challenging his conviction on the basis of multiple representation must show that a conflict of interest actually existed. A Sixth Amendment violation is not established by simply showing that the situation presented a potential for a conflict, since a "possible conflict inheres in almost every instance of multiple representation." The defendant must show that he and his jointly represented codefendants were actually in "adversary and combative positions." *Sawyer v. Brough,* 358 F.2d 70 (4th Cir. 1966). To meet this burden, the defendant ordinarily will point to such factors as factually inconsistent alibis, exculpatory statements by one codefendant tending to inculpate another, or substantial discrepancies in the weight of the evidence against different codefendants that would lead them to favor different defense tactics. See *Sawyer v. Brough,* supra.

Interference with counsel. State law may so restrict counsel's capacity to represent his or her client as to result in a denial of the effective assistance of counsel. Thus, *Ferguson v. Ga.,* 365 U.S. 570 (1961), found a denial of effective assistance in the operation of a statute which permitted defendant to make an unsworn statement to the jury but barred counsel from eliciting defendant's testimony through direct examination. Similarly, *Brooks v. Tenn.,* described at p. 78, held that the statute challenged there violated defendant's Sixth Amendment rights, as well as his Fifth Amendment rights, by preventing counsel from determining when to put the defendant on the stand. See also *Herring v. N. Y.,* 422 U.S. 853 (1975) (holding invalid, on Sixth Amendment grounds, a state statute giving the judge in a bench trial the authority to deny defense counsel a closing argument). A court order restricting counsel from fully assisting his client also may result in a denial of effective assistance. See, e. g., *Geders v. U. S.,* 425 U.S. 80 (1976) (holding invalid an order directing defendant not to consult with his attorney during an overnight recess that fell between the direct-examination and cross-examination of the defendant). The government may also deny effective assistance through the use of an informer who participates in client-counsel discussions. Compare *U. S. v. Levy,* 577 F.2d 200 (3d Cir. 1978) (violation where informer relayed defense strategy to the prosecution at its request) with *Weatherford v. Bursey,* 429 U.S. 545 (1977) (no violation where undercover agent "had no discussions either with his superiors or the prosecution concerning anything said at the attorney-client meetings" and his trial testimony related only to events occurring prior to the meetings).

CHAPTER 8

RAISING CONSTITUTIONAL CLAIMS

_____

43. TRIAL AND APPELLATE REVIEW: PROCEDURAL REQUIREMENTS

Procedural requirements and forfeited claims. While both federal and state courts must recognize federal constitutional claims, they also may impose reasonable procedural requirements on defendants raising those claims. All jurisdictions, for example, impose timing requirements for objections to unconstitutionally obtained evidence. Most jurisdictions require that objections to the admission of such evidence be presented by a pretrial motion to suppress. A pretrial objection is required because it assists in the orderly presentation of evidence by eliminating from the trial "disputes over police conduct not immediately relevant to the question of guilt." *Jones v. U. S.,* 362 U.S. 257 (1960). In many states, failure to make a pretrial motion to suppress will result in automatic forfeiture of the constitutional claim unless the defendant "could not reasonably" have made the motion prior to trial. N.J.Ct.R. 3:5–7. In others, the forfeiture will not be automatic even where a timely objection could have been made, but objections at trial will be considered only at the discretion of the trial court. Appellate courts have stressed that such discretion should be exercised liberally, but they also have been very reluctant to overturn a trial judge's refusal to consider an "untimely" objection. *P. v. Ferguson,* 135 N.W.2d 357 (Mich.1965). Those jurisdictions that do not require pretrial objections usually insist that objections to unconstitutionally obtained evidence be raised at the time the evidence is introduced at trial. Failure to make such a "contemporaneous objection" results in loss of the objection unless the trial court, in its discretion, deems it appropriate to consider a subsequent claim.

Procedural restrictions relating to the timing and form of objections also are imposed on other motions that may encompass constitutional claims—e. g., objections to the composition of grand or petit juries, and challenges to prosecutions based on a double jeopardy bar or a denial of a speedy trial. See Fed.R.Crim.P. 12(b) (requiring that all objections based on defects in the institution of prosecution be raised before trial). Failure to comply with these requirements will result in either an automatic forfeiture of the objection or a forfeiture subject to the trial court's discretion to consider a delayed objection. See Fed.R.Crim.P. 12(f) (failure to raise a required pretrial objection "shall constitute waiver thereof, but the court for cause shown may grant relief from the waiver"). While these forfeitures are sometimes described as "waivers," they do not require the knowing and voluntary relinquishment of rights commonly associated with waivers. Compare *Johnson v. Zerbst* (p. 372) with *Wainwright v. Sykes* (p. 406).

Constitutional limitations. If the state or federal procedural requirement is so arbitrary as to deny the defendant a fair opportunity to raise his claim, application of that requirement may itself constitute an independent violation of due process. *Reece v. Ga.,* 350 U.S. 85 (1955) (holding invalid a state law requiring that objections to the grand jury's composition be raised before indictment, where the defendant had been without counsel prior to indictment and appointed counsel then promptly moved to quash the indictment). The Supreme Court has rarely found it necessary, however, to examine the constitutionality of procedural requirements that arguably are invalid under these standards. In federal cases, the procedural requirements are promulgated by the Court itself and can appropriately be interpreted so as to avoid constitutional difficulties. In state cases, the Court may review a constitutional claim, notwithstanding a state court's refusal to consider that claim because of a procedural forfeiture, if the state procedural ground is not an "adequate state ground." *Henry v. Miss.,* 379 U.S. 443 (1965). A state procedural ruling will be "adequate" only if "the state's insistence on compliance with its procedural rule serves a legitimate state interest." Id. Thus, where a state rule denies a defendant a fair opportunity to raise a constitutional claim, the Court may simply find that the state court ruling does not rest on an adequate state ground and proceed to consider the merits of that constitutional claim.

Most of the state procedural rulings that have been rejected as not based on an adequate state ground have involved either a clear attempt to manipulate state procedural rules to bar consideration of defendant's constitutional claim or an application of a state rule in such a highly technical fashion as "to force resort to an arid ritual of meaningless form." *Staub v. City of Baxley,* 355 U.S. 313 (1965). See also *Wolfe v. N. C.,* 364 U.S. 177 (1960) (where the state court has discretion to excuse a failure to comply with a procedural rule, it may not exercise that discretion against considering federal constitutional claims while regularly exercising it in favor of considering "kindred" state claims). Where the state has relied on a standard application of a traditional procedural requirement, particularly one relating to the timing of objections, the Court has had no difficulty finding that the procedural ruling was supported by a legitimate state interest. Thus, in *Francis v. Henderson,* 425 U.S. 536 (1976), the Court concluded that several such interests supported a state requirement that objections to the composition of the grand jury (including a claim of racial discrimination) be raised before trial. Those interests included: (1) permitting the validity of the indictment to be resolved "before the court, the witnesses, and the parties have gone to the burden and expense of a trial"; (2) preventing defense use of a "sandbagging" strategy—i. e., "delaying the raising of the claim in the hopes of an acquittal, with the thought that if those hopes did not materialize, the claim could be used to upset an otherwise valid conviction at a time when reprosecution might well be difficult"; and (3) ensuring that the issue is raised while the persons responsible for the selection of the grand jury are likely to be available to testify and still have a reasonably fresh recollection of relevant events. See also *Henderson v. Kibbe,* 431 U.S. 145 (1977) (noting the value of the rule requiring that "counsel's views as to how the jury should be instructed be presented to the trial judge in time to enable him to deliver an accurate charge"); *Wainwright v. Sykes,* 433 U.S. 72 (1977) (noting the legitimate state interests served by a requirement of a contemporaneous objection to the admission of unconstitutionally obtained evidence).

Exceptions on appeal. As a general practice, appellate courts will review only those claims that properly were presented at trial. There are, however, some noteable exceptions. A small group of claims, viewed as going to the very power of the state to prosecute, commonly will be considered even if they were not presented in any fashion at the trial level. *P. v. Michael,* 394 N.E.2d 1134 (N.Y.1979). See, e. g., Fed.R.Crim.P. 12(b) (failure of an indictment or information "to show jurisdiction in the court or to charge an offense   *   *   *   should be noticed by the court at any time during the pendency of the proceedings"). These claims often are characterized as "jurisdictional defects," since the lack of jurisdiction renders the trial court's judgment "void" and subject to attack at any time. Most of these defects are not based on federal constitutional violations, although *Michael,* supra, held that a double jeopardy violation fell within this category.

Appellate courts also have the authority to consider "plain errors affecting substantial rights of defendants" though those errors were not pressed below. Fed.R.Crim.P. 52(b). Several appellate courts have shown a greater willingness to note potential "plain errors" of a constitutional dimension, particularly where the expansion of post-conviction relief (see §§ 44–46) makes it likely that those errors would otherwise be considered on collateral attack. *Alexander v. U. S.,* 390 F.2d 101 (5th Cir. 1968). Others have expressed a willingness, for similar reasons, to consider constitutional issues not raised below even when the likelihood of error is not so obvious. *S. v. Knoblock,* 170 N.W.2d 781 (Wis.1969). However, the trial record must be adequate for consideration of those issues notwithstanding their lack of development below. *Sykes v. U. S.,* 373 F.2d 607 (5th Cir. 1966) (noting that counsel's failure to raise a search and seizure objection at trial will almost inevitably produce an incomplete record since the appellate court can never know what justification would have been offered by the state if the search had been challenged).

44. POST–CONVICTION REMEDIES: FEDERAL HABEAS CORPUS FOR STATE PRISONERS

Introduction. The writ of *habeas corpus ad subjiciendum* is a judicial order directing a government official (e. g., a warden) to bring a person within his custody before the court so that it can inquire into the legality of that custody and discharge that person if the custody is deemed invalid. The writ is given constitutional recognition in Article I, § 9, which prohibits suspension of the writ "unless when in cases of rebellion or invasion, the public safety may require it." The constitutional mandate does not define the precise scope of the writ, and the first judiciary act authorized federal courts to issue the writ only on behalf of prisoners "in custody under the authority of the United States." It was not until 1867 that Congress, doubtful of the southern states willingness to adhere to federal law, authorized federal courts to issue the writ "in all cases where any person may be restrained of his or her liberty in violation of the Constitution." Under this provision, state prisoners could use the federal writ to challenge the constitutionality of the state convictions under which they were being held in custody.

Cognizable claims. Initially, the writ only permitted a prisoner to challenge a state conviction on a constitutional claim that defeated the "jurisdiction" of the state court. Although the habeas corpus statute referred generally to persons being held "in violation of the Constitution," the writ was viewed as incorporating the common law limitation that custody imposed under a final judgment of a court could only be challenged if the court lacked authority to issue that judgment. The earlier decisions thus dealt with such constitutional claims as double jeopardy violations and prosecution under a void statute. Over the years, the scope of the writ was expanded to include such claims as the denial of appointed counsel, with the Court reasoning that the trial court had "lost" jurisdiction when it failed to comply with the particular constitutional requirement. *Johnson v. Zerbst,* (p. 341). In *Fay v. Noia,* 372 U.S. 391 (1963), the Court finally concluded that the writ should apply to all constitutional challenges. *Fay* involved a challenge based on the government's use of an allegedly coerced confession, but the majority's wide ranging discussion of the history and role of the "Great Writ" clearly pointed to its availability to challenge all "restraints contrary to our fundamental law, the Constitution." Only ten years later, however, in *Schneckloth v. Bustamonte,* 412 U.S. 218 (1973), four concurring justices suggested that this conclusion should be reexamined. The concurring opinion disagreed with *Fay*'s analysis of the history of the writ and argued that *Fay* failed to give sufficient weight to the "costs" of federal habeas corpus review. Among those costs were the creation of an imbalance in the respective roles of the federal and state courts, the inefficient utilization of "limited judicial resources," and the loss of "finality" in criminal trials. The concurring opinion suggested that, perhaps, habeas corpus review should be limited primarily to claims "relating to [the] guilt or innocence" of the petitioner.

In *Stone v. Powell,* 428 U.S. 465 (1976), the Court retreated from the broad statements of *Fay* and moved in the direction of the *Schneckloth* concurrence. *Stone* ruled that a challenge to a conviction on the ground that the trial court admitted unconstitutionally seized evidence was not cognizable under federal habeas corpus unless the petitioner had been denied an opportunity for "full and fair litigation" of that claim in the state courts. The majority did not contend that a habeas court lacked jurisdiction to consider such a claim, but relied instead on the "equitable nature of the writ," recognized in *Fay* as granting the habeas court discretion to dispose of habeas applications "as law and justice require." See 28 U.S.C.A. § 2243. The majority reasoned that application of the exclusionary rule in a habeas proceeding made only a minimal contribution to the rule's effectiveness in deterring Fourth Amendment violations, and that contribution could not out-weigh the costs in-

volved. Those costs, the majority argued, included not only the usual costs of habeas review, as
noted in the *Schneckloth* concurrence, but also the
special costs that arise from the exclusionary rule,
which "deflects the truth finding process and often
frees the guilty." There was a need, however, for
consideration of search and seizure claims where the
applicant had not received an adequate opportunity
to litigate his claim in the state courts. This exception would serve as a safeguard against a state
court's failure to live up to its "constitutional
obligation to * * * uphold federal law." In
response to the suggestion that federal court review
was needed in all cases, the Court added that it was
"unwilling to assume that there now exists a general
lack of appropriate sensitivity to constitutional rights
in the trial and appellate courts of the several states."

So far, the Court has not added to the list of
constitutional claims that will not be cognizable on
habeas review if the petitioner had a previous
opportunity for full and fair litigation. Lower courts
have assumed that the *Stone* analysis also will apply
to other constitutional claims based upon a prophylactic exclusionary remedy (most noteably, *Miranda*
violations). *Richardson v. Stone,* 421 F.Supp. 577
(N.D.Cal.1976). In *Wainwright v. Sykes* (p. 466), the
Court found it unnecessary to decide whether "a bare
allegation of a *Miranda* violation, without accompany-
ing assertions going to the actual voluntariness or
reliability of the confession, is a proper subject for

consideration on federal habeas review, where there has been a full and fair opportunity to raise the argument in the state proceeding." Justice Brennan's dissent in *Stone* contended that the "groundwork [was] being laid for a drastic withdrawal of federal habeas jurisdiction" for all claims that are not "guilt-related." However, in *Rose v. Mitchell*, 443 U.S. 545 (1979), the Court rejected such a rigid classification of cognizable claims.

The petitioners in *Rose* challenged their convictions on the ground that there had been racial discrimination in the selection of the foreman of the grand jury that had indicted them. A divided Court held that their claim was cognizable on habeas review and distinguished *Stone*. The dissenters, arguing that *Stone* should apply, stressed that the petitioners' claim did not "implicate" the "need to protect the innocent from incarceration"; their claim went only to the validity of the grand jury indictment and not to the trial, where they had been convicted by a "fairly selected petit jury." The majority responded that there were other interests presented that justified consideration of a grand jury discrimination claim on habeas review: (1) since the court that oversees the selection of the grand jury is the trial court itself, there was "doubt" that discrimination claims "will receive the type of full and fair hearing deemed essential to the holding of *Stone*"; (2) allegations of grand jury discrimination involve charges that state officials are violating the direct command of the Fourteenth Amendment, as compared to *Stone*, "where the Court considered the application of a judicially created remedy [i. e., the exclusionary rule] rather than a personal right"; (3) while the deterrent value of the exclusionary rule was not significantly enhanced by application in a habeas proceeding, federal habeas review is likely to have a strong "educative and deterrent effect" on the state judiciary's grand jury selection procedure; and (4) the costs of quashing an indictment "are significantly less than those associated with suppressing evidence." Unlike *Rose*, most of the other post-*Stone* habeas cases considered by the Supreme Court have dealt with claims that went to the accuracy of the fact-finding process at trial. See, e. g., *Jackson v. Va.* (p. 80) (sufficiency of the evidence under the reasonable doubt standard); *Manson v. Braithwaite* (p. 278) (suggestive identification procedure allegedly violating due process). But note also *Crist v. Bretz* (p. 84) (double jeopardy violation).

Impact of prior adjudication. In *Brown v. Allen,* 344 U.S. 443 (1953), and *Townsend v. Sain,* 372 U.S. 293 (1963), the Supreme Court emphasized that cognizable constitutional claims would be considered on habeas review even though those claims had been fully adjudicated by the state court. The prisoner is entitled to an independent, federal court determination of his federal claim, and the state court ruling therefore cannot bind the federal habeas court.

Both *Brown* and *Townsend* noted, however, that the state court's findings of fact ordinarily can be accepted by the federal habeas court. Following *Townsend,* the federal habeas corpus act was amended to establish a presumption of correctness for state factual findings unless certain specified deficiencies existed in the state proceedings. See 28 U.S.C.A. § 2254(d); *Townsend v. Sain,* supra; *LaVallee v. Delle Rose,* 410 U.S. 690 (1973).

Impact of procedural "forfeitures." Prior to *Fay v. Noia,* supra, a defendant's forfeiture of his constitutional claim in a state court through failure to comply with valid state procedural requirements was viewed as precluding consideration of that claim on application for habeas corpus. In *Fay,* the defendant had failed to take an appeal, which state law viewed as a relinquishment of his constitutional challenge to his conviction. The state argued that the federal habeas court also was barred from considering that challenge since the requirement of an appeal was a reasonable state procedural rule. A divided Court rejected this position. The majority held that the "adequate state ground" limitation, which bars Supreme Court appellate review following a valid procedural forfeiture (see p. 394), does not apply to federal habeas corpus. The majority stressed that the "jurisdictional prerequisite [for issuance of the writ] is not the judgment of the state court, but detention *simpliciter,*" and therefore the exercise of

[*404*]

habeas jurisdiction should not be controlled by the basis for the state court's ruling. However, the federal habeas court did have discretion to deny relief to an applicant whose procedural default in the state proceedings reflected a decision to "deliberately bypass the orderly procedure of the state court." Denial of relief based upon a deliberate bypass was justified under the "equitable principles" that traditionally govern the exercise of habeas jurisdiction.

The *Fay* opinion did not explore at length what constitutes a "deliberate bypass," but it did stress that the determination of that issue should be in accord with the "classic definition of waiver—'an intentional relinquishment or abandonment of a known right or privilege.'" *Fay* found that there had not been a deliberate bypass in the case before it; the defendant had decided not to appeal his conviction, but only because he feared that he would receive the death penalty if successfully retried. The development of the concept of deliberate bypass otherwise was left to the lower courts. Those courts agreed that there was no bypass where counsel was unaware of the basis for a missed objection, but disagreed as to the assumptions that could be made as to counsel's knowledge where the record did not clearly indicate why no objection was raised. See *Wainwright v. Sykes* (p. 405) (opinions of Justices Stevens and Brennan, citing various lower court decisions).

The *Fay* view of procedural forfeitures, like the *Fay* view of cognizable claims (p. 399), was reconsidered and partially rejected during the 1970's. Although *Fay* referred to its deliberate bypass rule as a standard applicable to all procedural forfeitures, *Francis v. Henderson,* 425 U.S. 536 (1976), applied a somewhat different standard where a petitioner challenged his state conviction on a grand jury discrimination claim that he had failed to raise before trial as required under state law. Stressing the strong interests served by the state requirement of a pretrial objection (noted at p. 395), the Court held that habeas review would be available only upon a "showing of 'cause' for the defendant's failure to [object] * * * before trial * * * [and] also a showing of actual prejudice." In *Wainwright v. Sykes,* 433 U.S. 72 (1977), the "cause-and-prejudice" standard of *Francis* was held applicable to a petitioner seeking to raise a *Miranda* claim that had not been presented at trial in compliance with a state requirement of a contemporaneous objection. The *Wainwright* opinion noted its "reject[ion]" of the "sweeping language" of *Fay,* which had suggested a universal application of a deliberate bypass standard. Indeed, whether the deliberate bypass standard should remain applicable even in the *Fay* fact-situation was "left for another day."

The *Wainwright* majority cited three reasons for its refusal to apply the deliberate bypass standard in that case: (1) the contemporaneous objection rule serves several important procedural functions (e. g., permitting the "record to be made * * * when the recollections of witnesses are fresh") and therefore "deserves greater respect" than the *Fay* standard would give it; (2) the *Fay* standard "may encourage 'sandbagging' on the part of defense lawyers"; and (3) "failure of the federal habeas courts generally to require compliance with a contemporaneous objection rule tends to detract from the perceptions of the trial" as the "main event" rather than "a tryout on the road." The cause-and-prejudice standard, it contended, would not suffer from these deficiencies, yet would "not prevent a federal habeas court from adjudicating for the first time the federal constitutional claim of a defendant who in the absence of such an adjudication will be the victim of a miscarriage of justice." Since the *Wainwright* analysis is readily extended to other procedural rules relating to the timing of objections, the deliberate bypass standard is likely to be confined in the future to a very narrow class of forfeitures. Chief Justice Burger, concurring in *Wainwright,* argued that the deliberate bypass standard was only appropriate for forfeitures relating to decisions that require defendant's personal participation (such as the decision to appeal involved in *Fay*). Deliberate bypass is a proper standard in those cases, he noted, since the rights involved depend on "defendant's own decision" and can be relinquished only by a "knowing and intelligent decision by the defendant himself." See

[407]

also the discussion at p. 376. Arguably, the deliberate bypass standard also might apply to a defendant's failure to raise at trial a constitutional claim that goes to the "jurisdiction" of the trial court and is apparent on the face of the record. Cf. *Menna v. N. Y.,* and *Blackledge v. Perry,* discussed at pp. 410–411.

The Court in *Wainwright* did not attempt to give precise content to the cause-and-prejudice standard. It noted: "We leave open for future decisions the precise definition of the 'cause-and-prejudice' standard, and note here only that it is narrower than the standard set forth in dicta in *Fay v. Noia,* which would make federal habeas review generally available to state convicts absent a knowing and deliberate waiver." As for the case before it, in light of the substantial evidence of guilt introduced at petitioner's trial, there clearly was no possibility of "actual prejudice" resulting from the introduction of the statement now challenged by the petitioner. In a concurring opinion, Justice Stevens argued that the application of cause-and-prejudice standard in the *Wainwright* case was "consistent with the way [the lower] federal courts have actually been applying *Fay.*" Justice Stevens noted: "Matters such as the competence of counsel, the procedural context in which the asserted waiver occurred, the character of the constitutional right at stake, and the overall fairness of the entire proceeding may be more significant than the language of the test the Court purports to apply." See also *Jiminez v. Estelle,* 557 F.2d 506 (5th Cir. 1977) (suggesting that "cause" existed if counsel was unaware of well established grounds for objection that would be "controlling in the case," but also suggesting that such counsel would be incompetent under the Sixth Amendment). Of course, the meaning of the cause-and-prejudice standard only becomes important if the state court has imposed a procedural forfeiture; if the state court chose to ignore a procedural failing and considered petitioner's claim on the merits, the federal habeas corpus also will consider it on the merits, without regard to either the *Fay* or *Francis* standards. *Warden, Md. Penitentiary v. Hayden,* 387 U.S. 294 (1967); *Castaneda v. Partida,* 430 U.S. 482 (1977).

Impact of a guilty plea. The habeas remedy may be used to challenge the voluntariness of a guilty plea. If the plea is voluntary, however, it cuts off a challenge to most antecedent constitutional errors. See the discussion at p. 299, supra. There are, however, certain claims that survive even a voluntary plea entered with the assistance of competent counsel. In *Menna v. N. Y.,* 423 U.S. 61 (1975), the plea was held not to have "waived" defendant's claim that his prosecution was barred by double jeopardy. That claim survived, the Court noted, because it was not inconsistent with the factual guilt acknowledged by a valid plea; "a guilty plea simply renders irrelevant those constitutional violations * * * which do not stand in the way of conviction if factual guilt is validly established." In *Blackledge v. Perry*, 417 U.S. 21 (1974), a guilty plea did not bar consideration of petitioner's claim that the initiation of prosecution on a higher charge following a trial de novo violated due process (see p. 84). The *Blackledge* opinion shifted somewhat from the rationale in *Menna*. Petitioner's claim survived the plea, the Court noted, because it "went to the very power of the State to bring the defendant into Court to answer the charge brought against him." If the defendant had pled not guilty and had immediately raised the claim, there was no way that the violation could have been cured and a valid conviction obtained. In *Lefkowitz v. Newsome*, 420 U.S. 283 (1975), the Court held that a habeas court also could consider constitutional claims, notwithstanding a guilty plea, where the state had adopted a special procedure that permitted the defendant to enter a guilty plea while reserving the right to appeal any antecedent constitutional errors. In the several states where this procedure is used, the state prisoner is not limited to issues of the type noted in *Blackledge* and *Menna*, but may raise any cognizable claim that was reserved and appealed in the state courts.

Exhaustion of state remedies. Federal courts traditionally have refused to consider habeas applications of state prisoners who have failed to exhaust currently available state remedies. This qualification, now codified in the federal habeas statute [28

U.S.C.A. § 2254(b)], stems from considerations of federal-state comity rather than any inherent limitation upon the power of the federal courts. *Fay*, supra. In its most common application, the exhaustion requirement precludes consideration of a habeas application by a prisoner whose claim was raised at trial and is still subject to state appellate review. It also precludes consideration of claims that were not properly raised in the original state proceedings, but are still open to consideration by the state courts in post-conviction proceedings. *Ex parte Hawk*, 321 U.S. 114 (1944). However, "exhaustion of one of several alternative [state] remedies is all that is necessary." *Brown v. Allen*, 344 U.S. 443 (1953). If the applicant's claim was considered by the state courts on direct appeal, he is not required to initiate a state collateral attack even if the state post-conviction remedy would permit reconsideration of his claim.

Custody. The federal habeas corpus statute provides that the writ "shall not extend to a prisoner unless he is in custody * * *." The "custody-requirement" is derived from the procedural function of the writ as an order directing the jailer to bring his prisoner before the court, but it no longer is interpreted as requiring such immediate physical control over the applicant as the form of the writ might suggest. In *Jones v. Cunningham*, 371 U.S. 236 (1963), for example, the Court held that an applicant on parole was subject to sufficient "re-

straints" to "invoke the help of the Great Writ."
The *Jones* rationale also encompasses persons on probation. *Benson v. Cal.,* 328 F.2d 159 (9th Cir. 1964).
See also *Hensley v. Municipal Court,* 411 U.S. 345
(1973) (*Jones* applicable to petitioner released on his
own recognizance in conjunction with a stay of
sentence execution pending final disposition of his
habeas application). In *Peyton v. Rowe,* 391 U.S. 54
(1968), the Court held that a defendant serving the
first of two consecutive sentences was "in custody"
for the aggregate term of both sentences and therefore could immediately challenge the second sentence. *Braden v. 30th Judicial Cir. Ct.,* 410 U.S. 484
(1973), relying upon *Peyton,* noted that a defendant
serving a sentence in one jurisdiction, but subject to
a detainer from a second jurisdiction on a pending
sentence to be served there, can currently utilize
habeas corpus to challenge the conviction in the
second jurisdiction.

45. POST–CONVICTION REMEDIES—
FEDERAL PRISONER (28
U.S.C.A. § 2255)

Relation to habeas corpus. In 1948, Congress
adopted a statutory post-conviction remedy for federal prisoners, 28 U.S.C.A. § 2255, that was designed
to serve as a substitute for habeas corpus. The
primary objective of section 2255 was to shift the
burden of post-conviction review from courts in the
district of incarceration, where habeas petitions

were filed, to the court that originally imposed sentence. The section was not intended to alter the scope of the remedy available to federal prisoners, and the Supreme Court has held that section 2255 will be viewed as providing "a remedy exactly commensurate with that which had been available by habeas corpus." *Hill v. U. S.*, 368 U.S. 424 (1962); *U. S. v. Hayman*, 342 U.S. 205 (1952). With respect to constitutional claims, the section 2255 remedy is similar in most respects to the habeas corpus remedy for state prisoners, but there are certain significant distinctions.

Scope. Section 2255 extends to the same cognizable constitutional claims that may be raised by state prisoners on habeas corpus. *Stone v. Powell*, supra. It also extends to non-constitutional questions of federal law, but only where "the claimed error of law [is] a fundamental defect which inherently results in a complete miscarriage of justice and * * * presents exceptional circumstances where the need for the remedy afforded by the writ of habeas corpus is apparent." *Davis v. U. S.*, 417 U.S. 333 (1974).

Where the applicant's constitutional claim was previously decided on the merits, the court considering the section 2255 application ordinarily need not review that claim. *Castellana v. U. S.*, 378 F.2d 231 (2d Cir. 1967); *Sanders v. U. S.*, 373 U.S. 1 (1963). The principle of *Brown v. Allen* and *Townsend v. Sain* (p. 403), requiring independent federal determination of constitutional claims resolved in state courts, obviously has no bearing upon a section 2255 proceeding. Since the trial ruling in a section 2255 proceeding also was rendered by a federal court, that ruling need not be reconsidered unless it was based on a "deficient" factual adjudication or on legal principles that subsequently have been modified so as to possibly produce a different result. In determining whether a new factual adjudication is required, the section 2255 court applies standards largely similar to those established in *Townsend,* supra.

Where the constitutional claim could have been, but was not raised properly in the prior federal proceedings (either at trial or on direct appeal), the standards applicable are the same that would apply to similar procedural forfeitures in state courts. See the discussion of *Fay v. Noia* and *Francis v. Henderson* at pp. 404–409. See also *Davis v. U. S.,* 411 U.S. 233 (1973). Section 2255 proceedings also are governed by roughly similar rules relating to the availability of other procedures for raising constitutional claims. A policy comparable to that reflected in the exhaustion-of-state-remedies requirement (p. 410) is applied to section 2255 proceedings in the interests of "the orderly administration of the criminal law." *Bowen v. Johnston,* 306 U.S. 19 (1939). Thus, section 2255 motions will not be entertained during the pendency of a direct appeal.

[*414*]

Section 2255, like habeas corpus, also is limited by a "custody requirement," and the rulings expanding the concept of custody as applied to habeas corpus generally are also applicable under section 2255. It should be noted, moreover, that when the petitioner is no longer within federal custody, another post-conviction remedy, the writ of coram nobis, may be utilized to raise certain types of constitutional issues. See *U. S. v. Morgan*, 346 U.S. 502 (1954).

46. STATE POST–CONVICTION REMEDIES

Almost every state has one or more post-conviction procedures that permit prisoners to challenge at least some constitutional violations. A substantial group of states have adopted special post-conviction statutes, or court rules, roughly similar to section 2255. Many encompass all constitutional claims, while others may be limited to the same constitutional claims that are cognizable under section 2255. In states that utilize the common law writ, that writ may extend to all constitutional claims, the same claims cognizable on federal habeas, or only those claims that are viewed as establishing jurisdictional defects. *Ex parte Story*, 203 P.2d 474 (Okla.Crim. 1949). The writ of coram nobis is also viewed in several states as an appropriate remedy for presenting certain types of constitutional claims. *P. v. Cooper*, 120 N.E.2d 813 (N.Y.1954).

State courts generally will not reconsider on collateral attack cognizable claims that were raised and decided on the merits at trial and on appeal. Where claims were not raised previously, whether they will be considered depends on why they were not raised, with some states applying a deliberate bypass test derived from *Fay*. Many states also have followed the lead of *Jones v. Cunningham*, supra, and include within the custody concept persons not within the immediate physical control of the respondent. *In re Cawley*, 120 N.W.2d 816 (Mich.1963). Other states, however, provide much narrower remedies. They apply only to prisoners and permit consideration only of constitutional claims that could not reasonably have been raised at trial.

INDEX

References are to Pages

INDEX

INDEX

References are to Pages

INDEX

[*422*]

INDEX

References are to Pages

[425]

INDEX

INDEX

References are to Pages

INDEX

INDEX

INDEX

INDEX

[*436*]

INDEX

INDEX
References are to Pages

†